THE HEARING IMPAIRED CHILD
AND THE FAMILY

HUMAN HORIZONS SERIES

THE HEARING IMPAIRED CHILD AND THE FAMILY

by

Michael Nolan
and
Ivan Tucker

A CONDOR BOOK
SOUVENIR PRESS (E & A) LTD

First published 1981 by
Souvenir Press (Educational & Academic) Ltd,
43 Great Russell Street, London WC1B 3PA
and simultaneously in Canada

Reprinted 1983

ISBN 0 285 64920 5 casebound
ISBN 0 285 64921 3 paperback

Printed and bound in Great Britain by
Anchor Brendon Ltd, Tiptree, Essex

Contents

Acknowledgements

No authors operate in a vacuum and we have been fortunate enough to have had the opportunity of working at Manchester University with a stimulating group of people.

We have benefited from the support and guidance of Professor Ian Taylor, Director of the Department of Audiology and Education of the Deaf, and our work in this book has been influenced by him and by other members of the staff of the Department.

We wish particularly to acknowledge the many fruitful discussions we have had with two former colleagues, Kim McArthur and Christine Fulbeck. We also wish to thank most sincerely our wives Sheila and Katie for typing the manuscript and for their patience and encouragement throughout.

Geoff Thompson, of the University of Manchester Audio Visual Service, is gratefully thanked for providing some of the photographs, and the Department of Medical Illustrations, Manchester Royal Infirmary, for many of the illustrations.

Last but not least we thank the many parents and children with whom we have had the pleasure to work. They have taught us much, helping us to develop our ideas and techniques. We hope that in some small measure we have been able to help them.

Introduction

A hearing impaired child presents a family with a variety of problems and many challenges. We have attempted in our book to provide parents with a first source of information on the areas in which we know from our experience of working with families that they most need it.

Perhaps the problem for a particular family started when trying to obtain a satisfactory diagnosis for the child. You will see by reading Chapter 2, on the Assessment of Hearing, that this is not an uncommon problem, and we not only outline reasons for this but suggest ways of improving services. We strongly believe that any parents who are worried about their child's hearing should be given the opportunity of a full audiological assessment at a specialist centre, regardless of whether or not the child has passed a screening test. In our experience, parents are nearly always correct when they believe that their child has a hearing problem.

Parents who are considering having further children may find Chapter 1 on causes of deafness helpful. For detailed and personal information they should also consult a general practitioner who has access to the medical history and is able, where necessary, to arrange specialist advice.*

Throughout the book parents and professionals are considered as partners in the process of helping the hearing-impaired child to develop. Great emphasis is placed on the use of all of the child's remaining hearing, because our goal, and we believe the goal of parents too, is to make every effort to help the child develop speech and language.

*At Manchester, in our Department, almost one third of all sensori-neurally deaf children have been deafened by German Measles (Rubella). This source of deafness can be eradicated. But this will happen only when all parents encourage their teenage daughters to take advantage of the immunisation programme.

Chapter 5 on Hearing Aids emphasises the importance of the parents' role in the efficient use of amplification with children, and Chapter 6 describes our oral approach to language development. We know from our own work that even children with the most severe degree of hearing loss can and do develop spoken language. We believe that this is the means by which the hearing impaired child can be integrated into our society.

When problems arise, there will be many people who will be able to help the family of a hearing-impaired child. We have attempted to direct parents to these, and described the roles of various professional advisers. Parents are, throughout the book, encouraged whenever they have a problem or need information to ask and to keep asking until they obtain satisfaction. We have also provided suggestions for further sources of information.

Finally, we would like to impress on parents that their hearing-impaired child is first and foremost a child. This is something they should never forget. They must accept that their child has a disability, but always remember that they can greatly influence the extent to which that disability becomes a handicap. We live in exciting times; more children than ever before are being successfully educated with their normally hearing peers. This is a result of the positive and dedicated approach of parents, as much as of developments in technology and educational methods.

1 : Causes of Deafness in Children

One of the first questions parents of hearing-impaired children ask is: what is the cause of the deafness? This question is of considerable importance for parents, especially when the question of having another child is being considered. Yet it is not always an easy question for a clinician to answer, particularly in cases of sensori-neural deafness, which can be caused by any of a number of factors. Detailed investigations will probably have to be carried out before the clinician can attempt to answer. These investigations may include blood tests of mother and baby, urine tests of the baby, a thorough examination of the baby's ante-natal history and birth details, and a study of medical records in both families so as to check for any family history of deafness.

Before we can describe the various agents that may give rise to hearing impairment in children, however, it will be necessary to outline the structure and function of the hearing mechanism. This will help the reader to understand the various types of hearing loss, and how such losses are managed.

The Structure of the Ear
The structure of the normal ear is shown in a simplified form in Figure 1. As can be seen, the hearing mechanism is extremely complex, so the system has been set out in three parts.

The Outer Ear
The outer ear comprises the familiar auricle (or external ear) and the ear canal. The ear canal (or auditory *meatus*) is approximately 2½ cm. in length and is terminated at its inner end by a thin, strong, flexible membrane known as the tympanic membrane (or eardrum). This membrane completely closes off the ear canal and separates the outer ear

from the middle ear cavity. The location of the membrane protects it from damage caused by blows to the side of the head, and also helps to ensure that temperature and level of moisture near the membrane remain effectively constant. This is important for preserving the flexibility of the membrane.

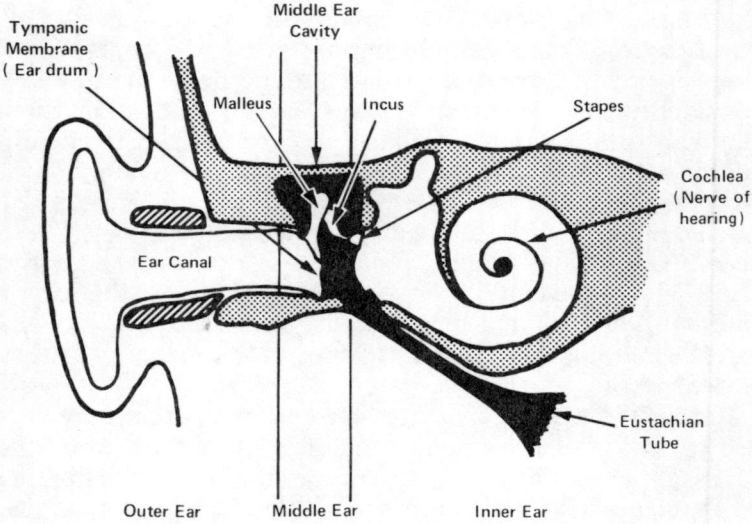

Fig. 1   The structure of the ear

The Middle Ear
The middle ear comprises a very small air-filled cavity beyond the eardrum, which contains three tiny bones or ossicles. These bones are known as the *malleus* (the hammer), the *incus* (the anvil), and the *stapes* (the stirrup). They are suspended across the middle ear cavity from the eardrum to the oval window, another smaller membrane that is situated in the bony wall between the middle and inner ear. The malleus is in constant contact with the eardrum. The incus is connected to the malleus at one end and to the stapes at the other end. The footplate of the stapes fits snugly against the oval window.

Figure 2 shows an enlarged picture of the ossicles. The shaded regions represent the contact areas between the bones. Remember also that the malleus is in contact with the eardrum and the stapes is in contact with the oval window.

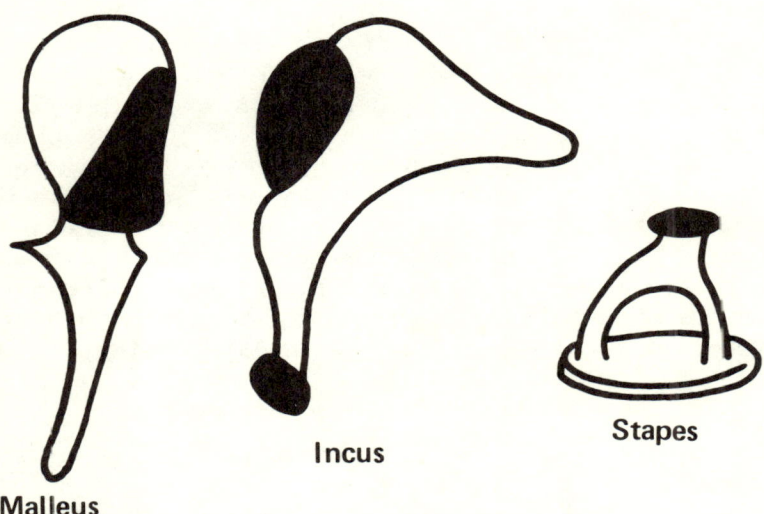

Incus

Stapes

Malleus

Fig. 2   The ossicles

The Eustachian Tube

The middle ear air-filled cavity is ventilated by means of the Eustachian tube. This is a narrow tube which runs from the middle ear to a space at the back of the nose (known as the nasopharynx). The Eustachian tube is normally closed, but opens when we swallow or blow our noses. Opening of the Eustachian tube allows a puff of air to enter the middle ear. A normally functioning Eustachian tube thus ensures a well ventilated middle ear cavity. We each have two Eustachian tubes, one ventilating each ear.

The Inner Ear

The link between the middle ear and inner ear is achieved by the contact between the stapes and the oval window. The inner ear itself is a complicated arrangement of tubes filled with watery fluid. Part of this arrangement (known as the *cochlea*) is concerned with our sense of hearing, and part (the *utricle* and semicircular canals) with our sense of balance. The cochlea lies just beyond the middle ear cavity and is shaped like a snail shell. The oval window is situated in the outer wall of its bony casing (i.e. in the party wall between the middle and inner ear). The cochlea contains very sensitive nerve fibres, each of which is considered to be sensitive to sound of a particular pitch. Those fibres that are sensitive to high pitched sounds are thought to lie towards the outer end of the snail shell structure, near the oval window, while those fibres that are sensitive to low pitch sounds are thought to lie in the innermost part of the spiral (the apex). All of the fibres come together in a bunch as they leave the cochlea, and constitute the nerve of hearing which conveys the information to the brain. The auditory nerve is thought to comprise up to 30,000 nerve fibres.

The Function of the Ear
The function of the ear is to convey to the brain precise information on the sounds emanating from our environment. In order to understand how this is achieved, we must first consider the meaning of the term 'sound', and the process involved when a sound is transmitted from a source (e.g. a guitar) to a receiver (e.g. the person listening).

Sound. What is it?
Most people, if asked to explain what sound is, would say something like 'it is something that we hear'. Now it is true that sound is perceived through our sense of hearing. But as an explanation of sound, the statement is far from adequate because it leaves unanswered the questions of *how* sound is produced, transmitted and perceived.

Sound may be defined as energy produced whenever any object is set into vibration. We are able to 'feel' heat energy from a fire. We 'hear' sound energy from a loudspeaker. All vibrating objects produce sound. If the properties of the sound are within the sensitivity range of the human ear, then we will hear it.

Sound perception – 'hearing' sound

To get some idea of how a person 'hears' a sound, let us consider the example of the sound made by a guitar, see Figure 3. When a guitar string is plucked it is set into vibration – it moves to and fro about its normal position many times every second. The string is able to do this

Fig. 3   A sounding guitar

because it receives energy from the person plucking it. As the string vibrates, it forces the air molecules around it to vibrate too. In fact it gives these molecules a tiny push each time it moves towards them, and a pull back as it moves back towards its normal position. The effect on the air molecules is much like that of a person gently pushing a child on a swing – the child moves to and fro, the adult pushing and gravity pulling back. Then the air molecules that are set into vibration by the string in turn act on their neighbouring molecules, setting them into vibration. So the effect travels quickly through the air – though it becomes weaker (smaller push-pull force) as the distance from the string increases.

An individual hearing the sound of the guitar does so when the sound vibrations travelling through the air eventually cause the air molecules lying along the person's ear canal to vibrate. The air molecules adjacent to the eardrum then vibrate, and in turn pass on the vibrations to the eardrum itself. Since the ossicular chain is connected via the malleus to the eardrum, any vibration of the eardrum results in vibration of the ossicular chain, with subsequent vibration of the oval window; which causes pressure changes in the fluid of the cochlea. This results in stimulation of particular nerve fibres (dependent upon the characteristics of the sound). When a nerve fibre is stimulated a tiny electrical impulse is generated. This impulse (information) travels up the acoustic nerve to the brain. In the present example it would be interpreted as the sound of a guitar string.

This simplified description illustrates the way in which all sounds are produced, transmitted, and perceived. It does not matter whether the source of sound is a loudspeaker, a bell, a person speaking or a car horn. *The sound produced is simply energy which sets up tiny push-pull forces in the air*. These forces are conveyed by the air molecules to the ear. As we grow up, our brains develop a familiarity with the sounds of everyday life, so that we learn to recognise a 'car' sound, a 'dog barking' sound, a 'baby crying' sound. *We learn to label the sounds which we hear*.

The Hearing Pathways

It will be seen from the above description that sound is conducted through the air, through the outer ear and eardrum and ossicular chain, by means of vibration. It is not until the sound reaches the cochlea that vibration is replaced by electrical impulse – through stimulation of specific nerve fibres.

It is thus conventional to describe that part of the hearing mechanism comprising the outer and middle ear, up to and including the oval window, as the *conductive pathway*; and the hearing mechanism beyond, including the cochlea and nerve of hearing to the brain centre, as the *sensori-neural pathway*.

Types of Deafness

If a child is to have normal hearing, the outer, middle and inner ear must function normally. Hearing impairment arises when disease, damage or abnormality occurs in one or more of these parts. If a problem arises somewhere along the conductive pathway i.e. in the outer or middle ear, the resulting deafness is known as a *conductive* deafness. If the problem arises along the auditory pathway of the inner ear, the resulting deafness is known as *sensori-neural* or *nerve* deafness.

Conductive Deafness

This type of deafness is caused by a 'blockage', or abnormal hindrance to vibration and hence to transmission of sound in the outer or middle ear. It generally results in a partial rather than severe degree of hearing loss. Nevertheless, such losses can and do affect children's language acquisition and school progress if present for long periods of time. As a rule it is possible to cure, or at least substantially remedy, this type of deafness.

Sensori-Neural Deafness

This type of deafness is caused by damage in the cochlea or nerve of hearing leading to the brain centre. Sensori-neural deafness can vary in degree from mild to total loss of hearing. Unfortunately this type of hearing loss is not amenable to medical treatment.

It is therefore considered permanent and must be managed accordingly. For example, it is necessary to fit children with suitable hearing aids if a significant sensori-neural hearing loss exists. Otherwise language acquisition (talking and understanding) will certainly be severely impaired.

Although detailed investigations into the cause of sensori-neural deafness will normally be carried out as soon as possible once the condition has been diagnosed, it is possible that the causative agent will remain unknown. Sample studies show that the cause of deafness in up to 50 percent of children with severe sensori-neural deafness remains unknown. It seems likely, however, that many of these children will in fact have been deafened by genetic (inherited) factors.

Causes of Sensori-Neural Deafness

Sensori-neural deafness can actually be present (i.e. the damage to a certain part of the inner ear can occur) while the baby is still in the mother's womb. This means that the child is born with a hearing problem. Such problems are generally described as congenital (i.e. with the child from birth).

Some children on the other hand may be born with a perfectly normal hearing mechanism, which is subsequently damaged by a particular noxious agent. In such cases the deafness would be described as 'acquired', (i.e. occurring after birth).

Congenital Sensori-Neural Deafness

The causes of congenital sensori-neural deafness fall into three main groups: the hereditary group, due to genetic factors; the prenatal group, resulting from damage to the inner ear of the baby as it develops in the womb; and the perinatal group, due to one or more of a number of possibly damaging factors that may affect the baby at or around the time of birth. It has been said on more than one occasion that this is the most dangerous time of a baby's life, and damage to the inner ear is certainly one of the risks to the infant during and soon after birth.

Hereditary Deafness

The term 'hereditary deafness', or 'familial deafness' is used when a child inherits deafness from its parents. When a baby is conceived it receives certain 'characters' from its parents, carried inside each cell on the *chromosomes*. Human cells carry 23 pairs of chromosomes – we receive 23 from each parent, which then pair up. The 'characters' carried by the chromosomes determine all our physical functions, including hearing. In fact, we have a pair of such characters, one on the chromosome inherited from our mother and one on the chromosome inherited from our father, though only one of these, the dominant character, is active and governs the hearing (or other function) of the child. The weaker character (called the recessive one) has no influence.

Normally hearing people generally carry two identical characters, both of which are consistent with normal hearing. It is possible however for a parent to be a carrier of a hearing character that produces sensori-neural deafness, even though he or she has normal hearing. In such a case it is possible that that parent's child will inherit this character, and be sensori-neurally deafened. The process of inheritance happens in the following ways:

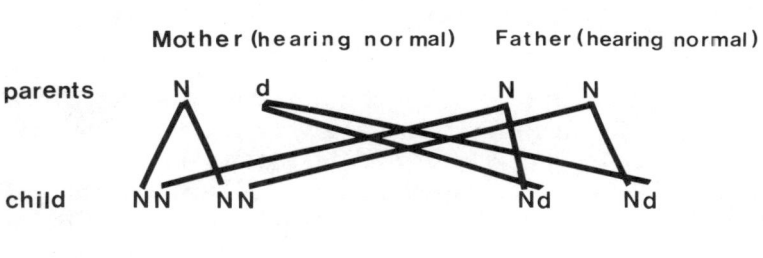

In this example a normally hearing mother has married a normally hearing man. In each of them, then, the dominant hearing character N is a normal hearing one; but in the case of the mother the recessive hearing character d is a sensori-neural deaf character. When they produce a baby, the child can receive one of a possible four combinations of hearing characters, as in the diagram. In all four cases – NN, NN, Nd and Nd – the child would have normal hearing because the dominant character N for normal hearing overrides the recessive d 'deaf' character. Hence in this marriage no children can be produced who are deaf due to inheritance.

It is however theoretically possible for both mother and father to be carriers while still having normal hearing. Although the chances of this happening are very small, they nevertheless do happen. In such a case the following would occur:

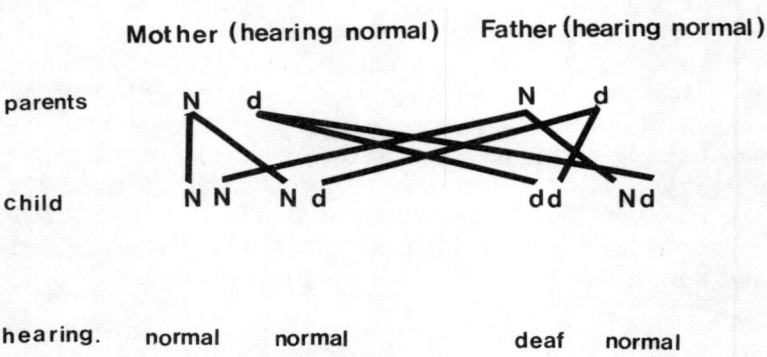

This time, three of the permutations – **Nd**, **Nd**, **NN** – would produce a normal hearing baby because the dominant normal hearing **N** character prevails. However in the baby inheriting **dd** deafness would result. This baby is furnished with deaf characters from both parents. Each time these parents produce a child there will be the same one in four (25 percent) chance of a hearing impaired child.

It may be seen from the above that such cases as this are very difficult to anticipate. There is no particular likelihood of a previous history of deafness in either family. And since the vast majority of adults with normal hearing carry a **NN** pair of characters for hearing, if either of the partners described had married such a normal carrier, no hearing impaired children would have been produced.

It is sometimes possible, from detailed family studies, to trace a family history of deafness through generation to generation, but in such cases the parents passing on the hearing problem are hearing impaired themselves, and the chances of conceiving a hearing impaired child are greater than in the previous example. The hearing impaired person in such cases carries a *dominant* deaf gene, unlike the recessive character previously described.

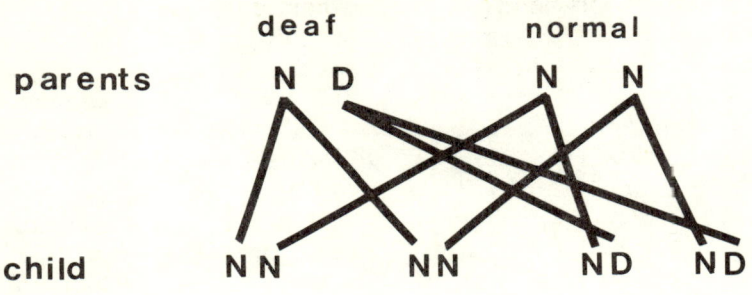

In this example, one parent is hearing impaired because the **D** character for deafness is dominant and overrides the normal hearing **N** character. The other parent is normally hearing. When conception occurs the resulting baby will inherit one of a possible four combinations of hearing characters from the parents. In every combination involving the dominant D deaf character, deafness will result because this character will suppress the normal hearing character. Therefore, in two cases out of four the child will be hearing impaired. Thus, each time a child is conceived in this partnership there will be a 50 percent risk of a hearing impaired baby.

Sex-Linked Deafness
The point was made earlier that we each have 23 pairs of chromosomes. These chromosomes carry the characters that determine our bodily functions. One pair of chromosomes have a special importance because they determine the sex of the child. They are therefore known as the sex determining chromosome pair. The other 22 pairs are

generally known as autosomes, and it is generally the case that information concerned with hearing function will be carried by the autosomes. It has however been found that sex-linked deafness (i.e. a sensori-neural deaf character carried on a sex determining chromosome) does occasionally occur. This is how it happens.

The male of the species has an **X** and a **Y** chromosome sex pair. The female has an **X** and an **X** chromosome sex pair. When a child is conceived it will inherit one sex determining chromosome from its mother and one from its father: the boys, being **XY**, inherit their **X** chromosome from their mother and obviously their **Y** chromosome from their father. Girls receive one **X** from their mother and one **X** from their father.

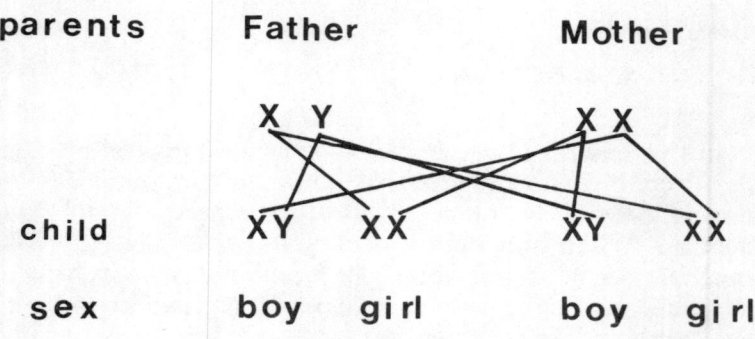

The hearing problem resulting from inheritance occurs in the following way.

Let us assume that a normally hearing father has a normal hearing character on the **X** chromosome (the **Y** chromosome is assumed not to carry hearing information). The mother who is also normally hearing is assumed to carry a normal hearing character on one **X** chromosome and a recessive **d** sensori-neural deaf character on the other **X** chromosome. She is therefore normally hearing because the normal hearing **N** character dominates the deaf **d** character in her case.

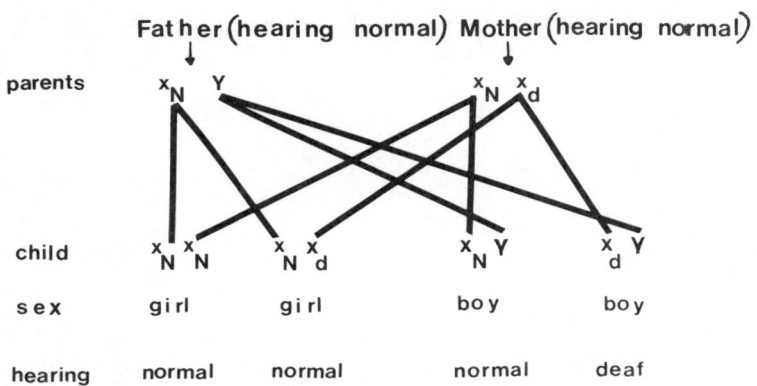

Any children conceived by this partnership will have one of a possible four chromosome permutations. Both possible permutations for girls **XX** will produce normal hearing because one **X** chromosome at least carries a dominant **N** normal hearing character. However, in the case of a baby boy, there is a 50 percent chance of a sensorineural deafness. This results from the fact that the boy is **XY**. There is no character on **Y** for hearing and the character on **X** therefore determines hearing in this case. The baby boy inherits his **X** chromosome from his mother and if he inherits **Xd** chromosome he will have a hearing problem.

Each time a baby is conceived in this partnership there will be an overall one in four chance (25 percent) of a hearing impaired child being born; and a one in two chance of deafness (50 percent) if the child turns out to be a boy.

Although during this section we have confined the discussion to inheritance of deafness, it is important for the reader to be aware that children can inherit a number of abnormalities or characteristics including deafness. Some of these may group themselves together, and if such a group of characteristics is inherited it is comparatively easily identifiable in a family because of the multiplicity of abnormality. Such groups of characteristics are generally known as syndromes: i.e. collections of symptoms, that are passed on through families together.

One syndrome that is a well known cause of inherited

deafness in children is Waardenburg's Syndrome. This is recognisable by a white forelock, that all affected subjects inherit.

Genetic Counselling

If parents of a hearing impaired child find themselves advised either that the cause of the deafness remains unknown, or that there are indications that the deafness is indeed hereditary, it is important for them to seek the advice of a genetic counsellor. This person is based at a local hospital, and is a specialist concerned with the study of inheritance. She or he will be able to offer guidance on the likelihood of the deafness being inherited, and on the chances that further children will inherit the deafness too. Such counselling will be particularly important if and when the child itself considers starting a family.

Causes of Sensori-Neural Deafness in the Pre-Natal period (during the time the baby is in the womb)

German Measles (Rubella Virus)

It is possible for a mother to contract the rubella virus for the first time during her pregnancy. If this happens, the virus is passed on and infects the baby. As far as the mother is concerned she suffers no more than minor discomfort from a slight fever and a rash. However, the consequences for the unborn baby can be catastrophic. This virus is particularly nasty and causes many handicaps in unborn babies, including severe sensori-neural deafness, blindness, mental retardation and heart defects.

The risk of rubella infection damaging an unborn baby depends very much upon the time during the pregnancy when the infection occurs. The risk is known to be most significant during the first 12-16 weeks and to decline thereafter. Sensori-neural deafness results from the fact that the virus effectively destroys part of the cochlea.

The most disturbing aspect of rubella deafness is that it can be prevented. Protection against rubella is freely available and given by means of an inoculation. This inoculation is being offered to all girls between the ages of

11 and 14 years through the School Health Service. It is also available to anyone else, particularly women in child-bearing years, from their GP. It should not be given during pregnancy, or within two months of intended conception.

The policy in the United Kingdom has been to try to protect the whole female population from this virus *before* they have children. Yet the public response to the inoculation campaign has been disappointing. The official figures for overall uptake in 1978 were 55 percent, although more recent provisional figures indicate an improvement on this number.

There is no doubt in our minds that parents and teachers must 'bring home' to their children and neighbours the dangers that this virus presents to an innocent and totally normal unborn baby; that the difference between having a normal baby and a deaf blind baby may lie in having, or not having, an inoculation.

We are of the opinion that couples should
a) ensure that the wife is protected against rubella prior to starting a family. The GP will advise on how this may be done
b) ensure that any teenage daughters do take up the offer of the inoculation through the School Health Service;
c) encourage their married friends and female colleagues to find out about the dangers of rubella, and what steps can be taken to prevent it;
d) although an inoculation against rubella will protect the majority of women against subsequent infection it is important to note that some women 'lose' their rubella antibodies (i.e. lose their protection against rubella infection). This may occur in a relatively short period after inoculation. Blood test can be carried out to check whether rubella antibodies are present. Such a test is generally given to all pregnant women during their first visit to the ante-natal clinic. It is our considered opinion that point a) above should be viewed as a means of ensuring that the woman is protected against rubella *prior to starting a family,* by arranging for a blood test with the GP.

Other Maternal Infections
Other maternal infections, such as cytomegalovirus and syphilis, can give rise to sensori-neural deafness in the baby.

Causes of Sensori-Neural Deafness in the Perinatal Period (at and around the time of birth)
We have already mentioned the fact that many people consider the time of birth as a potentially dangerous time for a baby. Some sensori-neural hearing problems are known to originate at this time in the baby's life.

Prematurity (baby born before the expected date)
Sensori-neural deafness does occur in a small number of cases of severe prematurity. However, this is becoming increasingly rare with greatly improved facilities for after-care, and our increased knowledge of the effects of drugs.

Anoxia
During a long and difficult labour, or soon after a difficult birth, it is possible for a baby to become short of oxygen. This has been believed sometimes to cause hearing impairment, although the actual way in which lack of oxygen could affect the hearing mechanism has not been identified. In studies carried out in our Department, it has been found that children who suffer cardiac arrest, i.e. whose heart stopped beating at birth, were more at risk with regards to hearing, than children with classical anoxia. It is encouraging to note that anoxia is becoming increasingly rare, because of great strides in the care of 'at risk' babies around the time of birth.

Neonatal Jaundice
At birth a physiological jaundice may occur owing to the relative immaturity of the baby's liver, coupled with the breakdown of red blood cells as the cell count falls from 7,000,000 per mm^3 to 5,000,000 in the first few weeks of life. This problem is likely to be more significant in premature babies. A substance known as bilirubin is produced as a result of the breakdown of the red blood cells. This

substance passes from the blood to the liver and is excreted. Any blockage or failure of the excretory system results in an accumulation of bilirubin in the blood. When this occurs the baby turns yellow and is said to be jaundiced. Deafness as a result of high levels of bilirubin occurs because of damage to the nerve of hearing at the brain stem. The condition is called kernicterus. The treatment of neonatal jaundice is phototherapy and exchange blood transfusion.

A neonatal jaundice as a result of Rhesus factor mismatch (incompatibility) can give rise to a much more severe form of this condition.

Rhesus incompatibility

If an individual's blood contains a substance called the Rhesus factor, it is known as Rhesus positive blood. If it does not contain this factor, it is known as Rhesus negative. Some people thus are born with Rhesus positive blood and others with Rhesus negative blood.

This can give rise to a problem when a Rhesus negative mother is carrying a Rhesus positive baby. During the time the baby is in the womb, its blood effectively comes into contact with its mother's blood, so the Rhesus factor contained in the baby's blood passes freely into the mother's bloodstream. Her body, however, regards this substance as poisonous, and reacts by producing another substance (antibodies) to combat it. These antibodies in turn then pass freely between mother and baby.

The concentration of antibodies remains low during the first pregnancy, offering no danger to the child. However, if there are subsequent similar pregnancies, the antibody concentration can rise, to destroy the baby's red blood cells and release a substance known as bilirubin into the child's bloodstream. It is possible, if no action is taken, for this substance to damage parts of the sensori-neural hearing system, once the child is born – that is, once the contact between the child's bloodstream and the mother's has been broken.

At one time this problem accounted for a significant number of children with sensori-neural deafness. However, there have been great advances in treating this condition in recent years. All mothers are now tested for the Rhesus factor during their first pregnancy, and the vast majority of 'mothers at risk' require no more than treatment (an injection) immediately after the first baby is born to ensure that no subsequent babies are damaged. Cases of Rhesus incompatibility causing sensori-neural deafness are now extremely rare.

Causes of Acquired Sensori-Neural Deafness in Children
Viral
Acquired sensori-neural deafness in children can result from an acute viral infection. Measles has been known to cause bilateral sensori-neural deafness, although this is an extremely rare occurrence. Mumps occasionally causes a hearing loss, but this almost always affects just one ear and leaves the other ear perfectly normal. Influenza has also been reported to give rise to sudden hearing loss. It appears that the damage to the hearing mechanism in all the above cases arises in the cochlea; and losses tend to occur suddenly at the time of infection.

Meningitis
Meningitis is an inflammation of the membrane covering the brain. It is probably the most common cause of significant acquired sensori-neural deafness in children.

Damage to the hearing mechanism usually occurs in the cochlea, although higher centres along the acoustic nerve may be affected. It is interesting to note that the incidence of hearing loss as a result of meningitis has been drastically reduced as a result of specific antibiotic therapy. In the case of bacterial meningitis, it is now estimated that as few as 3-5 percent of children affected are likely to have hearing problems.

At one time turbercular meningitis, which is now very rare in Britain, was treated with an antibiotic called Streptomycin. This drug is now known to be a cause of sensori-neural deafness when taken in large quantities. Alternative drugs are therefore used in such cases, and only a drastically reduced dosage of Streptocmycin, if any at all.

NOTE: The main point to appreciate about sensori-neural deafness is that it is permanent. If we say that a child has a sensori-neural deafness, we mean that irreparable damage has been done within the neural pathway. It is impossible at this time to transplant a cochlea, or implant a new auditory nerve.

Causes of Conductive Deafness in Children

The major causes of conductive deafness in children are related to blockages – for instance, by fluids or foreign bodies – in the outer or middle ear. This results in a dampening of the sound vibration, which effectively makes the sound too quiet to be heard. Deafness therefore results. The underlying problems causing this type of deafness can, in the vast majority of cases, be cleared up by suitable medical treatment, with the result that hearing returns to normal. The medical specialist who deals with diseases of the ear is the Otologist or Ear, Nose and Throat (ENT) Surgeon.

Generally speaking conductive hearing problems in children arise after birth, during infancy and childhood. There are however known cases of children born with congenital conductive deafness.

Congenital Conductive Deafness

This type of deafness arises in the womb during the time when the ear is developing. A variety of abnormalities may occur, including complete absence of the outer ear; the auricle present as a remnant only; occlusion of the ear canal (i.e. ear canal closed over with no visible eardrum); a total absence of ossicles. Very little is known about the cause in such cases. It has been found that many children are affected only in one ear, the other ear being normal. In such cases it is usual for clinicians simply to monitor the hearing in the good ear and do nothing about the affected ear until the child is older. Most children with one good ear appear to do satisfactorily in school, particularly when appropriately managed (e.g. preferential seat near to teacher). The decision as to whether an operation is needed (for instance, to open up a blocked ear canal) will be taken by the medical specialist.

Causes of Conductive Deafness after birth (i.e. during childhood)
Wax
Many people view wax as a cause of hearing problems, but it is in fact unusual for wax to impair the passage of sound along the ear canal, and deafness in children as a result of wax is rare. The only time that wax may give rise to a slight hearing problem is when it becomes hard and impacted in the ear canal. In this case a drop of warm olive oil will soften the wax and enable it to run out of the ear. Alternatively, your G.P. can remove the wax by syringing. Parents must not on any account poke objects such as cotton wool buds down a child's ear canal. Wax occurs naturally, in order to help carry dirt out of the ear and keep it healthy.

Foreign Bodies
Children do tend to put strange objects in the most odd places: buttons up noses, coins down throats, marbles, pebbles and matchsticks in their ears. It is unlikely that a foreign body placed in the ear canal (unless it totally blocks the canal) would cause a significant hearing problem, but if a parent does find that a child has been stuffing its ears with strange objects, the thing to do is to take the child to the casualty department of the local hospital.

Middle Ear problems – Eustachian tube dysfunction
Problems in the functioning of the middle ear give rise to the vast majority of conductive hearing problems in children.

You will recall that the middle ear cavity is air filled, and that it contains the ossicles which vibrate in response to eardrum vibration and thus 'pass on' sound to the nerve of hearing. It is imperative that the eardrum remain flexible, and that the ossicles vibrate freely if sound is to be transmitted efficiently through the middle ear.

The role of the Eustachian tube is an important one: to ensure that a constant fresh supply of air is directed into the middle ear space. This helps to maintain the middle ears in a state of maximal efficiency for sound transmission. If for some reason the Eustachian tube ceases to work effectively, a marked conductive deafness can result. This will generally occur in both Eustachian tubes simultaneously and cause bilateral deafness.

Eustachian tube blockage may have any of a variety of causes. Any infection around the back of the nose or near the top of the throat, such as a heavy cold, allergy, inflammation of the throat and nasopharynx, or enlarged adenoids, can result in the openings of the Eustachian tubes being obstructed and their functions being significantly impaired. And when this blockage persists, a watery fluid, which may range from thin to very thick, is produced in the middle ear space. This effusion causes a stiffening in the texture of the eardrum, and severely dampens the ossicular vibrations.

The problem faced by the ossicles may be likened to that of a person standing in a swimming pool. The person would find it relatively easy to walk about in an empty pool. If, however, the pool is then filled with water the person would find it far more difficult to move and would have to expend a great deal more energy to do so. It is similarly difficult for ossicles to vibrate in a fluid filled cavity. Middle ear effusion therefore results in a conductive hearing problem.

The treatment of middle ear deafness resulting from effusion varies according to the degree and underlying cause of the problem. It has been found that a large majority of cases clear spontaneously without treatment, or with simple treatment such as a course of medicine from the child's GP (e.g. decongestant, nasal spray). Other children require the specialist help of the ENT surgeon, who may decide to perform an operation with two primary aims in mind – restoring normal Eustachian tube function and removing the middle ear fluid. This operation may involve removal of adenoid pads (adenoidectomy), which can become enlarged and block the entrance to the Eustachian tubes. It will certainly involve drainage of the fluid from the middle ears. The surgeon does this by making a tiny incision (a slit) in each eardrum, through which he then 'sucks out' the fluid. Often he will place a tiny teflon tube (grommet) in each eardrum, so that the middle ear is ventilated through the ear canal. The grommets stay in position for a period of up to two years and generally 'fall out' naturally into the ear canal and then out of the ear. (Since they are so small, parents are unlikely to notice the grommets when they drop out.)

Children who undergo surgical treatment are followed up by the ENT surgeon over a period. It sometimes proves necessary to repeat an operation to remove further middle ear fluid, but in many cases the problem is resolved by one operation and does not occur again.

Mental Handicap and Hearing Impairment
The incidence of hearing impairment in the mentally handicapped is known to be far higher than in the normal population. Hearing impairment in such children can be either sensori-neural or conductive, and the causes are generally similar to those already discussed.

The most disturbing aspect of hearing impairment in the mentally handicapped is that it is so often missed – because audiological assessment and follow-up is simply not available, or because it is not held to be important. We believe that every effort should be made to ensure that *all* mentally handicapped children are thoroughly assessed for hearing, and followed up accordingly.

Down's Syndrome (Mongolism)
One group of children who are particularly vulnerable to hearing impairment are those with Down's Syndrome. It has been found in various studies that a large majority of such children do suffer hearing problems from an early age; yet a lack of response to sound is often dismissed as due to the 'mental handicap', and no thought is thus given to the question of hearing acuity.

The primary cause of deafness in Down's Syndrome children is middle ear dysfunction, that results in a *conductive* deafness. We have found that such children show markedly improved responses to sound following surgical procedures; and in cases where, because of other physical abnormalities (e.g. heart disease), operations are out of the question, or in cases where middle ear problems recurred after treatment but further operations were thought inadvisable, encouraging results have been obtained from the use of hearing aids.

We would encourage all parents of Down's Syndrome children to insist on a thorough audiological assessment should they have any doubts about their child's hearing acuity.

Conclusion

The fundamental difference between conductive and sensori-neural hearing problems lies in the fact that conductive problems can in a large majority of cases be cured, while sensori-neural problems are all viewed as permanent.

Parents will find that clinicians who are involved in the audiological assessment of children are interested not only in determining the *degree* of the hearing loss, but also in the *nature* of the problem. Suitable medical treatment of a serious conductive deafness will have a very significant effect on that child's auditory receptive ability. Similarly an appropriate hearing aid for a child with a sensori-neural deafness can ensure that the child is furnished with auditory experiences that are of fundamental importance to intellectual and emotional development.

2 : Assessment of Hearing in Children

Why test hearing?
People communicate with one another primarily by means of speech, and without this ability our lives can become extremely difficult. Talking is one of the things we do most 'naturally'. Children develop linguistic skills rapidly in their early years of life: amazingly progressing from babble to complex sentences in less than three years. But if speech is to develop, together with an understanding of language, it is necessary for the child to be able to hear the sounds of speech.

If a child is unable to hear some or all of the sounds of speech, language development in terms both of understanding and talking will be affected, though the severity of the problem will depend on the degree and nature of the hearing loss. *Clinicians are very conscious of the dangers that an unrecognised hearing problem can present to a child's subsequent linguistic development, and they recommend that all children be tested for hearing loss during the first year of life.*

Early diagnosis of a sensori-neural hearing problem and fitting of a suitable hearing aid certainly adds to a child's chances of developing speech. It enables the child to hear and enjoy many sounds in other people's speech that would be otherwise unheard – and such sounds at this stage are major sources of 'speech stimulation'. Further, the child is enabled to hear his or her own voice: and this too is a very important part of language development, for children learn to talk, not only through hearing other people's speech, but also by hearing themselves practising speech sounds. *Clinicians therefore want to identify hearing losses as early as possible and take the necessary action required to manage problems.* And since a conductive hearing problem is, as we have seen in Chapter 1, amenable to medical treatment and a sensori-neural problem is not, it is obviously very important to distinguish between the two. *Clinicians involved in the assessment of hearing in young children are therefore concerned with determining not only the degree of a hearing loss, but also the nature of the loss*.

A number of tests are generally carried out so as to furnish clinicians with the information they require. Since parents of hearing impaired children have rarely the technical knowledge to interpret the results of these tests when they are reported to them, it will be useful to describe the properties of sound in some detail before describing the tests of hearing used with young children.

The properties of sound
When a source of sound, such as a guitar string, is set into vibration it will move to and fro a certain number of times in every second. *Frequency is a measure of the number of cycles of vibration exhibited by a source of sound each second. Frequency is expressed in units of Hertz (Hz).* If a source of sound exhibits 1000 cycles of vibration per second, its frequency would equal 1000 Hz.

The range of normal human hearing extends from approximately 20 Hz to 20,000 Hz. However, the most important frequencies for speech discrimination are considered to be in the frequency range 200 Hz to 8000 Hz. The piano keyboard contains frequencies from 27.5 Hz to 4186 Hz. *Changes in frequency are generally recognised by a listener through changes in the pitch of the sound heard.* In a guitar, frequency changes according to the tension, thickness and length of string being plucked. A listener would be aware of such a change without having to see the guitar: the change would be apparent as the pitch changed. *Low frequency sounds have low pitch, and as frequency increases pitch becomes progressively higher.*

A particular sound has the property of *intensity* as well as the property of *frequency*. The intensity of a sound is related to the strength of the push-pull forces generated by the source of the sound. *Intensity is in fact a measure of the power of the sound*, which is responsible for the push-pull forces. If one considers a child on a swing, the power (strength) of the effort exerted by the adult determines the size of the swing's trajectory. A very gentle push results in a tiny to and fro movement – a vigorous push results in a much greater movement. In the same way, when the power of a sound source changes, the result is a change in the strength of the push-pull forces that act on the eardrum. The strength of these forces is generally called the sound

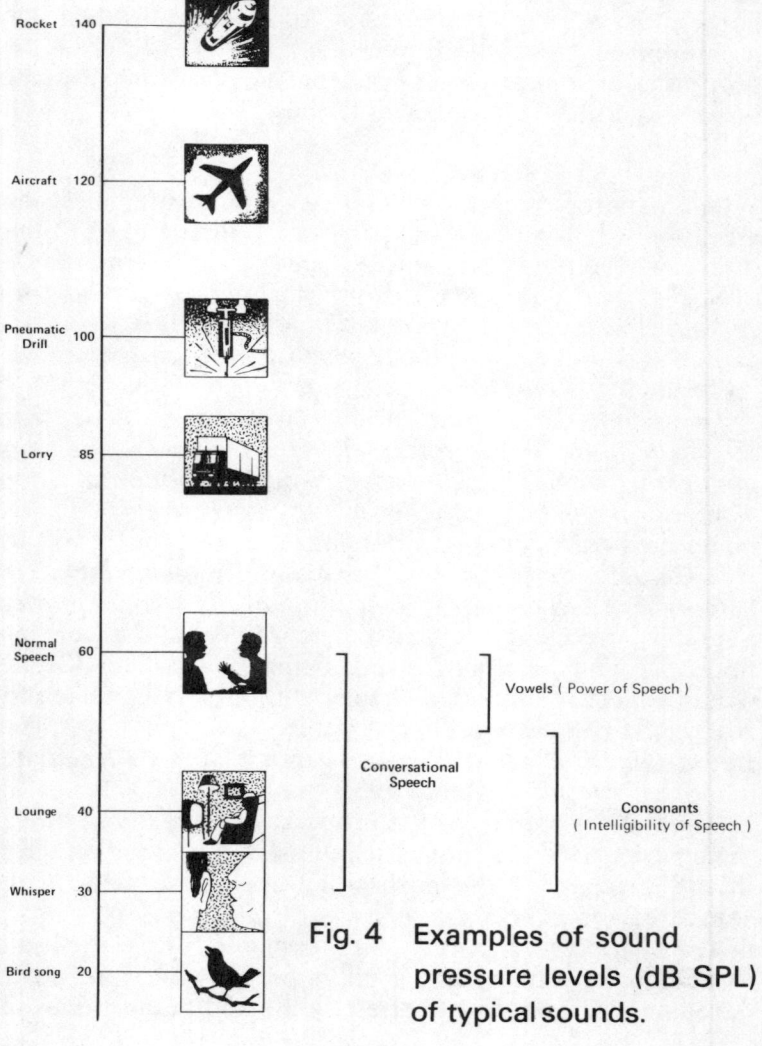

Fig. 4   Examples of sound pressure levels (dB SPL) of typical sounds.

pressure level, which is measured in units of Newtons per square metre.

The diagram (Figure 4) shows examples of sources of sound that we are exposed to during our everyday lives. It shows that *our ears are exposed to sounds covering a very wide range of sound pressure*, which the ear perceives primarily as changes in loudness. The quietest sound that the normally hearing person is able to perceive is approximately one ten millionth the strength of the loudest sound the ear can tolerate. Clearly such a range is far too wide for practical use. So a scale called the decibel scale has been adopted for expressing sound pressure (and therefore sound power). This scale compresses the ten million to one range of sound pressure into a 140 decibel range. That is 20 decibels is equivalent to a real change in sound pressure of times 10.

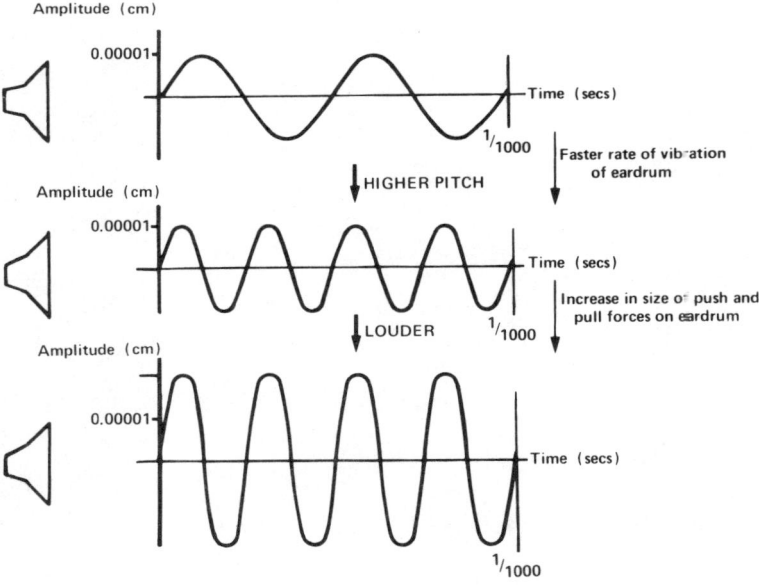

Fig. 5   Properties of sound

The starting point of the decibel scale, 0 decibel (0.00002 Newtons per sq. m.) is the sound pressure of the quietest audible sound. Conversational speech occurs at a sound pressure of 60 decibels (0.02 Newtons per sq. m.) and the sound pressure close to an aeroplane jet engine is approximately 120 decibels (20 Newtons per sq. m.). It is conventional to express sound pressure in decibels as 'dB SPL', so that a sound having a sound pressure level of 55 decibels would be said to have a sound pressure of 55 dB SPL.

Thus sound has properties of both frequency and intensity. These properties influence the manner in which the listener 'hears' a particular sound. Changes in the frequency and intensity result in pitch and loudness changes, as may be seen by reference to the diagram (Figure 5).

Hearing sensitivity as a function of frequency
The human ear is most sensitive to sounds in the frequency region 500 Hz to 4000 Hz (commonly called the mid-frequency region). This means that the ear requires less

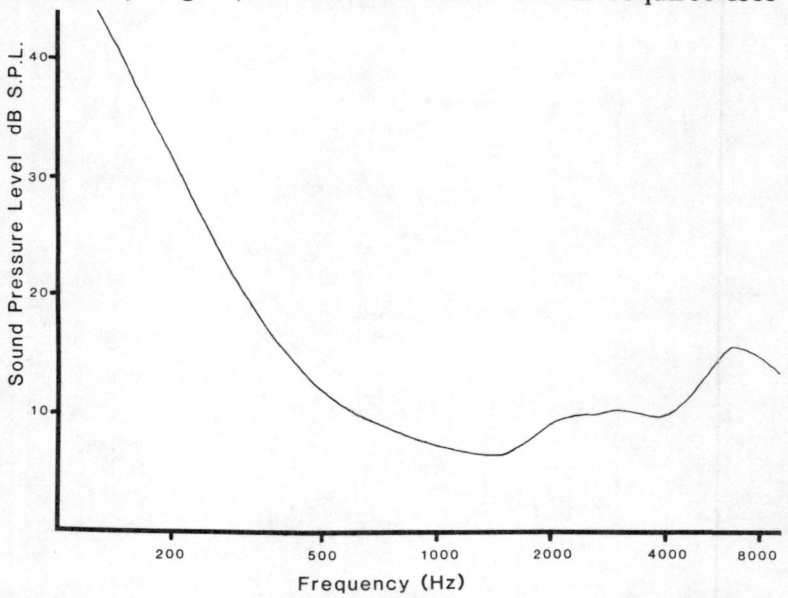

Fig. 6   Sensitivity of the ear when listening through the standard headphone.

energy, or a smaller push-pull force, to perceive mid-frequency sounds than it does to perceive the higher and lower frequencies. Thus it is not surprising to find that *the mid-frequency region contains the majority of speech sounds*. Such sounds are vitally important to us, because we communicate with one another through speech so our hearing needs to be sharp for these frequencies.

It is possible to show graphically the way in which the normal ear's sensitivity to sound varies according to frequency when listening through a standard headphone. The graph (Figure 6) is simply a means of illustrating the fact that a higher sound pressure (greater push-pull force) is required by the normal ear to perceive the low and high frequencies than to perceive the mid frequencies. The line on the graph traces the sound pressure levels that produce signals at the threshold of hearing for the normally hearing. *Threshold of hearing is the term used to describe the point at which the stimulus can just be heard.*

Normally hearing person hearing tests
The term 'normally hearing person' is used to describe someone whose hearing sensitivity is equal to that of the accepted norm. In audiology the term 'accepted norm' relates to the hearing levels of normally hearing, healthy, young adults aged 18 to 25 years. A large sample of such people have been tested via the standard headphone across the audible frequency range, and the average threshold values for the test frequencies adopted as the normal thresholds of hearing. The graph shown earlier was obtained in this way. *When a person is given a hearing test, his or her hearing levels are measured* (that is, the strength of the push-pull forces required to produce a sound at the threshold of hearing) *and compared with the accepted normally hearing values*. If the results are significantly different from the normal values, it is said that a hearing impairment is present. *Hence, hearing tests compare a particular person's hearing sensitivity with normal values for a range of test frequencies.*

Hearing impairment

The term 'deaf' has been used for many years to describe people with impaired hearing. This term is, in our opinion, inappropriate, because it conveys to the lay person a description of someone who hears no sound whatsoever. *There are in fact very wide ranges in the severity of deafness.* It is therefore far more appropriate to describe children with abnormal hearing as hearing-impaired.

When a young child has a hearing test, the clinician is primarily interested in determining whether or not the child's hearing for the speech frequencies is normal. The clinician will therefore test a child's hearing for each of the *specific parts of the speech frequency range.* The aim will be to answer the questions: *Does this child hear all the speech frequency sounds normally? If not, for which part of this range of sounds is the hearing impaired?* For variation in degree of hearing impairment can be very wide. Some children may have normal hearing for the low frequency speech sounds and a hearing impairment for the mid and higher speech frequencies; others may have impairment for all speech frequencies; whilst still others may have an impairment only in the mid frequencies of speech.

The importance of identification of hearing loss

It may be seen by reference to the diagram of the range of sounds that we are exposed to during our everyday lives (figure 4) that the sounds of speech cover a decibel range of approximately 30 decibels. This means that certain sounds of speech are stronger (have more energy) than other sounds. In fact the sound pressure of the strongest vowel 'aw' as in *talk* is over 30 times that of the weakest consonant 'th' as in *the.* It is possible to study speech sounds using specialised equipment, and such studies have shown that the *powerful sounds of speech are the vowels* which are listed in Table 1. Most of the energy generated when a person says a word is contained in the vowel part of the word. *Vowel sounds are primarily low to mid-frequency sounds. The other category of speech sounds are the consonants, which are weaker and lie in the mid to high-frequency region.*

These sounds are listed in the table for reference. Thus when a person says a word, some of the sounds comprising the word may be as much as 20-25 decibels stronger than other parts of the same word. (Figure 7)

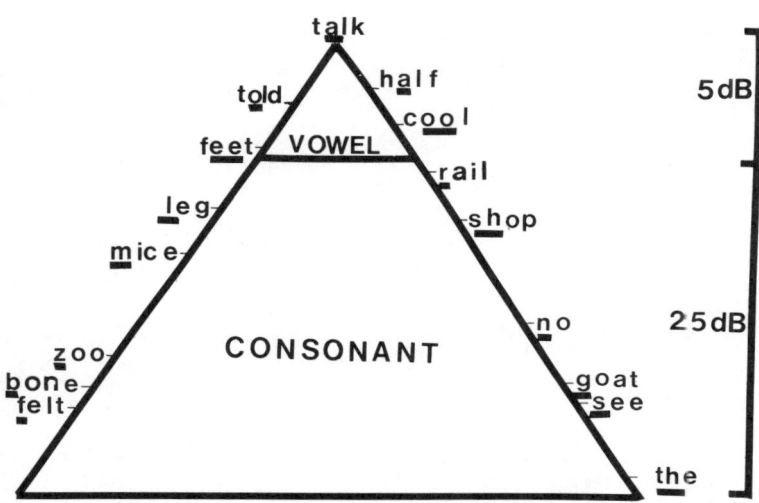

Fig. 7   Examples of speech sounds.

Sounds of speech

We have highlighted the fact that spoken words are made up of vowels and consonants, the vowels being the stronger and hence perceived at a louder level. If someone said to you:

The boy is going to the shop you would probably have a clear picture in your mind of a child with a basket and some money, running an errand for his mother. You could clearly understand the statement. However, if instead the statement was:

--e -o- i- -oi-- -o --e --o- you would probably have little if any idea of what was being said. This statement is simply the original with all consonants removed. Thus, although vowels have power, they do not provide us with much clue to meaning when heard in isolation: in other words they have a limited contribution to speech intelligibility.

Table I

VOWEL SOUNDS (powerful)	CONSONANTS (weaker in strength)
see	pet
sit	bet
ten	tea
bat	cat
arm	got
hot	child
caught	June
put	fat
food	veil
cup	thirst
bird	the
ago	soap
page	zip
mow	shield
high	vision
how	house
boy	mum
near	not
rare	finger
pure	leg
	red
	yes
	watch

If we listen to the statement again, but this time without the vowels:

Th- b-y -s g--ng t- th- sh-p, the meaning is far more

apparent. The statement has again acquired intelligibil ty. So it is clear that consonants are extremely important in speech, in that they provide the key to the intelligibility of spoken words.

It is therefore vitally important for clinicians to assess a young child's ability to hear both vowel and consonant information. This is why parents will observe that a range of test stimuli of differing frequency content will be used during a hearing test.

The major aim of any diagnostic hearing test is to determine the levels of hearing for the various speech frequencies. If certain speech frequencies are inaudible to the child it will be necessary to consider providing suitable amplification (hearing aid) in order to expand his or her experience of speech sounds.

Testing the hearing of young children

Introduction
Two categories of hearing test are used in the assessment of young children. The first category are known as *screening tests. The aim of this type of test is to identify children with abnormal hearing*, without actually measuring their levels of hearing or determining the nature of any hearing problems. Screening tests are simply pass-fail tests, which are usually carried out by health visitors in local Health Centres or Child Health Clinics. The first screening test of hearing should be carried out between the ages of six and nine months.

The second category of tests are known as *diagnostic tests*. These test are undertaken at a specialist Audiology Clinic, following failure of screening test. The clinic may be located in an Ear Nose and Throat Department of a hospital, in a Regional Specialist Audiology Centre such as the one at Manchester University, or in an Area Child Health Clinic. Such tests are usually applied by audiological specialists who have considerable experience in testing the hearing of young children. *The aim of the diagnostic test is to determine both the degree of hearing loss across the speech frequencies, and the nature of the loss.*

Screening Procedures

The basic aim of the screening procedures is to identify the children with impaired hearing. The first test should be applied to all babies during the first year of life, so that those who have a hearing problem can be helped both medically and educationally at the earliest possible moment.

Although most areas in Britain do apply screening procedures to young children, certain areas still rely on screening only those babies on the 'at risk register', that is those babies whose hearing is at risk because of a family history of deafness, rubella infection in the mother during early pregnancy, or birth complications. This policy assumes that babies who are not 'at risk' will have normal hearing: yet more than half of the babies with sensori-neural deafness diagnosed in our Department have deafness of an unknown or unpredictable nature, and would not have been listed as 'at risk' with reference to hearing. *We would strongly urge all parents to ensure that their children have a hearing test between the ages of 6 and 9 months, regardless of whether the child is on an at risk register.*

The screening test of hearing, 6-18 months

The first screening test of hearing applied to babies is commonly called the distraction test. This test is based on the fact that once children have reached the developmental stage of being able to sit up, with good back and head control, they will turn the head and pinpoint (localise) a sound source in the horizontal plane (i.e. at a height approximately level with the ear). Children generally reach this developmental milestone between the ages of 6 to 9 months. So around this age an appointment card will be sent out by the health visitor inviting the mother and baby to attend the local centre where hearing tests are carried out. Since the sole aim of this initial test is to identify children with hearing impairment, the test is simply a pass-fail one and is generally applied by two health visitors who have received training in the screening of hearing of young children.

Test stimuli

Since hearing tests are designed primarily to assess children's ability to hear the speech frequencies, over low, mid and high frequency ranges it is necessary in the screening procedures to use frequency-specific stimuli in each of these ranges: that is stimuli that produce purely low, mid or high frequency sounds. The distraction tests that are usually used contain sound stimuli specific to the parts of the frequency spectrum relevant to speech, and are designed to be attractive and motivating to a baby. The sounds that 6-18-month-old babies best respond to are sounds that have meaning for them: the human voice, rattles, chime bars. So a voiced sound such as the vowel 'oo' (as in shoe), rhythmically presented, will be used to assess response to the low frequencies; a G chime bar to test mid frequency response; the consonant 's'(air gently blown over the top of the tongue and between the teeth – with no voicing), again rhythmically presented, to test high frequency response. A specialist piece of equipment, the Manchester University high frequency rattle, was specially developed in our department to assess high frequency response.

It is possible to record sound visually, on a machine known as a spectrograph. This machine is able to draw a picture of a sound showing the frequencies that make it up, so by looking at spectrograph images of the test sounds, we can confirm that they do test the specific parts of the speech frequency spectrum for which they were intended.

It is always good policy to present an arousal stimulus during a screening procedure: it is as such a stimulus that the cup and spoon are often used during a distraction test, the spoon being scraped gently against the side of the cup. This stimulus is particularly effective with young children because it is associated with food! But the spectrograph of the cup and spoon shows why this stimulus cannot be counted as a test item. It contains a very wide range of frequencies, so it is possible for a child to hear only certain components of the cup and spoon normally, and still respond (turn); that is, the baby can pass the test while having a hearing impairment. The arousal item is used instead at the beginning of a test to relax the child, and check whether he is able to turn and localise a familiar sound.

Parents may feel at first that the 'waving of rattles' and 'sounding of chime bars' behind a child is a rather crude way of assessing hearing. However, because the sounds employed are chosen specifically because they are appealing to a baby and at the same time frequency specific it should now be clear that they do constitute a scientifically reliable check of a child's hearing across the speech frequency region.

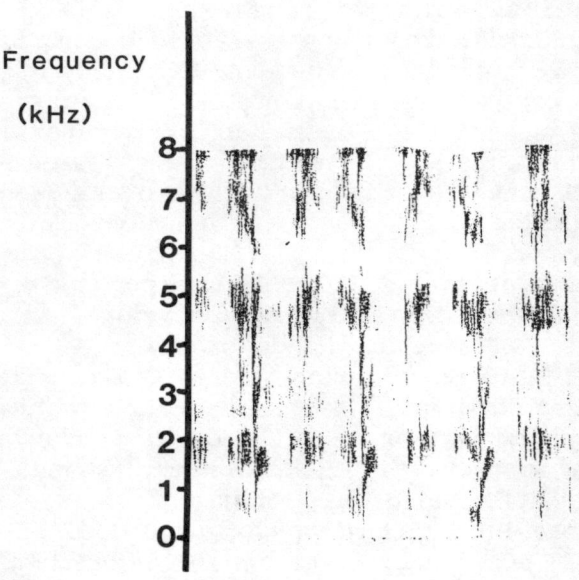

Fig. 8   Spectrograph of the sound of the cup and spoon.

The test procedure
The series of photographs (Plates 1 – 7) illustrates the test procedure adopted during the distraction test. The baby sits on her mother's knee in a slightly forward position, and is supported at the waist. Clearly, the baby must be developmentally ready for this – able to sit up and to turn the head

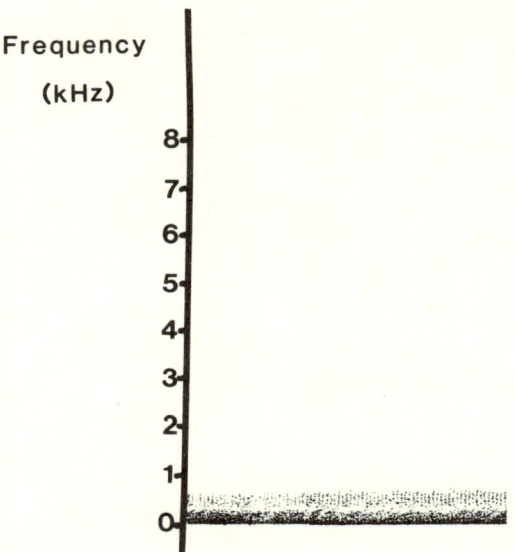

Fig. 9   Spectrograph of the vowel "OO'.

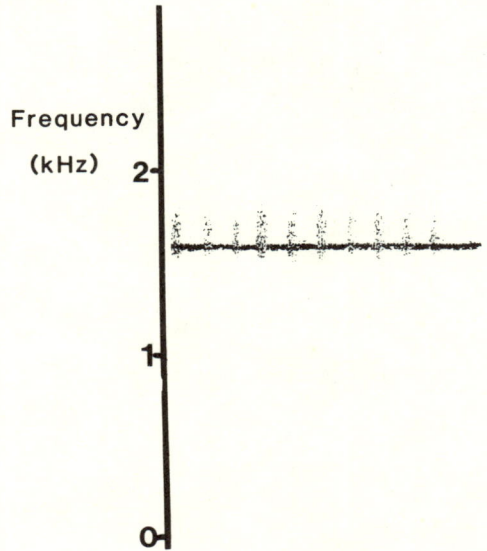

Fig. 10   Spectrograph of the G chime bar.

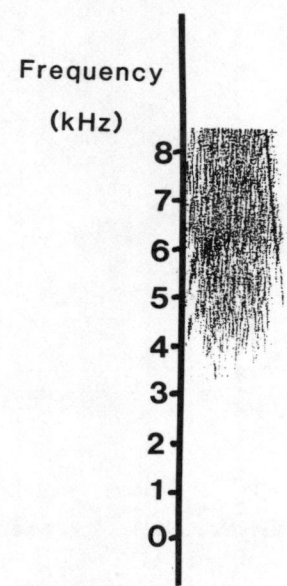

Fig. 11 The Spectrograph of the sound 'S'.

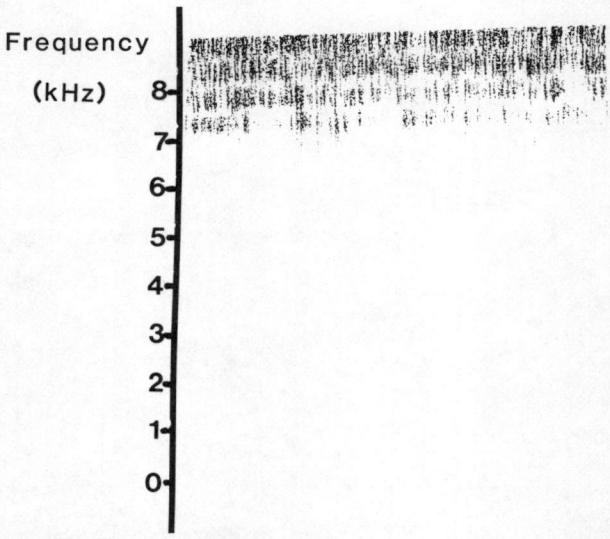

Fig. 12 The spectrograph of the Manchester University High Frequency Rattle.

before the test can be applied. Younger babies such as the one shown in Plate 5 (four months old) are too immature because they have very limited head control (the head tends to flop on to the chest) and are unable to sit without considerable support. They would therefore have great difficulty in turning, particularly to quiet sounds, so testing at this age is unreliable.

The developmental level of the eight-month-old baby girl (Plate 6) clearly highlights the rapid progress children make in their early months of life. The baby has good head control, can sit unsupported and is able to turn her head without difficulty. This child is developmentally suitable for the initial screening test. It is interesting to note however that babies of this age do have localisation difficulties with sounds presented above the head. (Plate 7) This is why the test stimuli are presented on a plane level horizontal with the ear.

Once the baby has settled in the clinic (which by the way should be a quiet room free from extraneous aural or visual distractions, such as from traffic), the test may proceed.

One health visitor will attract baby's attention to the front using, for example, a small toy. The second health visitor will move into position at the rear, three feet from the child, as in the photographs. At the front the toy being used to attract the baby's attention will be removed – perhaps by hiding – and at that instant the sound stimulus will be made at the rear, at a fixed minimal level: this is the level at which normally hearing babies would just perceive it. The child must respond by turning and accurately locating the stimulus. Two responses on each ear for each stimulus must be observed if the child is to pass the test.

The correct application of the test is extremely important. The person in the front must not overstimulate the child in such a way that she is totally absorbed with the toy and will ignore the stimulus. On the other hand the testers must ensure that the child is responding reliably to sound and not to vision (by seeing the tester in the rear out of the 'corner of the eye', because the tester has moved too far forward), smell (tester wearing 'strong' perfume), vibration (tester moving carelessly on a hard floor), or by anticipating that the stimulus is to be presented. It is also important for the tester to ensure that the stimuli are presented at minimal levels. These factors are impressed upon health visitors during their training, and subsequent referesher courses.

If a child fails the initial screening test, it is our recommendation that a further test be applied within a fortnight. Should the child still fail, then referral to a specialist audiology centre should be made routinely.

Although the distraction test may appear to be rather simple, experience has shown that when applied correctly it is in fact very effective indeed in identifying hearing impaired children. On the other hand we know that some children with impaired hearing do pass this initial test. This is not a fault of the test design, but a problem of slipshod testing. Hence we recognise a great need to maintain standards of excellence in screening procedures – the Manchester Department, through the Ewing Foundation, employs an Adviser full-time to train and advise clinicians involved in the screening procedures.

The most important point for all parents to remember is that if they are at all worried about their child's hearing, they should insist on a full audiological investigation at a Specialist Audiology Centre, irrespective of whether or not the child has passed a screening test. Our experience is that when parents are concerned about their child's hearing, in the vast majority of cases they are correct. We wish to see young children referred to us in these early months of life, so that a clear picture of their hearing sensitivity can be obtained. We are happy to see them, and when in some cases it is possible to demonstrate to the parents that the child's hearing is satisfactory or that only a temporary problem (e.g. congestion) exists, we do not see the testing as a time wasting exercise. We see such early testing as a very important role of an Audiology Centre, far more satisfying than seeing a child for the first time at three years of age with no speech because of an unrecognised hearing impairment. Parents, if they are at all concerned about their child's hearing, can with confidence insist that their GP arrange for a full audiological investigation.

This investigation really should take place at a specialist

centre. Many GPs have little or no expertise in assessing the hearing of young children, so that they are ready to test a child who is causing parents concern despite passing screening, by snapping fingers close to his ear, jangling keys, or crumpling tissue paper behind him. Such stimuli are both too loud (that is, not minimal and hence audible to many children with hearing impairment) and too wide in frequency range (that is, they contain all speech frequencies equally) to be accurate indicators of hearing impairment. Indeed if one compares the frequency content of the sound of 'jangling keys' (Figure 13) with those used in the distraction test, the differences are obvious.

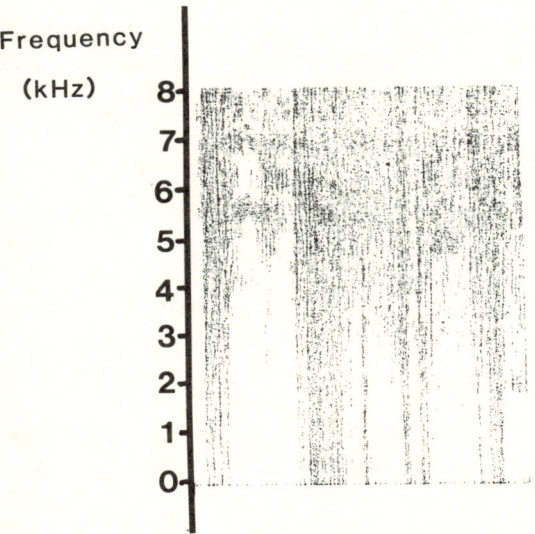

Fig. 13   The spectrograph of the sound of jangling keys.

The co-operative test of hearing. 18 – 30 months
As children grow and mature, it is necessary to apply more sophisticated screening tests. Children in the age range 18-30 months are able easily to inhibit (ignore) sounds as they are presented in the distraction test, so use is made of the normally hearing child's growing understanding of spoken

language. The child is seated at a table, or if he is timid on mother's knee, and the clinician gradually gains a rapport with him, through play. Once the child's confidence has been gained, the tester moves out of vision and into a routine of very quietly spoken requests, presented at three feet from each ear, to which the child's response is measured. For instance, if the child is playing with a set of balls, he may be asked to '**put it in the box**', '**put it on the stick**', '**give it to mummy**', '**put it on the table**', as in the photographs of this test (Plates 8 – 10)

The child's ability to hear the high frequency consonant sound 's', G chime bar and the high frequency rattle would be separately assessed, using distraction techniques, but possibly with the child seated at a table rather than on mother's knee. The application of the test would otherwise be the same as in the distraction tests already described. This approach, combining distraction with verbal techniques, reduces the problem of inhibition sometimes encountered with children in this age category.

The child's ability to localise sound at a distance is assessed by gradually raising the sound level from a chime bar or other noise maker toy, and noting the response.

It is important for parents to realise that children vary widely in their ability to respond to the co-operative test. Failure to complete it is not therefore necessarily proof of hearing impairment. Some normally hearing children of eighteen to twenty months may not be able to understand and follow commands in the way described: this is not an indication of backwardness, simply confirmation that the test range is wide. Clinicians are well aware of this fact, as they are of the negative stage which many two-year-olds go through, when any request to carry out a task is met with a firm NO! In all such cases the distraction test would also be applied as a double check on hearing acuity.

Failure in this age group, as in the earlier one, should be followed by a direct referral for a thorough audiological assessment.

Performance test 30 – 40 months
Children mature very rapidly and by the age of approxi-

mately 30 months screening of hearing may be achieved by use of the Performance test. This test involves the child in a game of some sort, such as putting small wooden men in a wooden boat. The child is trained to wait until the command 'go' is spoken by the tester, then to place a man in the boat. The signal is presented at a minimal level with the tester out of vision at three feet from the ear. The spectrograph of 'go' shows that it is a test of low frequency. The child must respond reliably to two minimal 'go' signals on each ear, to pass. The test is then repeated, using the stimulus 's' as a test of the higher speech frequencies. The tester will again train the child, perhaps by saying '**Now I want you to listen for Sammy Snake. When Sammy says "s" put the man in the boat.**' Having carried out the test a number of times with the child, the tester then positions himself out of vision at three feet, as in the photograph (Plate 11) and presents the stimulus 's' at a minimal level. The child must respond reliably to two minimal signals 's' on both ears to pass for high frequencies.

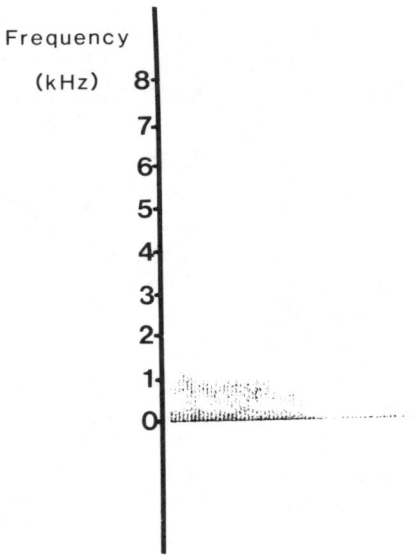

Fig. 14   The spectrograph of 'go'.

If a child fails the performance test he or she should be referred for a detailed investigation.

Pure tone audiometry. 36 months plus
When children reach the age of three years, it is generally possible, with skilful handling, to train them to carry out a 'Pure tone audiometric test of hearing.' This the very same hearing test that adults are given, and it can be treated as a natural development from the performance test: once a child has the ability to wait, and then perform an action (such as putting a man in a boat) in response to the command '**go**', it is a relatively short step to performing the same action in response to a whistle via a headphone.

A pure tone is simply a sound of one frequency, perceived as a whistle, its pitch becoming higher as the frequency increases. It is theoretically possible to measure a person's hearing levels for every single speech frequency: 200 Hz, 201 Hz, 202 Hz, all the way to 7998 Hz, 7999 Hz, 8000 Hz by use of pure tones. But this would be obviously impractical, so we do not test hearing for each individual frequency, but at 'frequency stations' along the speech frequency range. Tests are generally carried out for the frequencies 250 Hz, 500 Hz, 1000 Hz, 2000 Hz, 4000 Hz, 8000 Hz.

The pure tone test of hearing therefore provides the clinician with a very clear picture of a child's hearing levels across the speech frequency range. The machine employed in the test of pure tone audiometry is known as an audiometer. This machine is built to satisfy very stringent specifications, to enable the hearing levels of the person being tested to be compared with the accepted norm. We know that the sensitivity of normal hearing people varies with frequency: the graph in figure 6 showed the variations in strength of the push-pull forces required by a normally hearing person just to hear a particular tone. So the audiometer is designed in such a way that the signal produced during screening is at the accepted norm level for each test frequency. Hence, if a child is able to hear all the test tones at the screening level, we conclude that he has normal hearing.

The test is applied as shown in the photograph (Plate 12).

The child is seated at a table facing the tester with the audiometer between them. The child is fitted with headphones and the tones are presented in one ear. In our department, young children are trained to respond to a tone by putting a ball in a box or a man in a boat as in the performance test. **'I want you to listen for the whistle. When you hear it, put the man in the boat'**. Two reliable responses for each test stimulus must be observed if the child is to pass the test. Once one ear has been tested the tones are directed into the other headphone, and the test is repeated.

Parents sometimes express doubts about the reliability of pure tone hearing tests in young children: 'He was placed in a room on his own. The woman told him to say yes when he heard the whistle. She closed the door and operated the machine from another room and observed him through a one way mirror. I could see he did not understand what he was to do. He was lost!'

Such comments as these concerning a four year-old child, highlight the need for play techniques, with mum close at hand if reliable results are to be obtained with young children. We encourage parents to stay close to their child, to reassure and encourage.

The screening test of hearing of pure tone audiometry is applied to children at various ages during their school lives: often in infant school, then at seven years of age and again in the early teens. Older children respond best to the test by tapping on a table, illuminating an indicator light or simply saying 'yes' in response to the tone.

Failure of the screening test for pure tone audiometry should lead automatically to referral for detailed investigations.

Diagnostic Procedures
The aim of a diagnostic test of hearing is to ascertain actual levels of hearing and the nature of the hearing problem. Diagnostic procedures therefore involve a number of tests.

Parents will generally find that the first thing a clinician will do at the beginning of a diagnostic session is to ask questions about the child: relating to pregnancy, the birth, illnesses since birth, whether the child suffers from frequent colds, whether there is a family history of deafness. This information will assist the clinician in his subsequent investigations, particularly where a hearing loss is present and possible causative agents are being investigated.

The first step after the initial interview will be to apply the formal hearing test. This test will be one of the screening procedures described earlier – the particular test depending on the child's age and stage of development – but adapted for diagnostic purposes. In a diagnostic test the level of the stimulus is gradually raised from the minimal level, until the child responds. In the distraction, co-operative and performance tests the clinician will measure the stimulus level at which the child responds on a special machine known as a sound level indicator, which indicates the strength of the push-pull forces required by that child to hear that stimulus (Plate 13). The level is then recorded and a note made of the stimulus used. If, for example, the diagnostic procedure was a performance test around the word 'go', the clinician would present the stimulus 'go' at a gradually increasing level until a reliable response was observed. This level would then be measured, checked for consistency and recorded.

In the diagnostic procedure using a pure tone audiometric test of hearing, the signal level for a particular pure tone is read directly off the signal level dial. The audiometer used in such tests is designed so that, for a particular test tone, the signal level produced by the headphone is at the normal level of hearing when the signal level dial is set to zero. This means that the result of a hearing test on a normally hearing person would produce hearing levels of zero for each test tone. This is done purely for convenience: the clinician is interested in determining whether or not a particular child has normal hearing; and, if a loss is present, how much above the norm the hearing level is. Thus if a child has a hearing level (threshold) at 30 decibels on the signal level dial, his hearing is 30dB worse than the norm (hearing at 0dB). Since it is conventional to record hearing loss as measured on an audiometer in dB HL, a child with a loss for a particular test tone of 30 decibels, would be said to hear at 30dB HL.

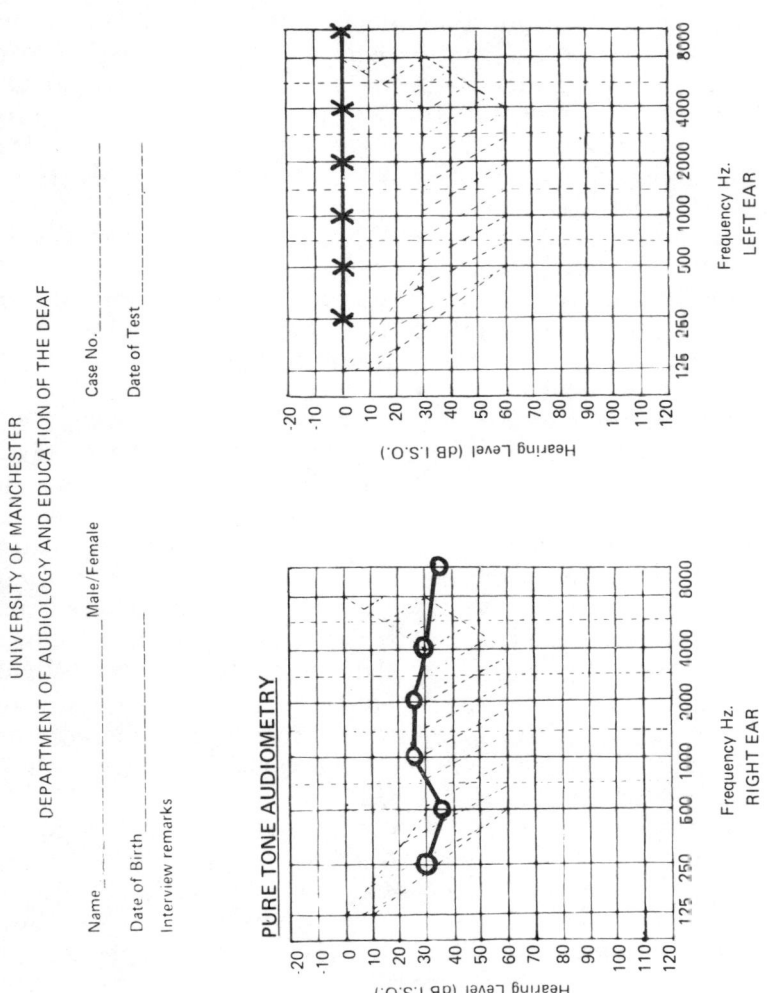

Fig. 15 An example of an audiogram.

The results of the pure tone audiometric hearing test are recorded on a form known as an audiogram. This form comprises a horizontal axis on which the test frequencies are listed, and a vertical axis corresponding to the reading of the signal level dial of the audiometer. The threshold of hearing for each test tone is simply read off the signal level dial of the audiometer and recorded on the audiogram form. An 'O' is used to denote results for the right ear and an 'X' is used to denote results for the left ear. The example (figure 15) shows a child who has a loss on the right ear of 30dB HL at 250 Hz, 35dB HL at 500 Hz, 25dB HL at 1000 Hz, 25dB HL at 2000 Hz, 30dB HL at 4000 Hz and 35dB HL at 8000 Hz. The hearing on the left ear is normal.

In clinical practice, responses are taken as being within normal limits, and therefore consistent with normal hearing, for signal level dial readings of up to 15dB HL.

Tests used to discover the site of the hearing problem
Once the clinician has applied the formal hearing test he or she will try to determine the nature of the problem. You will recall that hearing problems fall into two categories: conductive problems, which are associated with congestion and/or infection of the outer and middle ear and are often amenable to medical treatment; and sensori-neural problems (or nerve deafness) associated with damage to the cochlea and nerve of hearing (inner ear), so no treatment is possible and the problem is considered irreversible. It is obviously vitally important for the clinician to determine the type of loss at the earliest possible moment, so that suitable management strategies can be implemented.

There are three types of hearing loss with which children may present: a pure conductive loss, a pure sensori-neural loss, or a combination of both types of loss (i.e. a sensori-neural loss with a conductive loss on top) which is generally termed a mixed loss. In the case of mixed problems, the clinician will try to organise treatment as soon as possible to clear up the conductive component, because this then enables the child to make full use of the remaining hearing, possibly with help from a hearing aid.

The clinician therefore applies a number of tests so as to

determine whether the loss is conductive, sensori-neural or mixed.

Pure tone audiometry
In a diagnostic procedure involving the use of an audiometer (used with children over the age of three years) a child will hear pure tone signals (whistles) through headphones placed over the ears. When a pure tone is produced by a headphone the signal travels down the ear canal and sets the eardrum into vibration. The vibrations are then conducted across the middle ear by the ossicles (the three tiny bones of the middle ear) to the cochlea, where conversion into an electric impulse takes place. This impulse then travels along the nerve of hearing to the brain where it is interpreted as a whistle. This means that when a hearing test is carried out the integrity of the whole of the hearing mechanism is being tested. Sound has to travel through the outer ear, the middle ear and the inner ear, as is the case in our everyday lives, and it will not be clear at that stage whether the reason for the loss lies in the outer, middle or inner ear. Such tests are termed air conduction tests of hearing, and they measure a child's total hearing.

The clinician will, with children who are sufficiently mature to carry out the pure tone audiometric test by headphones (air conduction), go on to apply a similar test using a small vibrator, which is placed on the mastoid bone behind one ear, to test bone conduction. The child hears the same whistles as before, but this time from the vibrator rather than the headphones. He is instructed to perform a task similar to that used in air conduction testing – putting a ball in a box, or tapping on a table – each time he hears the tone. This test is known as pure tone audiometry for bone conduction. The signals produced by the vibrator by-pass the outer and middle ear system. (Plates 14, 15) They make the skull vibrate, and this stimulates the cochlea and hence the nerve of hearing directly (the inner ear). So air conducted signals travel through outer, middle and inner ear while bone conducted signals simply travel through the inner ear.

A normally hearing person will hear the air and bone conducted signals at the same level on the signal level dial of the audiometer; i.e. air conducted level OdB HL, bone conducted level OdB HL.

If a child shows a loss for air conduction and normal levels for bone conduction, the indications will be that the pathway to the brain centre for bone conduction is normal and not damaged. Hence, the inner ear is normal. As the air conduction level is abnormal the loss must lie in the outer or middle ear, so the loss must be conductive in nature.

If a child shows an equal loss for air and bone conducted signals, indications would be that there must be damage in the inner ear pathway (because the bone conduction sensitivity is depressed) and the outer and middle ears must be normal. This loss would be sensori-neural in nature.

If a child shows a loss for air and bone conducted signals with a greater loss for the air conducted signals, a mixed loss is indicated. This means a loss resulting from a problem in the outer or middle ear which affects the air conduction level but not the bone conduction level; and an added loss resulting from a problem in the inner ear, affecting air and bone conduction levels equally (see example in Table II).

Table II

	OUTER-MIDDLE EAR LOSS	INNER EAR LOSS	TOTAL LOSS
AIR CONDUCTION	a	b	a + b
BONE CONDUCTION	–	b	b
NORMAL HEARING	a = 0	b = 0	
CONDUCTIVE LOSS:	a = 30 (e.g.)	b = 0	

AIR CONDUCTION = 30 dB
BONE CONDUCTION = 0 dB

SENSORI-NEURAL LOSS:	a = 0	b = 40 (e.g.)	

AIR CONDUCTION = 40 dB
BONE CONDUCTION = 40 dB

MIXED LOSS:	a = 20	b = 40	

AIR CONDUCTION = 60 dB
BONE CONDUCTION = 40 dB

Example of how different hearing losses result

The bone conduction test of hearing is a very useful aid in helping to identify the nature of a hearing problem. However, it is only one of a number of tests that will be applied during the diagnostic session, and the clinician will consider the results of all tests before coming to a firm decision. One of the limitations of the bone conduction test with young children is that it cannot be applied unless they are developmentally mature enough to carry out a pure tone audiometric test. The majority of children under the age of three years will not be tested by this technique. In such cases it will be necessary to rely more heavily on the results of other tests.

Another problem of testing by bone conduction is that the bone conductor sets the whole skull into vibration, and both ears are stimulated at the same level regardless of the position of the vibrator on the head. This means that the clinician cannot put the vibrator behind the right ear and test this ear, and then repeat for the left ear as is possible in the headphone testing.

So a technique known as masking has to be employed in order to determine the bone conduction levels of each ear. This involves introducing a continual noise into one ear while the whistle is introduced in the other ear (test ear) in the normal manner. Young children find this procedure very difficult and many are unable to perform reliably on this test until the age of seven years.

Masking is also necessary in air conduction testing if there is a significant difference between the hearing levels of the two ears. This is because for high signal levels it is possible to hear the signal in the opposite ear to that being tested. If the difference between ears is greater than 40 decibels, the clinician will have to apply masking to the better ear so as to ensure that this ear does not hear the signal and so confuse the results for the poor ear.

Thus although pure tone tests are extremely useful with young children, they are sometimes limited in their effectiveness by the maturational development of the child.

The Electroacoustic Impedance Bridge
Once the formal hearing test, including bone conduction

testing where applicable, has been applied, the clinician will go on to another test, known as an impedance bridge test. This involves a machine known as an electroacoustic impedance bridge, which has been developed to aid the clinician in discriminating between conductive and sensori-neural hearing problems by telling the clinician whether the outer-middle ear part of the hearing system is functioning normally. It therefore provides information on whether a child has a conductive component in the hearing loss.

The machine comes in various configurations, depending upon the manufacturer. However, all systems comprise a probe unit (as shown in the photograph, Plate 17), with a small rubber tip attached to its end. This tip is placed at the end of the child's ear canal during the test. The probe unit is composed of three tubes: one is connected to a source of sound which feeds a low pitch tone down the tube towards the eardrum; the second is connected to a very small microphone which measures the sound being reflected from the eardrum; and the third is connected to a pump which enables the clinician to apply small amounts of pressure on the outside of the eardrum, thus making it stiffer than normal.

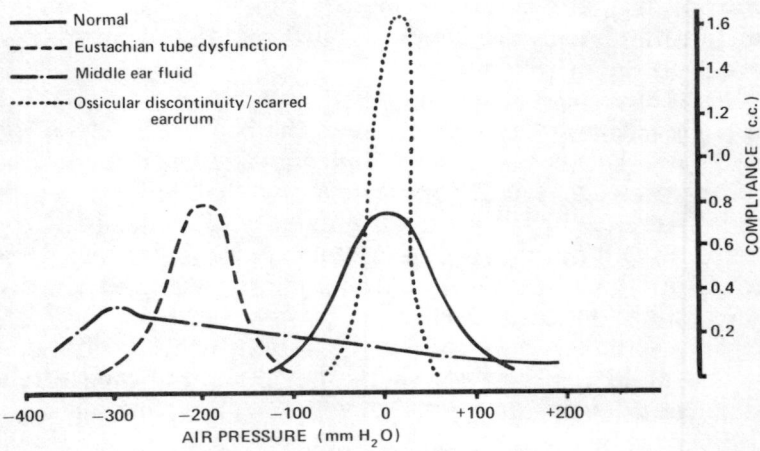

Fig. 16 Impedance bridge results for normal and pathological ears.

In a normal ear, the sound travels down the ear canal through the eardrum and is conveyed across the air filled middle ear cavity by the ossicular chain to the oval window. This is the conductive pathway of the hearing system. Very little sound is normally reflected from the eardrum because it is flexible and relaxed and therefore able to convey sound very efficiently.

If a problem exists anywhere along the conductive mechanism, to make the eardrum become stiffer, the result will be that more sound will be reflected by the eardrum than normal, and thus less sound will cross to the cochlea and nerve of hearing, so a hearing loss will result. The electroacoustic impedance bridge measures how much sound is being reflected from the eardrum, and therefore determines how efficient the middle ear is at conveying sound to the cochlea. This information enables the clinician to determine whether or not a *conductive* loss is present.

The measurement of middle ear function by means of the electroacoustic impedance bridge is a quick and easy test to perform. The measurements are objective, in that the child has to do nothing more than sit relatively still on mum's knee or on a chair, and it may be applied to children of all ages. In our clinic it is used routinely on all children from a few months of age.

In order to carry out the test the child is seated on the mother's knee. If the child is wriggly, and rather tentative about having the probe placed at the end of the ear canal, we ask mother to cuddle him into her, with his head resting on her chest. Parents can feel confident that no discomfort is caused by the test: we apply it to ourselves every day before the clinic, to make sure it is functioning properly, so we speak from experience. Some young children object to *any* strange object being placed in their ear canal, but few children object so violently that the test cannot be carried out.

The child's ear is examined to check that the entry to the ear canal is not blocked with wax. Then a suitably sized rubber probe tip is selected and pushed on to the end of the probe unit. This unit is often incorporated into a head set which is placed over the child's head as shown in the photograph (Plate 16). Alternatively, a hand-held probe unit may be used, which is simply held against the ear at the entry to the ear canal (also shown for reference). The probe is carefully placed in the ear canal and an airtight seal must be obtained before the measurement proceeds. The clinician will check whether this has been achieved. For the test, the clinician simply presses the pump to change the stiffness of the eardrum, and the machine automatically records the variation in the amount of reflected sound as the stiffness varies. A particular shape of pattern will be produced on the chart recorder, according to the condition of the conductive mechanism of the child's ear. The various patterns that are observed with different conditions of the conductive mechanism are shown in figure 16. From these patterns it is relatively easy for the clinician to identify disorders that affect the conductive mechanism in children.

Speech Tests of Hearing
The tests of hearing that have been described thus far are all aimed at furnishing the clinician with information on the degree of hearing loss, and the functioning of the conductive mechanism of the hearing system. Another important measure, that can be applied to children over the age of two and a half years, is a speech test of hearing. Such tests provide the clinician with information on the child's ability to hear and comprehend speech, and are clearly very useful since hearing speech is without doubt one of the most important functions of our auditory system. Furthermore, such tests provide the clinician with information on the overall reliability of the test battery.

The speech test of hearing that will be applied to a child will depend primarily on the child's age and language level.

The Kendal Toy Test
The first test, carried out with young children from the age of about 30 months, is one such as the Kendal toy test. This uses a selection of toys, the names of which should be familiar to most normally hearing children of this age. There are three sets of fifteen toys in the test and the usual

procedure will be to choose one set of toys for a particular child. Each set of 15 items comprises 10 test items and five distractors. The photograph (Plate 18) shows how the test is usually applied: first, each toy will be taken from the box and shown to the child. The clinician will probably ask the child to name the toy – **'What's this?'** – just to check whether the child is familiar with it. **'Yes it's a duck isn't it. Put him on the table.'** Each item is placed on the table in front of the child. The tester then moves three feet away, out of vision, and asks the child to point to different items on the table. **'Have you a magic finger to point with? Right. When I say – show me the mouse, I would like you to point with your magic finger to the mouse. Good. Now listen hard, I am going to speak very quietly'.** The clinician will thus determine the level of voice required by the child accurately to identify the items. The voice level will be measured on a sound level indicator. Then the test will be repeated on the other ear.

It is important for parents to realise that the child is *not* expected to name the items during the test, but simply to give evidence of hearing the clinician by pointing. Such a test is thus particularly effective with children who have speech difficulties.

Here is an example of one of the sets of toys.

TEST ITEMS: knife bath soap tin bus
                  pipe car boat pig brush
DISTRACTORS: wheel jar comb pin duck

It will be seen that the items are grouped according to vowel sounds. You may recall that vowels are essentially low-mid frequency sounds, while consonants fall into the mid-high region of speech, and that consonants are also weaker in strength relative to the vowels. So children with hearing problems frequently have most difficulty in hearing the higher frequency consonant sounds, and therefore often confuse words such as **'bus'** and **'duck'** because they can hear only the vowel sound clearly. The skilled use of the Kendal toy test can provide a clinician with extremely valuable information about a child's hearing. If a child requires a raised voice level in order to perform reliably on the test, this would suggest hearing impairment because normally hearing children are generally able to point to the test items at very quiet voice levels. However, no firm decision on hearing loss will be made until the results of all tests have been obtained.

The Manchester Picture Test

As a child grows older it is possible to apply more sophisticated speech tests. One such test is the Manchester Picture Test, which comprises eight sets of 10 picture cards, one of which is shown in Plate 19. Each card contains pictures of four objects, and the child is asked to point to one specified object on each card. This test may be applied to children from the age of approximately four years. It is designed to test a child's ability to discriminate specific vowel and consonant sounds of speech. Each set of 10 cards tests the child's ability to hear five specific vowel sounds and five specific consonant sounds. If for example the vowel sound to be tested is – e – , as in the word well, the test card will contain pictures of a ball, a wall, a doll and a well. The child would have to hear – e – in order to identify the well, because this vowel sound occurs only in this word on the card.

If the consonant sound being tested is – d – , as in dish, the test card will contain pictures of a tin, a pin, a dish and a fish. Here again only the test word contains the required – d – consonant sound. Hence the child would have to hear – d – in order to identify the dish.

The tester will apply the test for certain fixed voice levels (measured on a sound level indicator), and monitor the child's performance with change in voice level. If voice level has to be raised to a high level before the child scores accurately on the test, the results will support a diagnosis of hearing impairment.

Speech Audiometry

When children reach the age of about seven, their speech discrimination ability is usually tested using speech audiometry, in a test that is also used for adults. The child listens through headphones, which are connected to a tape recorder, to lists of pre-recorded monosyllabic words (e.g. home, catch), presented at a prescribed level to one ear at a time. The child is asked to repeat each test word in turn, and the clinician scores the response in marks out of three.

If, for example, the test word was **house** and the child responded with **house** he would be awarded three points. If the response was *mouse* (i.e. he heard two of the three sounds in the word accurately) he would be awarded two points. If the response was *c*ow he would be awarded one point. If the response was *five* no points would be awarded. A test list comprises ten words, and each test list is therefore scored out of thirty. The clinician will examine the variation in discrimination score with signal level, and compare this with the normal hearing pattern. This comparison provides information on whether the child's performance is consistent with normal hearing, or with hearing impairment.

Decision Making

Once the diagnostic procedures have been completed, the clinician will consider the results of all the tests. If both the conventional hearing test and a speech test have been applied, for instance, the clinician will check for consistency. And the impedance bridge measurement will aid in deciding on whether there are any conductive problems that should be dealt with before any sensori-neural ones are tackled. By this time, the clinician should have a clear picture of: a) the degree of hearing loss; and b) the nature of the loss. So a decision can now be made about the steps that can be taken to help the child.

If there is a conductive element in the hearing impairment, the first thing the clinician will do is arrange for an Ear, Nose and Throat (ENT) examination at the local hospital. It is our policy to review children immediately after ENT treatment, and to check whether improvement has taken place.

In cases where sensori-neural problems are indicated, the clinician will probably inform the parents of the position, discuss its implications and arrange for immediate help from the parent guidance service. During the short interim period that will elapse between the diagnostic session and the first follow-up appointment, the clinician will be organising suitable hearing aids and earmoulds, and briefing a teacher of the deaf about the child.

NOTE: The diagnostic tests of hearing that have been described above are ongoing, and become more sophisticated as the child grows up. They are capable of identifying both the degree and the nature of a hearing problem from a very early age. So, although many of the tests may appear simple, parents can feel confident that they are appropriate and reliable and that they will enable clinicians to plan a strategy of management.

Recent Developments

Over the past few years a number of new procedures for measuring hearing and identifying neurological disorders have been developed. One new procedure is known as Electric Response Audiometry. This may be applied in any one of four ways, but the most suitable for young children is known as Brain Stem Electric Response Audiometry (BSER), which involves placing three tiny electrodes on the head – one on the forehead, one on the scalp and one behind the ear on the mastoid bone as shown in the photograph (Plate 21). These electrodes sense tiny electric signals generated by the nerve of hearing in response to sound stimulation. However, sophisticated and expensive equipment which is available only in a few centres, and has to be operated by specially trained technicians (see Plate 22), is necessary for this type of test, so at the present time screening or diagnosis of hearing by this method on a large scale is impractical. A great advantage of this test is that it may be applied to children from a few days old, and hence can help to identify hearing impairment at the earliest age. However, it does not provide very much information on low frequency hearing, nor does it distinguish clearly between conductive and sensori-neural hearing problems. Furthermore, it is necessary for the child to be quiet during the test, or the results can be totally meaningless. So such tests as the BSER will not replace the traditional tests, but are best used in conjunction with one or more of the tests described earlier.

One area where BSER-type measuring can be particularly useful is with handicapped children. Children who, because of physical or mental handicap, are unable to respond reliably on conventional hearing tests can be tested on BSER and in this way, some estimation of hearing level can be obtained. In such cases measurement of the integrity of the conductive mechanism can also be made, by using the impedance bridge test. An estimation of the child's general awareness and reaction to sound will also be considered before a decision on hearing level is made.

Tests used with neonates – Physiological reactions to sound
The cluster of physiological responses provoked in a new born baby (neonate) by a sudden sound, involves changes in heart beat rate, respiration rate, head movement, body activity, muscle tone, head jerk and eye blink. Studies have been carried out in America, and more recently in the United Kingdom, using such physiological reactions of newborn babies to sudden relatively loud sounds as indicators of hearing integrity.

Recent developments in microprocessor systems have enabled a system known as an auditory cradle to be developed, which measures certain physiological reactions to sudden sound stimulation of a newborn baby. The most suitable time to apply this test is about four days of age, while the infant is still in hospital.

This type of test is however not a replacement for the later conventional tests applied at 6-9 months. It cannot measure actual hearing levels, nor diagnose the nature of the problem if one exists. And it is possible for babies with certain types of hearing loss to pass the test. So the test is really an 'at risk indicator'. Babies who fail on such a test should be closely monitored, and given thorough ongoing conventional audiological assessment, particularly at six months.

Parents should remember however that *all* babies should be thoroughly tested around this time, regardless of any earlier hearing investigations.

Age of diagnosis
There is no doubt in our minds that throughout the United Kingdom the age of diagnosis of hearing impairment in children is at present too high. This is not a fault of the tests presently employed, but a fault in the application of such

tests and a lack of awareness among clinicians of how often parents who suspect deafness, even in children who 'pass' screening, are correct. We would therefore repeat our plea that parents insist on referral to a specialist audiology centre if they have any doubts about their child's hearing, regardless of whether the child has passed screening. We believe that correct application of the aforementioned tests, together with direct referral in cases causing parents concern, will bring the age of diagnosis down considerably.

3 : Some Common Early Reactions to Diagnosis

Why did it happen to us?
When you have it confirmed that your child is indeed hearing-impaired, whatever your prior suspicions and however well you may feel that you have prepared yourself for the news, you will probably feel crushed, empty and alone. No doubt you are frightened by the enormity of the problem and feel inadequate at the prospect of the help your child will need. You may also feel betrayed, let down in the face of all your expectations through pregnancy that were building up to the arrival of a normal, healthy baby. When the baby arrived, that is probably exactly what he or she seemed. Then, as the weeks and months went by perhaps you noticed his lack of responses to common everyday sounds, but continued to hope against hope. Now you feel you have lost the normal child you planned for, indeed thought you had. Your first need may be to mourn.

First, let us say that parents may *feel* inadequate to deal with their problems at this stage. We believe that they are far from inadequate. Parents (or primary care workers) are the *only* people who can really help their child in his early steps towards communication.

On the other hand we believe that parents need, and should have, plenty of help from a skilled guider-counsellor. So if no teacher specialising in parent guidance comes to visit you automatically in the next few weeks after diagnosis, write to the local education authority and ask for a visit. If such help is not provided in your area, contact local councillors and MPs and point out that what is now quite a widespread service to parents in this country and elsewhere, is not provided. As you are helped and guided, so your confidence, possibly shattered by the news of your child's handicap, will grow and you will be better able to give your child the help he needs. *You* are with him all day long, after all; *you* will talk to him, sing to him, *you*, with the help of his hearing aids, will stimulate his language development.

In the early days after diagnosis you may feel that you are not getting much practical advice, since the counsellor will be concentrating on support rather than on specific aspects of the child's development. However he or she will undoubtedly be aware of the pressing need to learn speech and language, social and other skills, and so will be advising on the fitting and use of the child's hearing aids.

Pressing though stimulation needs are, they take second place until families feel ready to cope with what they may initially feel is an insurmountable hurdle.

We have seen many reactions by parents to what they see as a major tragedy. Here is one parent's description:

'Empty really. My wife just broke down. I would have liked to as well, but it would have looked stupid both of us walking through Manchester like that. One of us had to be normal you know. Times are, when things are quiet you think why? – why? and no reason.'

This parent is asking why he and his wife have been selected in this way. It must seem a very harsh world at this time and, even though we go to considerable lengths to show 'why' it happened, parents are unlikely to feel any better even when we have an answer. The point is that they had expected, and looked forward to, the birth of a normal child. To find that their child is handicapped is a shattering of these expectations.

Certain causes of deafness can be identified, as we have shown in Chapter 1, and it may be important for you as parents to know this, in terms of the eventual management of the situation. Perhaps it is even more important for this knowledge to be available in later years for the child himself, so that when he asks 'Why am I deaf?', 'What if I have children?' you will have some positive information for him. However, in the early days after diagnosis the question may not really be 'What is the cause?', so much as 'Whatever the cause why did it happen to us?'

The first phase of any guidance and counselling programme therefore aims to help you overcome your first reactions, and come to terms with the problems of bringing up a child who has a sensory handicap. It is about finding new expectations, new hope; and here we can say with absolute certainty that there are now more possibilities for hearing-impaired children, more chances for their being educated alongside their hearing peers, than ever before. This is not merely due to recent changes in educational policy, but a consequence of developments over many years as hearing-impaired children have gained ever higher levels of educational and social attainment. We will return to the subject of schooling later, but at this point we want simply to highlight the fact that today's parents of a hearing impaired child have room for at least cautious optimism about the future. Early diagnosis, efficient amplification with hearing aids and an encouraging home environment are three major ingredients for good progress in the child. To this your child brings his own ability and personality – as does any child, hearing-impaired or not.

You should feel free to talk to your guider/counsellor, to air any worries, to work through feelings of guilt, fear, confusion or inadequacy. We do not believe this to be a luxury but a vital necessity if you, his family – parents and brothers and sisters – are to be united in the determination to help him to progress. This positive approach will be of inestimable importance to the child in the early years. We shall say more later about counselling, and about 'who helps', but at the time of diagnosis parents need most a trusted counsellor, someone to whom they are not afraid to talk, someone who really listens to what they have to say. This trust has of course to be earned, and professionals in this field are trained to be aware that empathy, not an officious attitude, is likely to help them achieve this sort of relationship.

'I think the biggest thing about parent guidance is you are not on your own. I suppose we have all had our problems, one way or another, and it is nice to think you can pick up the telephone and know that there is somebody there you can talk to if you are not happy about something. I think that is the biggest thing I found, that there is somebody actually interested in your child's welfare and doing something to help them. I don't know how people cope who have nothing at all, because I don't think I could have done.'

It is very easy for professionals in this field to get bound up in technicalities – technicalities relating to hearing aids, or to aspects of teaching the child – and hence not to notice the need of parents for 'someone to talk to about your feelings'. If you find this to be the case, all we can say is: If you demand the time and attention of a counsellor it is a perfectly reasonable demand. Perhaps the child is in fact your first child, perhaps normal child development is something about which you know little. To a certain extent we all practice on our first child and bring a more relaxed and practical approach to subsequent children, but if the first child is handicapped it will be much more difficult to know whether he behaves this way because he is a child or because he is a hearing impaired child? You have a right to ask. Many problems become serious, particularly in the area of social development, simply because parents are not given appropriate advice at the times when problems are presented. So read all you can about deafness, demand counselling time and do not hold back your questions, ask! Take the advice *you* believe to be the soundest, and apply it to the handling of your child.

'In a way really when you have had a child and it is your first child, you are not experienced in bringing up children anyway and perhaps of course you have never met a deaf child or a deaf person before. You have no idea what deafness is. I think it takes years to dawn on you what it is and what it means. And the techniques you are shown in parent guidance . . . now they seem second nature, but really they are not, you have got to learn them.'

Clearly the person who is involved in helping a family with a hearing-impaired child needs to have a sensitivity to all the needs of the family. This goes beyond the skills and specialised training one would normally see as the qualifications of a teacher of the deaf. Many parental needs are not even expressed verbally, yet need to be visible to those trained and experienced in counselling and guidance.

Workers involved in counselling families with handicapped children have reported reactions of shock, grief, resentment, relief, anxiety, bewilderment and many other emotions around the time of diagnosis, and sometimes later on too. Perhaps you have experienced some of these feelings. It is likely that you have. But you were not necessarily overwhelmed by them. Whatever the case, we think that you should receive support through the difficult emotional period; and we also hope that you will receive a whole programme of practical suggestions for the management of your child. We do not even see you moving on from a need for emotional support to a need for practical help. Techniques for coping with emotional reactions to having a handicapped child are inextricably linked with the techniques of ongoing support needed in the education and development of the hearing-impaired child. Added to this, parents and counsellors need each to retain an openness about information on the child and the implications of his particular handicap for future development.

One mother has written that 'A handicapped child is a handicapped family'. This undoubtedly has some truth in it, because there will inevitably be changes in relationships and activities in any family as a result of the birth of a handicapped child. And the concept will surely be useful if it points professionals to consider the whole family rather than just the child. But we feel that there is also a real need for stressing not what is abnormal about your hearing impaired child, but his many normal attributes. He is a normal child with a sensory handicap.

It has also been said that parents of handicapped children tend to suffer from a reaction called 'chronic sorrow' – particuarly if the child is severely impaired. In our culture sorrow is often concealed, and this concealment can on occasions be so extreme as to be mistaken for symptoms of mental illness. So whilst professional workers often stress the tendency of patients to deny the reality of a child's handicap, they may neglect to report something that may in fact be more common: their tendency to deny their sorrow.

Yet no two families react in exactly the same way and this suggests a further principle to us: and that is that you as parents need *individual* support. Whether what you are feeling is disbelief that your child has any problem (often along with criticism of the test procedures), shock and numbness, fear for the child's future; whether you are searching for a miracle cure in transplants, or acupuncture, or special operations – you all need individual and sensitive support.

People also do not realise how frequently the reaction of parents to a diagnosis of deafness is, in fact, relief: relief that you have achieved a diagnosis that confirms what you have thought for a long time, relief that it is deafness and not some worse form of handicap. At the Department of Audiology and Education of the Deaf, University of Manchester, in the period 1968-1974 the age at which most children were diagnosed as hearing impaired and enrolled on the parent guidance programme was two and a half years. It was alarming that the screening procedures had failed to detect the majority of these babies. Yet it was found to be almost universally true that the mothers had suspected that their babies were hearing impaired very early on. We have seen nothing to suggest to us that the current situation is any better. We place great emphasis on the views of parents about their children, and it has been suggested that prior to, and on a separate occasion from the screening test, parents should be asked if they feel that their baby hears normally. If the answer is no, in addition to the screening process, these children should be seen by an expert in testing the hearing of babies.

If you think that your child is hearing impaired, or know of someone else who feels this about their child, press for an appointment at a specialist audiology centre. Do not be put off by anyone, be they health visitor, general practitioner or hospital doctor. If you, the parent, feel that your child is hearing impaired, he almost always is:

'We were convinced that he had a hearing problem long before he was diagnosed. I felt when he was diagnosed – well thank God somebody has finally appreciated the problem. I felt very concerned about it, obviously, but the main thing was that at least now it is diagnosed something can be done about treating it.'

'I began to feel that people – I mean my own mother and

different people – were saying I was stupid to be thinking there was something wrong with him, he was perfectly normal and I really began to think that there was something other than a hearing problem and that it was a mental thing with him – I am sure I was relieved that it was what we had suspected and nothing more.'

'There was a sort of resistance from our parents, on both sides, to the fact that there was anything wrong with him. We felt we were battling, not only against the first doctor who said his hearing was normal, but it was also our families who said "Oh no he's just a slow talker". So you see we met resistance all the way along.'

The child mentioned in this last paragraph was finally diagnosed at almost four years of age.

Parents get repeated assurances that everything is satisfactory, when it most definitely is not. We can assure you that you will not be the first parent of a hearing-impaired child who has been told:

'It will only be wax.'
'You worry too much, he's all right.'
'Don't worry, he's just a slow talker.'
'He's normally hearing' (after keys have been jangled within in his area of vision).

Relief at diagnosis, then, may be your first reaction. But you may not necessarily have an easy adjustment because of it. The last child mentioned above was undergoing all the frustrations that only lack of communication skills can bring. The parents had unwittingly made inappropriate responses at various stages in his development. He was not easy to handle at home and terrible in the shops. His mother reported that on one occasion prior to diagnosis she had been at the end of her tether and tried to 'lose' him in one of the shops in Manchester. She said 'You know that's one thing about deaf children – you can't lose them, can you?'

Yet very soon after aids had been fitted and the family had received counselling, that child was unrecognisable. He became a pleasure to shop with and much easier to handle. The lack of an early diagnosis had meant that mother and child simply did not know how to respond appropriately to each other. It had also delayed the development of the child's communication skills.

The time around diagnosis has been termed a crisis time. But it would seem to us that the early years are indeed a succession of crises, and that ongoing support and counselling are essential if the family are to be helped to face them.

Stress

Readers can readily see from the comments we have already made that there are many areas where stress may arise for the family of a hearing impaired child. What the vast majority of such families are trying to come to grips with is a whole new area of expertise. They are learning how to handle hearing aids, how to understand the limits of their efficiency as well as how to persuade a young child to wear them – the stress associated with unreliable aids or inadequate earmoulds can alone be enormous. Add to this the stress in trying to explain your child's problems to friends and relatives when you are not really sure of their complexities yourselves, fears for your child's future and tensions between family members. Later on you may feel stress as a result of the child's lack of, or apparent lack of, linguistic progress. It is very hard for parents to persist with linguistic input when for long periods they seem to be unrewarded. And there is no doubt that stress you feel as a family can and will be communicated to the hearing impaired child.

Any professional worker who is hoping to help you will need to work towards a reduction of the factors that cause stress, and to respond appropriately in areas where stress cannot be avoided. One parent has suggested that the *external* stresses on the family are what should be emphasised, rather than the more usual concept of the *internally* stressed 'handicapped family'. She points out the paradox that the services – educational, medical and social – are supposed to help handicapped children and their parents, but may actually make them wretched. Among the examples are teachers who give parents unrealistic tasks – tasks they feel they cannot achieve, so this makes them feel

guilty or inadequate. Also criticised are doctors, psychologists and local authority bureaucrats, who do not give
parents adequate information, or give it in an unintelligible
way, or make decisions about handicapped children without
consulting their parents.

Researchers have reported many criticisms of professional practice around the time of diagnosis, practice
which could well be stress inducing. The heaviest criticism
seems to have been reserved for doctors, which is not
surprising since it is often doctors who are the first to tell the
family that the child has a hearing impairment. Parents
over-react at this stage, and they may certainly be unrecep-
tive to information: many parents report not being able to
remember what is actually said on the day of the diagnosis,
however simply it was put. But the research literature is full
of accounts of casual and hasty diagnosis, abruptness and
apparent lack of interest, failure to offer information about
the type, degree of impairment, and possible causes. There
are so many reports that it would be impossible for all to be
attributable to the 'emotional states' of the parents. If you
feel that you and your child have been treated casually, or
hastily, or if more is demanded of you than you can really
achieve, let the services know about it. Services will assume
they are absolute perfection unless you let them know
otherwise.

The authors would like to see the following family support
model adopted throughout the services. It incorporates all
the major specialisms which may become involved with the
hearing impaired child and his family.

In our opinion there is an obvious need for the services for
parents and their children to be co-ordinated, and for one
person to be responsible for the guiding and counselling of
the family. This principle is in line with the recommendation
of the Warnock Committee which inquired into the education of handicapped children.

What we do not want to happen is for this triangle to turn
upside down so that the services which are designed to help
you actually bear down on you and make you feel worse. It
is very important that we professionals sort out our

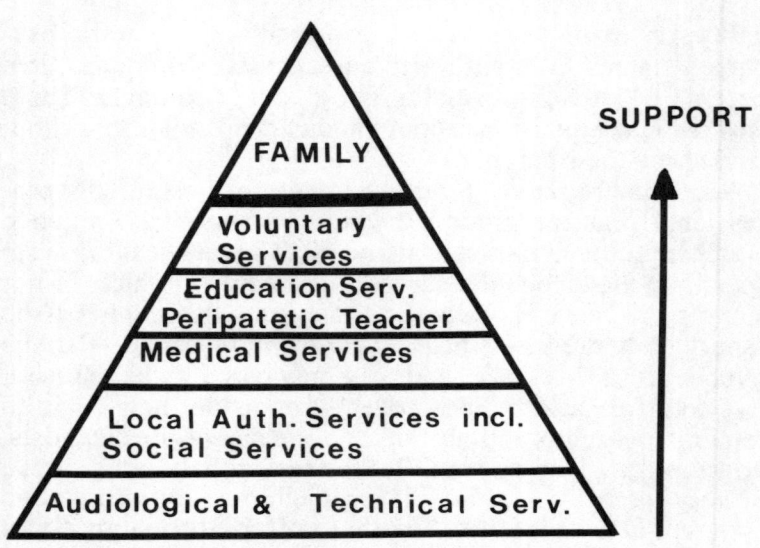

respective roles, and if we do not do it ourselves you must push us to do it. We know that parents may be unnecessarily called to appointments for hearing retests locally when the child's care has been passed over to a specialist audiology centre; and that repeat appointments are made at Ear, Nose and Throat clinics when the loss has already been established as sensori-neural with no involvement of the middle ear, or when the state of the middle ear could just as well be monitored at the routine audiology retests (bearing in mind that with young children the audiology picture is built up only gradually, over a number of years). On occasions minor conditions are monitored at a specialist audiology or ENT clinic when the condition might be monitored locally at much less cost, both financially and in travelling time for the family. These comments are not meant to be a threat to any specialist's authority or responsibility for the management of his patient in the way he thinks best, but rather an appeal for teamwork. We should all ask ourselves the question, 'Do we really need to see this child routinely?' For your part you can ask yourself whether the appointment appears to be beneficial for you or your child, and if you think not, ask why it needs to take place and expect a clear answer. It is a fact of life that children with handicaps need to be checked for other possible problems. But for many families there is a real problem in trailing their children from one specialist centre to another.

This issue we see as quite separate from the one we call 'diagnosis shopping', where the parents themselves seek extra opinions from specialists. There are indeed children who are taken from one centre to another: from Manchester Audiology Department to the Nuffield Speech and Hearing Centre in London, to the Audiology Unit at Reading and so on. Though you may occasionally think that the first specialist has 'got it wrong', this kind of diagnosis shopping is often simply hoping for the miracle – that the next specialist will say the child is not deaf at all, or that there is some miracle cure for this type of deafness. If you find yourself in danger of this kind of shopping, ask yourself the questions 'Do I really need further opinions about my child? Am I really sure he is deaf and just delaying acceptance of this fact, and therefore delaying the steps necessary to help my child make progress?' Always ask the audiologists and doctors who test your children to explain and demonstrate what has been found. If they say that aids or special treatment are required, ask them to describe the aids or treatment and what benefits they expect from it.

Stigma

The concept of stigma is used to refer to a personal attribute that is, or is felt to be, deeply discrediting or undesirable in the eyes of other human beings. Irvin Goffman, an American sociologist, uses the word to cover the problems that handicapped people have with their identities, with how they see themselves. If handicapped people do indeed suffer from stigma, perhaps their families, as one mother has suggested, are stigmatised 'once removed'.

We all know of examples of a hearing impaired child being taken into a shop and the shopkeeper saying 'Oh poor love' and giving her free sweets and fruit, just when the mother is trying to teach her that we go into shops to buy things and that we use money to do this, or to train her to eat sweets only after tea. The mother is put in the stressful position of having to tell the shopkeeper that she doesn't allow sweets before tea.

Try to react to situations such as this one as if your child were normally hearing: if the shopkeeper gives away his stock to all children, then join the queue and accept it. But if he does not give it to normally hearing children, then do not accept it for your hearing impaired child.

Blame and Guilt

One of the most common reactions of parents to handicap in a child seems to be a feeling that they are somehow to blame for it. You may ask yourself the question 'Is it my fault?' Or you may extend the question to 'Is it my husband's fault?' or 'Is it the doctor's fault?' One mother for instance informed us that she had had normal children by her first husband, implying that she felt her second husband was somehow responsible for her hearing handicapped child. This attitude had undoubtedly put a strain on the marriage, and it was very helpful for this family to have an appointment with a genetic counsellor who was able to clear up their misconceptions.

The possibility of experiencing guilt feelings extends right through your child's life. In a way we have already touched on this when we wrote about stress. If you cannot get your child to wear his hearing aids all day you feel guilty, particularly if you see Mrs Jones' Mary wearing hers happily. If the moulds are poor, the aid whistles and you cannot set it to the correct level, you again feel guilty, for not being able to set the aid as instructed by your adviser, although the quality of the earmoulds is largely outside your control. Don't suffer in silence, ask for help! It is sometimes difficult to get hearing impaired children to wear hearing aids, but there are a few tricks that come in handy occasionally, like putting the aid in and quickly involving the child in playing with his favourite toy, or putting it in and immediately going off for a walk, or ensuring that cords etc. are well concealed from pulling fingers. But whatever happens do not worry, your child's hearing aid will certainly not be the first to end up in the goldfish bowl, however 'accidentally'.

We want you to provide as many situations as possible where communication is required between you and your child; but don't feel guilty because some activity you are undertaking does not involve him. Take a relaxed attitude to communication. Learn to 'read your child', get to know what he is interested in and wants to communicate about, and you will have an excellent starting point. Remember that communication involves taking turns, so give the child his turn too! If you are tense about whether or not you are providing 'meaningful linguistic stimulation' for the child, then this tension will be transmitted to him and you may kill the very thing you are trying to nurture. Enjoy him as a child for himself, since as with all children he is not a baby or even a child for long. He will benefit more from the close warm loving bond between himself and his family than from anything else that is done to or for him. If you start from this point then communication will grow outwards.

We are of course aware of the double-bind involved in saying to people who cannot possibly avoid tension, 'Don't be anxious – be relaxed with your hearing impaired baby'. But it may help some parents to hear about someone we know, the mother of very severely hearing impaired twins. We saw them recently in their first half-term holiday after entering school. They looked so smart and grown up in their school uniforms, and we thought how different they were from the frustrated babies we had first seen four years previously. So we asked the twins' mother if, with the benefit of hindsight, there was anything in the way she had handled or managed the children, that she would have changed, if she could. She replied that she would have done the same things, but that if she had known how well they would grow up she would have been far more relaxed and less anxious about doing them.

4 : Who helps! Support Available to Parents

The process of identifying the hearing handicapped child is often, unfortunately, a long drawn out one. So it is helpful to parents, and to other professionals who see the family later, if the parents know *who* they saw for diagnosis and what was said. We would suggest that all parents, when they see any kind of specialist, write things down, because memories at these times are notoriously inaccurate, and it is only by being clear about your child's situation that you can make the best of the services available.

If there is real teamwork operating, as soon as the diagnosis is made, arrangements will follow for the child's aids to be fitted and for the family to receive the counselling and guidance of a peripatetic teacher of the deaf (this is a teacher who visits the home, sometimes called the advisory or visiting teacher of the deaf.) The first session with the teacher may actually take place at the time of diagnosis, if he or she works in close liaison with the diagnostic team. The teacher has special qualifications to help hearing impaired children, in addition to normal teacher training, and may have undertaken further training in parent guidance and counselling – although it must be said that the majority of peripatetic teachers will not have done so. The peripatetic teaching service has in recent years been the most rapidly expanding area of service in the field of special education of hearing impaired children.

Not all of these teachers are involved with pre-school children, though many are. Of 16 Education Authorities surveyed by one of the authors in 1977, 11 had no specialisation in the service for hearing impaired children (so the teachers covered a 'patch' and were involved with all hearing impaired children in their area, whatever the ages of the children), three had pre-school specialists plus general coverage, one had pre-school/infant plus junior/secondary specialists, and one large authority had many specialisms.

This apparent lack of organisation can be accounted for partly by geographical and other problems. In a rural county for instance specialisation is difficult because of the large distances involved and area coverage seems to be the only answer; but with some authorities it can only be accounted for by lack of organisation and direction. It does not seem possible to us for teachers to be guiding and supporting families of pre-school children, with the depth of knowledge that this entails, and still to keep step with all that is going on in infant, junior and secondary schools. There is a real danger in these situations that the teacher will fail adequately to support any of the children in his or her care, or will support some at the expense of others. We would like to see specialisms developing more widely, if only the rather crude ones of pre-school, primary and secondary.

We have already mentioned that there is an increasing number of severely hearing impaired children who have been integrated into normal education. Most of these have benefited from early diagnosis, good amplification and good home-training, so we do not regard this policy as a cheap alternative for local authorities. Such children are unlikely to succeed without the active and continued support of the peripatetic teacher, who should be monitoring progress closely, undertaking specific teaching tasks and advising non-specialist staff. The teacher may visit parents at home or may invite them to attend additionally at a clinic where the teacher is based. Not only do hearing impaired children at home need extensive support from a peripatetic teacher, but children in normal schools need a wide variety of his or her support skills. This means, in our view, that peripatetic teachers cannot efficiently support tens, let alone hundreds of hearing impaired children, as some are doing at this time. If you, as a parent of a hearing impaired child, get infrequent, irregular, or no visits at all from a peripatetic teacher, we suggest that you complain to your Education Department.

In a good service, therefore, there will be a number of positive moves being made right from the time of diagnosis, including fitting of hearing aids for the child and advice for the parents on speech and language interaction with the young hearing impaired child. The counsellor will however not offer too much advice at once, but consider carefully when to give information (he may give the same information several times if he feels it hasn't been grasped or retained), when to listen and when actually to involve you in an interaction situation with the child. We do not believe that parents can be given a *single* course of training. What we do has to be geared to the child's own development, because problems tend to arise in, or relate to particular developmental stages: it is no use, if Mary is having the most awful temper tantrums now, to say 'What a pity we don't get on to tantrums for another six weeks!' If we were asked to select the most fundamental principle of parent guidance, we would say: to respond to the needs of the family at that instant in time. As you will realise, this calls for a first rate knowledge base on the part of the teacher and a very high degree of flexibility.

The time early after diagnosis will certainly be a busy time: visits for tests, for impressions to be made so that earmoulds can be produced, for hearing aids to be fitted; but the peripatetic teacher is usually on hand to help it all along smoothly. People do report delays in fitting procedures, particularly in having earmoulds made, but we can report that the situation is certainly improving. It is ironic that the expensive hearing aid is often kept waiting for the inexpensive earmoulds to arrive!

Partnership – Parents and Professionals
The relationship between the members of the family and those who guide and counsel them needs to be one of partnership. We do not say this in an academic sense, but in a real sense of meeting of minds to share problems and to work together to achieve appropriate solutions. So we believe that the counsellor needs to have an empathetic rather than a sympathetic attitude – to feel with you rather than for you. You may get any amount of sympathy, but empathy may be in short supply! We are also convinced that it helps to have a single main counsellor; or, if there must be more than one, that at least they act in accord in both principle and practice.

There is always a chance that you will receive conflicting advice from professionals. There is more than one way of tackling many of the problems facing the parents of hearing impaired children, so you may even benefit from a variety of approaches. But generally speaking we feel it is consistent advice that is most likely to build confidence in you and your family. So if the people advising you constantly disagree on the best approach you may need to make a decision about whether or not you continue to see them all in the future. Choose an adviser you can trust, rely on and believe in, and if necessary say goodbye to the others.

The Court Report, which contained the recommendations of the Court Committee on the future of the Child Health Services in Britain, concludes that our services for children should reflect the importance of the family in all aspects of child health. There needs to be a close partnership between parents and professional staff. Another recommendation which has the support of the government is the setting up in each Health District of a District Handicap Team. This would consist of a paediatrician, a nurse for handicapped children, a social worker, a psychologist and a teacher. They would be able to call on other specialists in particular handicaps – in the case of the hearing impaired, an audiologist, Ear, Nose and Throat consultant or teacher of the deaf – where the need arose. We see here an ideal opportunity for linking education and medicine. From the medical diagnosis of disorders which are likely to be handicapping, there should be a natural progression into educational help aimed to provide an opportunity of offsetting the worst effects of the handicap. We all need to work to ensure that partnership between professionals, and between professionals and parents, is more than just a word.

In relation to the developing hearing impaired child, there should be an element of partnership in *all* the decisions that affect him and his future. These might involve modes of communication, attendance at nursery classes, eventual school placement and so on. So we see it as our task to provide you, the parents, with as much information as possible: we would arrange visits to a variety of educational settings, provide you with written information material, organise short courses and discussions so that your parental decisions can be thoroughly informed decisions, and our professional advice and opinion sought rather than forced upon you. Given that this form of briefing does take place, we have found that parents are very realistic about their child's prospects and about his needs from the educational system. The main limiting factor is usually the range (or lack of it) of educational provision available locally. In the short run, without a great deal of knowledge of the educational system, you may not be able to influence this, but undoubtedly in the long run parents and parents' organisations can influence what is provided by an education authority, and pressure for better facilties will certainly help future hearing impaired children.

The Wider Family Network and Friends

When the child is diagnosed you will quickly sense the need for extra 'work' with him. This is undoubtedly required if the shortfall in his language input is to be made good. However there is a real danger that other family relationships will suffer because of the extra attention devoted to the hearing impaired child. It is not uncommon to hear a normally hearing sibling say 'I wish I was deaf and then perhaps you would listen to me,' or 'You've always got time to play with her, never with me.' In this way you may find yourselves creating in the other child an enemy in place of a possible ally. Your time must be shared fairly if conflicts are not to result.

There are a number of ways of managing the problem. You may for instance make opportunities for interaction with the hearing impaired child by arranging times when the normally hearing child plays with neighbours' children, or is at the nursery or playgroup, or is engaged by the other parent. If the ages of the children are close, many activities can be carried out together. Essentially, the normally hearing child must feel as little as possible that the hearing impaired child is the centre of all attention, the focal point of every family activity.

A similar conflict can effect the husband-wife relationship. It has often been said, after a marriage break-up, that so much attention was concentrated on the hearing impaired child that the couple felt they hardly knew each other. They had grown apart because all efforts were concentrated on the child, all conversation was about the child. If you are aware of the problem, you can work to avoid this happening.

If for instance you can claim that you never leave your child to go out with your spouse, we would view this not as true devotion to the child but rather as a failure to realise that the marriage relationship also needs attention. We shall refer to this again in the chapter on common problems. At a practical level, however, if you claim that ordinary baby-sitters cannot cope with your child, we would suggest that there would be few situations in which any friendly person who has a child of their own would not be capable of handling a hearing impaired child. Of course it is better if the sitter is known to the child, but this applies to the sitter for any young child.

If you feel very strongly that an ordinary mum could not cope with your child, perhaps the time has arrived for the local parents of hearing impaired children to band together to sit for each other. For it is an important aspect of any child's training to learn gradually to be separated from you. Your child must learn that on occasions you will leave him, but that *you will always come back*. Relatives who see the child frequently can be of great assistance here. And it is better to adopt the policy of planned separation earlier rather than later, perhaps starting with only a few minutes whilst visiting a shop or a neighbour.

It is very likely that your friends and neighbours will be keen to help and yet embarrassed or nervous about what to expect and what to do. Perhaps they think that because the child cannot hear very well, it is pointless to talk to him. (Perhaps you thought this yourselves a little while ago.) You should point out that the child does hear things through his aids, and that he should be spoken to normally. It is helpful if the neighbours see you playing with and talking to the child. You should not on the other hand go into a whole host of technicalities – or the neighbours may never want your child round to play, thinking he is far too specialised for them to cope with!

So it is best to give information when it is requested. For example, a neighbour says 'When Jenny was round at my house her aid was whistling so I thought it was broken and turned it off. Was that right?' This neighbour has not come across acoustic feedback and does not know the tips for dealing with it – check that the mould is in the ear properly and if so turn down the aid a little etc. But these can be quickly learned, and this is the opportunity to teach them. We all want our children to be accepted easily by our friends and neighbours and when they are the experiences can be really uplifting. One neighbour said to the mother of a hearing impaired child, 'When Mary was here the thing in her ear fell out.' She was asked what she did and when she replied 'I stuck it back in of course,' the child's mother almost cried in gratitude for the 'normalness' and 'natural-ness' of the response. She was also able to get in a good teaching point when the neighbour continued 'It was tricky but I managed it.' She showed her how to pull the pinna towards the back of the head and latch the earmould in the ear.

One of the biggest dangers with a hearing handicapped child is that the family becomes isolated, adding to the isolating nature of the deafness itself. But when you are outgoing, your children become so too. They should be encouraged to visit and play with friends, and to have them home. Adults are amazed at the ease with which young children can communicate with one another.

Neither you nor your child will be helped by ignorance (in the sense of lack of information) in the general public. The media, including television programmes, have given a certain amount of attention to deafness, but unfortunately ignorance still abounds. So though it may be hard for you to talk about your child's handicap, it will be very helpful if you can, particularly to people with whom the family is in frequent contact.

Parents' Organisations
Parents can be of inestimable value to each other, in terms

of both practical and emotional support. In Britain, there is a large organisation of parents of hearing impaired children called the National Deaf Children's Society (N.D.C.S.), with a head office in London and branch organisations throughout the country. The N.D.C.S. plays a very important role in representing the interests of families with hearing impaired children. It also publishes useful literature for parents, including a lively magazine for parents called *Talk*, and organises courses and conferences throughout the country. The organisation puts a good deal of effort into educating the general public about the needs of hearing impaired children. They see this, as we do, as a very important prerequisite if hearing impaired children are to take their place fully in the hearing world. N.D.C.S. also have a research committee and fund research into various aspects of deafness.

At a local and practical level N.D.C.S. have started a scheme they call 'Dogsbodies'. The Dogsbodies are mothers of older hearing impaired children, or interested volunteers, who attend a short course and then act as volunteer help to families with hearing impaired children. They can baby-sit, for instance, or look after the other children whilst the mother attends a clinic appointment with the hearing impaired child.

The Social Worker
Most social workers are generic, that is they deal with a full range of problems and do not specialise in any. But there are in some parts of the country specialist social workers for the deaf who provide a range of services for hearing impaired people. You might enquire as to whether there is one available to you. Such a specialist will know just what support services there are for the hearing impaired locally. If your social worker on the other hand is not a specialist, you may have to do some of the research on services yourself.

Most of the provision is related to the school-leaver or adult, but there are special aids and allowances available to children too. For example, if your child is two years old, and severely hearing impaired, you can apply for a Child

Attendance Allowance. A severely hearing impaired child does require a lot of attention and stimulation and the allowance is intended to help enable you to provide this. The leaflet on the Child Attendance Allowance is NI 205, available from the local Social Security Office. You will be visited by a doctor representing the Attendance Allowance Board, and it is helpful if you make sure that the doctor is made fully aware of the severity of the child's handicap – a back-up letter from the Audiology clinic or from a child's visiting teacher can help.

If however you feel that the allowance is a charity you can do without, you might just ponder the possibility that if saved it could provide the spare aid the National Health Service do not provide, so that your child will never never be without a functioning aid; that it may provide additional educational toys for you to use with him; or that, if you otherwise feel you have to work to help the family budget, it might give you the opportunity to spend more time with the child. All these are good reasons for accepting the allowance as a *right*, a right you would want to support for other parents with handicapped children.

Pre-School Playgroups Association
The Pre-School Playgroups Association can give you useful information on local playgroups, including guidance on helping a child to settle into his playgroup; or support and training to start one.

Toy Libraries
Throughout the country there are now toy libraries, where parents can borrow toys which are of educational value to their child. The Toy Libraries Association also produced a very useful booklet called *'Hear and Say' – Toys for Children with Hearing, Speech and Language Difficulties*. Some of the toy libraries also organise play-schemes.

The Local Education Authority (LEA)
We have already described the special role of the Local Education Authority's visiting teacher of hearing impaired children, but we want to mention the general role and

responsibility of the LEA to provide education for every child, appropriate to his age, aptitude and abilities. If a child is aged two or over and his parents believe that he requires special education which he is not receiving (and it is our firm belief that the education of hearing impaired children of this age should wherever possible be in the home) then they have the right to ask the Local Education Authority to have him assessed. Parents also have the right to attend the child's assessment, and to be given information on the nature and extent of the disability, and on the child's needs in terms of education.

When decisions are being made about a child's educational placement, Authorities should (although it is not law that they do) follow the procedures laid down in the Department of Education and Science (D.E.S.) *Circular 2/75 Special Education (S.E.)*. Forms are completed by the teacher (S.E.1), the Clinical Medical Officer Child Health (S.E.2), and the Educational Psychologist (S.E.3). There are places on all the forms for parents to make their views known. Finally form S.E.4 is filled in by a representative of the Authority, summarising the findings of forms 1-3 and recording the decision about whether special education is required, and if so where the child should be placed. Things do go wrong, parents are not always adequately consulted or even adequately informed of what is going on, but we believe that the above procedures if adhered to form the basis of a satisfactory assessment procedure. The educational provision for hearing impaired children is also the responsibility of the local authority, and in Chapter 9 we discuss in some detail the support provided for hearing impaired children in normal schools, in special classes in normal schools (sometimes called partially hearing units) and in special schools.

The Audiology Technician
Most big hospitals have an Audiology department, often attached to the Ear, Nose and Throat Department. You may be sent here to collect hearing aids and batteries, and possibly to have earmoulds made for the child. If the department has a paediatric audiology facility the child's

initial audiological assessment may also have taken place here. In a good department the Physiological Measurement Technician, who has special training, will keep a good range of spares for the child's aids and it should be possible for him to borrow an aid of the same type when his breaks down, unless his is a very unusual or specialised type of aid. It should also be possible to get enough batteries to save you attending too frequently, and to obtain a spare receiver for the child's aid. In many places you will meet a skilled technician who cares whether your child has the correct equipment and makes special efforts to help. If however you find that spares are never available, the moulds are never satisfactory, or there is never a spare aid of the same type, then you should not hesitate to complain directly to the technician in charge, and also to the peripatetic teacher who should be able to advise you of further steps to take.

The Otologist or Ear Nose and Throat Surgeon
This doctor specialises in the treatment of certain diseases which can give rise to hearing problems. He will be based in the ENT department of the local hospital, and it is usual for him to see all hearing impaired children in his area, including children with sensori-neural deafness. This is necessary because it ensures that no *conductive* hearing problems are overlooked. He may also see your child with the peripatetic teacher when retests of hearing are being carried out.

The Health Visitor
We have put the health visitor last, not to indicate that she is least helpful, but rather to draw attention to her role. A good relationship between parents and health visitor can be extremely useful where it is found that the child has problems, provided that there is also close liaison between the specialists dealing with the handicap and the health visitor. We believe the major role of the health visitor in respect of hearing impairment is to identify the child during the screening process, and to provide support after diagnosis while relationships are built up with workers from the specialist services for hearing impaired children. Problems

only arise where inappropriate advice is given on the basis of a superficial knowledge of the special problems of deafness and its remediation. What we have already said about liaison between professionals would apply here.

5 : The Hearing Aid: How To Get the Most Out of It

The Hearing Aid
The term 'hearing aid' is used to describe a wide range of equipment, both naturally occurring and man made, which amplifies or increases the intensity (loudness) of certain sounds. In earlier times people used animal horns and sea shells to improve hearing. Since then, technology has advanced and sophisticated hearing aids have been developed.

Many people think of a 'hearing aid' as either a rectangular box worn on the chest with a lead running to the ear (the body worn hearing aid), or a small unit that fits in or behind the ear (the 'in the ear', ear level or post aural hearing aid). There are, however, a wide range of hearing aids in use with hearing impaired people, and in this chapter we shall describe some of these systems. We shall use the term 'conventional hearing aid' to describe the most commonly used types of hearing aid, which pick up sound that is travelling through the air and make it louder: that is, the body worn and post aural aids. Other hearing aid systems include some that have been in use for many years, and some that are very recent introductions into the field of amplification. All of the systems described are designed to improve the auditory experience of the hearing impaired. In children the quality of hearing experience is of very great importance, because without effective experiences of the sounds of speech they will have very little chance of developing speech and language.

The need for a hearing aid
Children learn to talk and develop an understanding of speech through hearing the sounds of speech. Language development proceeds most rapidly in the early years of life, progressing from simple babble to complex sentences in the short space of about three years. If a child's hearing is such

that some or all of the sounds of everyday conversational speech are inaudible, then that child's speech and language will be severely restricted. This is the main reason why it is so vital for all children to have a hearing test early in life.

When a child is found to have a hearing impairment, the clinician will decide whether or not a hearing aid is warranted. It is almost certain that in the case of sensori-neural deafness, where no improvement in hearing is possible, an aid will be recommended. In conductive conditions the clinician may well decide to wait, for in many such cases recovery occurs spontaneously or following medical treatment.

The clinician's primary concern is to *ensure that a child makes full use of the residual (or remaining) hearing*. Therefore, if the fitting of a hearing aid is felt to be the only way of ensuring that the child will hear some of the sounds of conversational speech, a hearing aid must be fitted.

A child's ability to make use of his residual hearing depends to some degree on the severity of the hearing loss. From our experience with hearing impaired children, we have found that spoken language does develop, even in children with very severe hearing losses, provided that *efficient amplification is given at an early age and the parents are given support and guidance*. However, it is vital to realise that the handicap of sensori-neural hearing impairment is a serious one. A hearing aid will not restore a child's hearing to normal, in the sense that the child will hear as the normally hearing hear. The hearing aid will give the child experience of sound that would be otherwise unheard, hence it plays a very valuable role in the child's sensory stimulation and contributes greatly to subsequent development of language.

Selecting a suitable hearing aid
The type of hearing aid issued to a particular child will depend primarily upon the degree and nature of the hearing loss, and the age of the child. Parents often ask whether their child should have one or two hearing aids. This will depend upon the degree of loss in each ear. However, should the losses be such that amplification in both ears would benefit

the child, then we would always provide two aids. When one is fitted with glasses one expects to have sight improved in both eyes, not one. Similarly with hearing losses; we feel that both ears should be aided if this is desirable and practically possible. Adult hearing aid users have indicated to us on many occasions that the quality of hearing through two aids is far superior to that through one.

There are two main designs of hearing aids in use with children: the *body worn aid* and the *post aural aid* (see Plates 27 and 30). There are many models of both, variously designed to help people with different degrees of hearing loss; and the clinician who selects the hearing aid for a hearing impaired child will consider the full range from both commercial and National Health Service (NHS) sources. All hearing impaired children in the United Kingdom are provided with conventional hearing aids free of charge. There is therefore nothing to be gained in purchasing conventional hearing aids privately. (This does not include radio aid systems, which are discussed later in the chapter.)

The clinician, as we have said, has at his disposal the whole range of conventional body worn and post aural types to choose from, although he is expected to give some priority (not technical) to aids on the Government call-off contract arrangement. In general, the body worn aid is better suited to very young children, partly because it is much easier than the post aural type to secure firmly to the child (see Plate 30). It is therefore less likely to be damaged or lost during everyday play activities. Furthermore, the amount of amplification available from a body worn aid is, generally speaking, greater than that available from a post aural aid. This is primarily a characteristic of the ear mould, which will be discussed shortly. Since *the reception and development of language is the goal that parents and professionals are working towards in hearing impaired children, factors influencing the reception of speech and language far outweigh cosmetic aspects of hearing aids at this time in the child's life*. The aim should be to ensure that the child uses his residual hearing to the full, so as to have every opportunity of developing speech and language. Hence, the majority of severely and profoundly deaf children are fitted with body worn hearing aids in the early years of life. Consideration will be given to the issue of post aural aids as the child gets older. Technically speaking it is possible, at this later stage, to fit children with post aural aids, even if they have the most severe losses.

Concern has been expressed that high levels of amplification could further damage the residual hearing of profoundly deaf children. There are conflicting opinions on this, but there is no conclusive evidence to suggest that damage is caused where amplification is carefully applied. We would justify such amplification, on the simple grounds that without it a child would not have the opportunity of hearing enough speech to develop his own speech and language. Carefully applied amplification with regular follow up does in any case ensure that any slight change in hearing will be noted. There are those who would ask what use hearing is, if it is not to aid the development and use of communication skills?

When the clinician is making his decision on which type and model of aid is most appropriate to a particular child, he will be trying to choose one that produces a sound environment most closely resembling that of the normally hearing person. Once a particular model of hearing aid has been selected the clinician will arrange for the provision of suitable earmoulds.

The earmould
The type of earmould required will depend upon whether the hearing aid is of a body worn or post aural type. The distinction may be seen in the diagram (figure 17) and photograph (Plate 26) of the earmoulds used with body worn and post aural hearing aids. The earmould for use with the body aid has a circular ring clip in the back face. This locks on to the receiver and supports it during use. The post aural mould is somewhat simpler, having only a tube running through it which carries sound from the ear hook of the aid down towards the eardrum.

The main purpose of the earmould is to feed sound from the hearing aid down the ear canal towards the eardrum. The mould therefore couples the hearing aid user to the hearing aid. *Each individual hearing aid user requires his or her own personal earmoulds.* These will be made at the audiology clinic or hearing aid centre where the hearing aids are issued.

Earmoulds are manufactured by either a one-stage or a two-stage process. Both processes involve a technician taking an impression of the child's ear (see Plates 24 and 25). The material used for impression taking is generally a soft rubbery substance such as silicone rubber. This is introduced into the ear by hand or injected with a syringe. It will harden within the space of a few minutes without discomfort, and then be removed.

Children do sometimes show distress during impression taking sessions, especially at the early ones. This is a very natural and understandable reaction to a rather strange procedure. But with careful handling and encouragement the vast majority of children soon become accustomed to the ritual and show no distress on subsequent occasions.

After the impression has been taken and removed, it will be processed into the final earmould. In one-stage processes the impression itself acts as the final earmould, so all that is required is for tubing and possibly a ring clip to be fitted before the moulds are ready for use. This is generally done on the spot and avoids any delay in fitting the hearing aids. In two-stage processes, which account for the majority of children's earmoulds, the impression will be sent to a specially equipped laboratory where the final earmould will be manufactured.

Detailed research studies carried out in the Department of Audiology and Education of the Deaf, University of Manchester, have shown that soft acrylic, silicone rubber and vinyl earmoulds are best suited to children. *Parents should therefore try to ensure that their children are fitted in one of these materials if this is practically possible.*

There will obviously be a time interval between impression taking and earmould fitting in the two-stage process. However, this should be of the order of only one week and certainly no longer than two weeks.

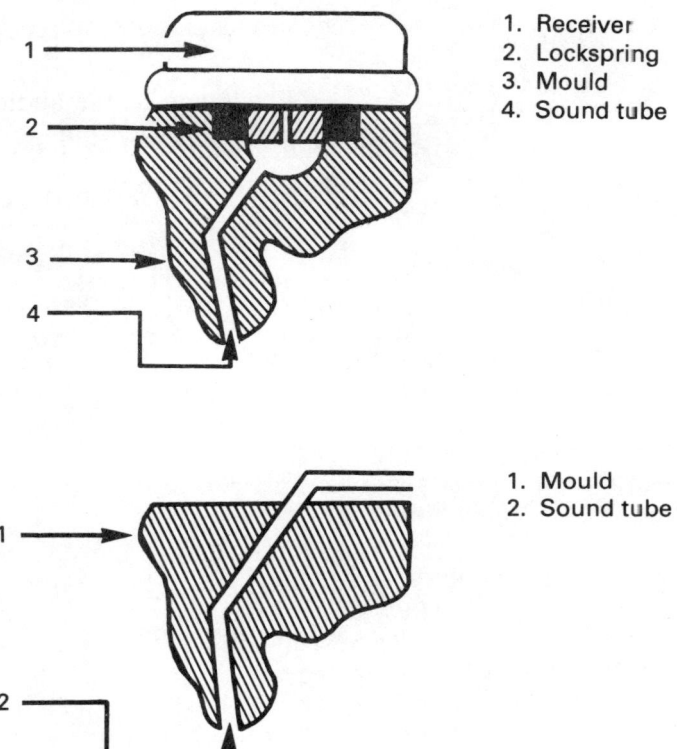

1. Receiver
2. Lockspring
3. Mould
4. Sound tube

1. Mould
2. Sound tube

Fig. 17 Earmoulds for bodyworn and postaural hearing
aids.

Once the earmoulds are ready for use, the hearing aid will
be set and fitted by the clinician.

Setting the hearing aid
A child's hearing aids will be adjusted and set by the
clinician, so that those sounds of normal everyday conversational speech which the aid can amplify are presented at
a comfortable level for the child. This is not an easy task and
parents should always take note of their child's reaction

when wearing an aid. If a child shows an adverse reaction, perhaps by crying when exposed to certain loud sounds, this indicates that the hearing aid is producing sounds too loud for the child to tolerate. This may be due to a problem known as *recruitment*, which means that the subjective loudness of any sound grows at a very rapid rate so that the child is able to tolerate sounds only within a relatively narrow loudness range. This problem can be overcome by setting the hearing aid so that the loudest sound delivered does not exceed the discomfort level. However the child may be issued with specially designed aids known as *compression hearing aids*. These deliver the range of everyday sounds to a child at a comfortable level, while retaining the quality of the signal. Such aids are desirable for children suffering from recruitment, because gross adjustment of the output limitation control switch on a conventional hearing aid will reduce the quality of the information being received.

Problems of recruitment in children are generally recognised at diagnosis or during the fitting of the hearing aid. However, on occasion they do not become apparent until the child has begun to use the hearing aids in everyday life. It is therefore important for parents to keep an eye on their child's use of hearing aids and to report any adverse reactions to the clinician or visiting teacher of the deaf.

If a child is to derive maximum benefit from his hearing aids it is vitally important that the aids are used efficiently. Efficient use will depend to some degree on the clinician who selects and sets the aids; to some degree on the parents who are responsible for the day to day use of the aids; and to some degree on the professional workers who will advise the family until the child enters school. Efficient amplification therefore requires a concerted team effort.

It must be possible to set the hearing aids at the required volume setting without producing acoustic feedback.

Acoustic feedback

Acoustic feedback is a characteristic high pitched whistle that sometimes occurs in a hearing aid, caused primarily by 'leakage' of sound as a result of poorly fitting earmoulds.

Sound leaks out of the ear canal from around the earmould and is picked up by the microphone. It is then reamplified and directed through the earmould again, more leakage results and so on. In other words a 'feedback loop' is formed, and produces the high pitched whistle. A hearing aid that is producing acoustic feedback is obviously performing inefficiently and speech heard through it will be distorted. The problem must be remedied by provision of a new earmould. Meanwhile, the only way to remove feedback until a new mould is produced, is by turning down the volume control, but this will clearly result in the child receiving less linguistic stimulation.

Parents often find it very difficult to obtain satisfactory earmoulds for their children. There is no doubt that the provision of good quality earmoulds depends on the expertise of local technical services, and that this varies according to which part of the country you live in. Parents must not, however, be put off, they must insist on a new earmould should their child's mould prove unsatisfactory. *You are not being a 'nuisance' if you ask for further impressions and moulds to be made. So where very high gain settings are required, for instance, insist on silicone rubber moulds, as the most likely to give the required acoustic seal, and always insist on a good fit. Good earmoulds and good amplification are a key to your child's prospects for linguistic development.*

The problem of acoustic feedback may also arise in body aids, because of sound leakage at the coupling point between receiver and earmould. This is not as significant a problem as an unsatisfactory earmould, but certainly contributes, particularly in cases where high output levels are being used with severely and profoundly deaf children. The difficulty can very easily be overcome by replacing the plastic sealing washer on the receiver with a thin layer of 'blutac'. This material is positioned as shown in the photograph (Plate 23) around the base of the receiver. Care must be taken to ensure that the sound hole of the receiver is not blocked. Once the 'blutac' is in position the receiver is pushed firmly on to the earmould and an excellent acoustic seal at the coupling point will result.

Encouraging the wearing of the hearing aid.
Once the procedure of selection, setting and initial fitting of
a hearing aid has been completed, the next step is to get the
child to accept and wear it. It is vital for parents to encourage
their child to wear the hearing aids consistently, as soon as
possible: remember that the aids will provide the child with
experiences which are at the very root of language development. We continually emphasise to the parents of the
children attending our clinic the importance of the hearing
aids, and guide them through this initial 'breaking in' period;
and we find that the children in fact adapt very quickly.

In the first few days of use, children may often pull out
the receiver of a body aid, or pull off the post aural aid
completely. However a calm, cool, unconcerned strategy of
immediate replacement – 'Oh dear, it's fallen out' – com-
bined with distraction of the child's attention to a toy or
perhaps a drink will soon overcome this problem. It takes
children a little time fully to appreciate the value of a hearing
aid, and this period will clearly vary from child to child.
However, it should be weeks rather than months. The most
positive policy is to engage the child in various sound-making activities. Give her experiences of talking – hold the aid
microphone close to your mouth, cover your eyes, say
'peep', and uncover your eyes 'bo'. Repeat, covering the
child's eyes. Sing to the child. Encourage her play with
noise-maker toys, such as drums, chime bars or simply a
hammer banging a wooden peg. Give the child experiences
of everyday domestic noises – cutlery chinking, the sound
of water gushing out of a tap. Experiences of sounds such
as these will certainly be the most positive factors in
encouraging the child to wear the hearing aid. (See Plate
41).

If a child shows clear and consistent rejection of a hearing
aid and it proves impossible to gain acceptance, this
indicates that a real problem exists. Some children, as we
have already mentioned, have loudness tolerance problems.
In other cases a sharp earmould may be causing a sore ear,
or the child may suffer from an allergy to the earmould
material which causes itching in the ear. Another possibility
is that instead of giving out an intolerably loud sound, the

aid is emitting no useful sound at all. Hence, it is equally important to ensure that the output is adequate, as it is to ensure it is not too great. There is, in other words, no point in starting off on an aid at too quiet a level with the idea of gradually working up, because at very quiet output levels the child will be unable to hear any sound and will therefore have no motivation for using the aid. All these factors will require discussion with the clinician who fitted the hearing aid.

Everyday use of hearing aids with children.
It is a fact of life that young hearing aid users rely very heavily on their parents to ensure that their aids are used to their full potential. Children generally are not able to set their own aids, or even to fit them during the early years of life. Furthermore, they very rarely indicate when a fault arises, even when it results in reduced, distorted or even total lack of output from the hearing aid. Therefore, the parents and later on the teachers have the responsibility of ensuring that hearing aids are well maintained and used to maximum effect.

So that the adult can ensure that a hearing impaired child derives full benefit from his hearing aids, it is imperative for him or her to have a basic understanding of what a hearing is and what it does. It is vital to be familiar with the separate building blocks, or units, that comprise a hearing aid; and to be able to pinpoint minor faults and rectify them without recourse to a technician. Hearing aid centres should have spare aids, so that a child need never be without an aid altogether – but a replacement is not always of an appropriate type, and any deficit of this kind becomes an additional handicap. Even adult hearing aid users report that, when for some reason they are without an aid for a period (as when it breaks down on holiday), they are set back in perception terms by far more than the length of time they were without the aid. For young children deprived of their aids as they are acquiring language, the effect might be critical.

The Conventional Hearing Aid
Both conventional body worn and post aural hearing aids are in fact made up of a group of individual units or building

blocks (see figure 18) connected to one another in a particular order.

The units that comprise a conventional hearing aid are: a microphone; an amplifier; a battery; a lead; a receiver; an earmould. Each unit plays a vital role in the overall functioning of the hearing aid, and the aid will not function satisfactorily should a fault develop in any one of the units. *The aid is only as strong as the weakest link in the chain of building blocks.*

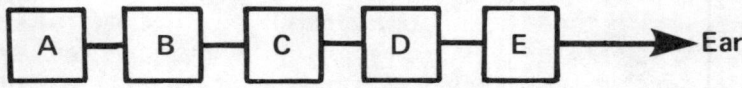

The units comprising a conventional wearable hearing aid.

A — Microphone, amplifier, other controls i.e. the 'hearing aid' box of either body or post aural type.

B — Battery

C — Lead

D — Receiver

E — Earmould

Fig. 18   The conventional wearable hearing aid.

Although in physical appearance the body aid may look quite different from the post aural aid, they are in fact basically the same. The major difference is in the size of the components that constitute each system: the body aid case houses battery, microphone and amplifier and is linked by a relatively long lead to the receiver and earmould, while the post aural aid case houses *all* components, with the exception of the earmould.

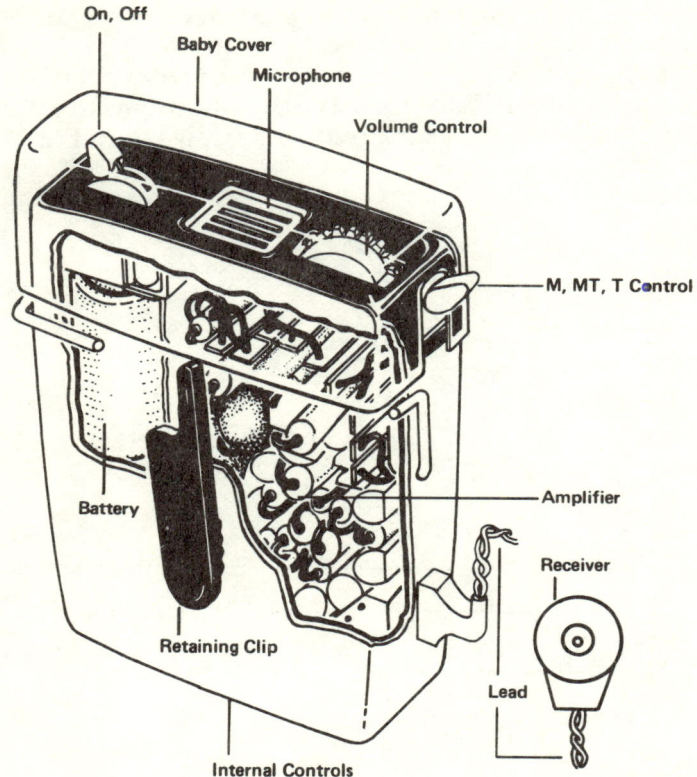

Fig. 19   A conventional body worn hearing aid.

The mode of operation of a conventional hearing aid

A hearing aid is designed to pick up many of the sounds of everyday life, and to increase the intensity, or loudness, of these sounds. The basic principle involved is shown in the illustration (figure 21).

What actually happens may be described in the following way: When we speak to one another, as we have already seen, our vocal organs generate tiny forces that alternately push and pull the air molecules surrounding these organs.

These air molecules pass on the push-pull forces to their neighbours, and the forces therefore travel out from our mouths through the air. Eventually these forces may fall on our eardrums, and if they do, they cause the drums to vibrate and, if our hearing is unimpaired, we perceive the vibrations as sounds of speech.

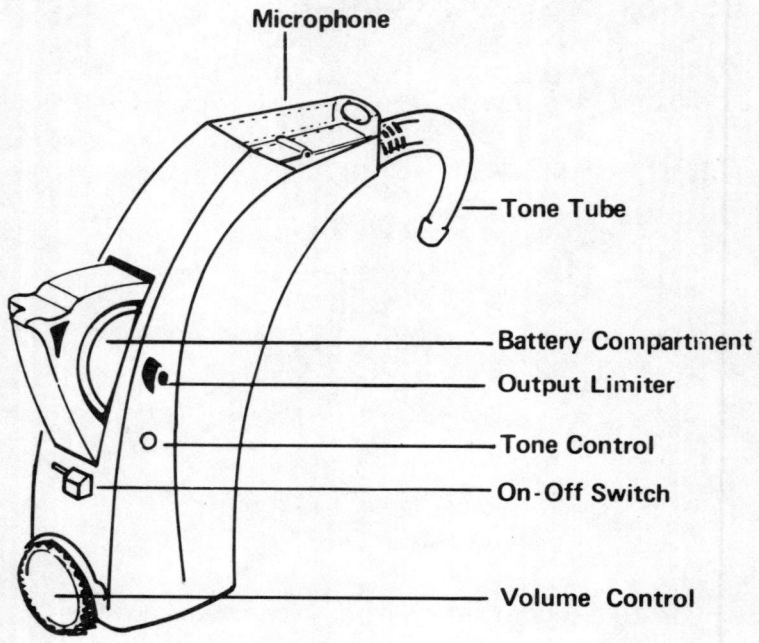

Microphone

Tone Tube

Battery Compartment

Output Limiter

Tone Control

On-Off Switch

Volume Control

Fig. 20   A conventional post aural hearing aid.

Any other object that vibrates will, like the vocal chords, produce push-pull forces of sound.

Supposing that our hearing on the other hand is impaired, the push-pull of the vibrations may need a boost before we can perceive them as sounds. This is what a hearing aid can do.

The first building block of the hearing aid is a *microphone*. Its job is to sense the tiny push-pull forces travelling through the air, and to convert them into electrical signals. These electrical signals are then boosted, or amplified, by the *amplifier* in the hearing aid. Bigger electrical signals now travel along the hearing aid *lead* to the *receiver* unit. Here they are converted back into their original push-pull-force form, that is the receiver sets the air molecules around it into vibration. The forces are, however, now bigger than those sensed by the microphone in the first place, because of the amplification in the hearing aid. They are directed through the *earmould* towards the eardrum, on which they have a bigger push-pull effect than would have occurred without amplification. To the hearing impaired child, to whom the original sound was inaudible without the aid, the sound may now be audible.

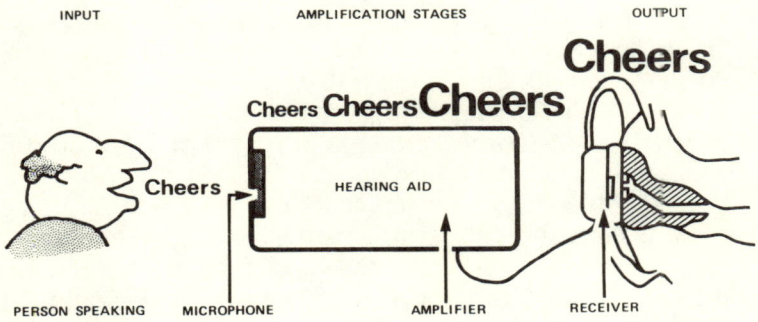

Fig. 21 The basic mode of operation of a hearing aid.

Conventional aids, body worn and post aural, all work on this principle of sensing and picking up sound travelling through the air, amplifying it and then directing it through the earmould to the user's eardrum.

All of them also need a source of power. Just like a radio, television or a tape recorder, a hearing aid is driven by electricity, and it will not work unless a source of electricity is provided. The hearing aid *battery* is this source. The battery is therefore as important a component of the hearing aid as any other.

The building block units of conventional hearing aids.
It may be useful at this point to consider in detail each of the
basic units of the hearing aid system, together with the
relevant control switches.

The microphone.
As you can see from the diagram of the body worn aid (figure
19), the microphone is generally positioned on top of the
hearing aid case. It will thus be directly below the chin when
fitted in the normal wearing position. Its job, as we have
already seen, is to pick up the sound waves travelling
through the air and convert them into electrical signals. So
the microphone needs to be a very sensitive instrument, and
although designed to stand up to general everyday wear and
tear, it is liable to damage, particularly from the bumps and
bangs of the child user's play activities. *It is therefore good
policy to protect hearing aids from unnecessary damage*,
such as for example that caused by being dropped on the
floor. A nice looking harness, such as shown in the
photograph (Plate 43), together with a hearing aid securing
clip, will ensure that the aid is held firmly and will not fall
out when the child bends down.

It is clear from the diagrams that both body worn and post
aural aids have design features inappropriate to child users:
they have, as a rule, been designed for adult users, not
children, and manufacturers are only now beginning to
confront these problems. In the body worn aid for instance,
the siting of the microphone is directly below the chin. In
addition, since it is so important for the child to have the best
possible opportunity of hearing his own voice – that is, to
get the auditory feedback necessary to language development – the microphone will normally be an upward facing
one. However, when a young child is eating or drinking there
is a good chance that food or drink will fall down on to the
microphone grill and that after relatively little use the grill
will become so blocked, or fluids will so damage the
microphone, that the aid will no longer work (Plate 37).
Hearing aid manufacturers have recently begun to issue
baby covers made from clear plastic to clip over the top of
the aid, not only to protect the aid from everyday enemies

such as food, water, sand and paint, but also to prevent the children from tampering with the controls on top of the aid (Plate 30). Such covers have no significant effect on the amplification produced by the aid.

If the model of hearing aid used by your child does not come with a baby cover, you can babyproof it yourself by wrapping the aid tightly in cling-film sandwich wrap (Plate 35). Remember to pull the cling-film tightly over the microphone grill. In the long run however, it is to be hoped that hearing aid manufacturers will realise the shortcomings of these design features and consider the use of satellite microphones for young children.

Problems of food spillage do not arise with post aural aids of course, because the aid is worn behind the ear. However, there is a much higher risk of damage to post aural aids from falling than to body worn aids. This is because young children's ears are soft and small and often have difficulty supporting the weight of a relatively large instrument, particularly during the rough and tumble of play. Try using surgical tape to secure the aid in place, should it fall continually out of the ear.

The microphone of the hearing aid may be switched in and out of the system by means of the M-MT-T switch that is situated on the casing of conventional body worn hearing aids. This switch enables the child to use the aid in one of three ways, though generally speaking the aid will be set to the M setting, which means that the microphone is picking up sound waves, converting them into electrical signals and directing them to the amplifier in the ordinary way already described. When this switch is set to the T setting, on the other hand, the microphone is no longer sensitive to sound and the aid will pick up sound only if used in an *inductive loop system*, such as may be used in a classroom. This system will be described in detail later – see page 123. For the time being, it is sufficient to remember that *that aid will not pick up ordinary sound if the switch is set to the T position.*

The MT setting enables the microphone to pick up ordinary sound waves in the vicinity of the aid, and also to pick up information from the inductive loop system at the same time. However, the amplification for a particular volume setting will be less with the aid on MT setting than on the M setting. *It is therefore important to set the aid to M setting unless a loop induction system is in operation.*

Most post aural aids have only an M and a T setting. In such cases the M setting should be used unless information is being presented via an inductive loop system.

The amplifier

The hearing aid amplifier is constructed from transistors and is situated in the casing of the aid. The basic principle of its functioning is shown in the diagram (figure 21): the amplifier increases the magnitude of the electrical signals coming from the microphone, and the degree of amplification, as well as the range of signals amplified, will depend upon the setting of the controls. As in a radio or record player amplifier, the amplification can be selective of lower, higher or middle range frequencies.

The On-Off switch

The on-off switch controls the power to drive the amplifier. It is very important to switch the aid off when not in use, otherwise the batteries will run down and their power will be wasted.

The volume control

The volume control switch increases or decreases the amount of amplification produced by the amplifier. Generally speaking, on most body worn aids, the volume controls are numbered. The clinician who fits the hearing aid will advise the parents on the required volume setting. *Parents should ensure, by regular checks, that the aids are set to the required setting.* If a child has two aids, it is quite possible for the volume settings to be different on each. The clinician will decide this on the basis of the hearing loss in each ear and the response characteristics of the aid, which may be different for the same volume control setting. It is a good policy to place a sticky label inside the casing or on the back of the aid with the required levels for each aid and the ear into which it is to be fitted. There will thus be no confusion.

We have already made the point that conventional hearing aids have some design features unsuitable for young hearing aid users. One of these is that many post aural aids have no markings at all on the volume controls, so it is necessary to mark the control with quick drying paint at the setting required by the child. Parents should always ensure that this is done when the aids are fitted, otherwise they will find it impossible to set the aids at the correct level in the future.

The tone control

The tone control switch enables the clinician to vary the relative amplifications of the range of frequencies handled by the amplifier. As a result, subjects with various shapes of hearing loss can be helped by the same hearing aid. There are generally three positions on the tone control switch, N, H and L. The N control means that the aid is working normally. The H control is a low frequency or bass cut, and the L control is a high frequency or treble cut. The tone control will be set by the clinician and should not be altered.

Many modern aids now have internally situated tone controls. In such cases it is clearly impossible for the control to be disturbed. With aids that have an external, manual tone control, it is important for parents to ensure that it is always set to the required position.

Output control limitation

Hearing aids, as a rule, incorporate a control to set the maximum amplification that the aid can deliver (output limiter). This control will be set by the clinician. It is situated internally and requires a special tool to alter it. Once set, it should not be altered except by the clinician. This control protects children from unwanted amplification of loud sounds such as doors banging, heavy lorries and road drills that could cause distress if they were greatly amplified by a hearing aid.

If a child continues to show distress reactions to sounds after the aids have been fitted, it is important that the fact be reported to the clinician. He will investigate and remedy this problem.

The battery

The hearing aid battery can and does have a very significant effect upon the performance of the hearing aid. Unlike the other units, the battery must be replaced regularly, or the amplification delivered by the aid may become so low that the sound will be below the child's hearing threshold.

A body worn hearing aid is powered by either one or two penlite batteries. The post aural aid is powered by a single button sized battery. These batteries are shown in Plate 36.

When a body worn hearing aid is in use, it will gradually drain the resources of the battery. The output from the aid therefore falls gradually, as the power of the battery decreases. It is very important to ensure that the output from a child's hearing aid remains steady at the level recommended by the clinician. It is therefore imperative that the parents change their child's hearing aid batteries regularly. Interested readers can refer to the table below and see that the battery life in many hearing aids is very short indeed. indeed.

Table III

HEARING AID	BATTERY REPLACEMENT PROCEDURE
MAICO WINDSOR EL. Mk. II	THREE TIMES A WEEK (MONDAY, WEDNESDAY, FRIDAY).
PHILIPS 8140, 8146 *(Except PP Receiver)	ONCE A WEEK (MONDAY). *TWICE A WEEK (MONDAY, THURSDAY).
BW 61	TWICE A WEEK (MONDAY, THURSDAY).
BE 11, 12, 13, 14, 15,	ONCE EVERY THREE WEEKS.

Suggested battery changing guidelines.

One major reason why parents must change children's hearing aid batteries regularly is that the children themselves are unable to compensate for any decrease in output resulting from a gradually decaying battery source: if the children were mature enough to adjust their own aids, and eventually, when the battery was of no further use, to judge when to change it, this would increase battery life. However, young children are unable to do this, so their parents must ensure that the output from the aids remains steady at the volume setting recommended.

Ideally parents should familiarise themselves with the output level required by their child. This means developing a daily routine of switching the aid on, holding the receiver to the ear and listening. This procedure familiarises parents with the power output required by the child, so that they will recognise when the output of an aid has dropped to an unacceptable level. Guidelines on battery changing routines can only be approximate, because the lifetime of a battery depends on a number of factors: such as hours of use daily, volume setting, age of the battery. However, the guidelines should alert parents to the need for regular battery replacement.*

The button shaped battery used to power post aural hearing aids is usually a mercuric oxide cell – zinc air cells, which are identical in appearance, are now in use as well, but in the United Kingdom only on a small scale. The button cell, as it is commonly known, has a different discharge characteristic to the penlite cell. Whereas the penlite cell output fades away slowly with time, the button cell remains at the same power level and then breaks down suddenly. This means that the output from the post aural aid remains steady over a relatively long period of time; and in addition that it

*Parents may be interested to know that it is now possible to obtain an audio-visual alarm system which indicates when the battery of a hearing aid is in need of replacement. This alarm is contained in a small plastic box which is connected to the hearing aid. The alarm emits a bleeping tone and flashes a warning light when the battery voltage has dropped to an unacceptable level, and remains on until a new battery is inserted. Further details may be obtained by writing to the Department of Audiology, University of Manchester.

is very easy for the parent to determine when the battery needs replacing, because the aid simply stops working.

And now a word of caution about the button sized battery, as yet another example of a design feature not geared to child hearing aid users. The battery compartments on post aural hearing aids are easily accessible even to young, inexperienced but exploring fingers, so that it is very easy for a child to remove the battery, swallow it himself or drop it on the floor for even younger fingers to find. The button batteries are smooth, small and round (see Plate 34) and therefore only too easily swallowed. And the mercury cell is a source of potentially fatal poison should it leak while in the child's stomach. Studies have indicated that corrosion of these batteries in the gastric juice is quite rapid, so leakage may occur in less than six hours. It is thus essential for parents to ensure that spare batteries are kept in a safe place away from children; and if they find any evidence that the child is tampering with the battery compartment, to secure the compartment firmly with surgical tape.

It is also important to check when replacing a hearing aid battery that the new battery is in good condition. This can be done in a body aid by fitting the battery correctly in the manner indicated in the battery compartment, switching it on, setting to maximum volume, and holding the receiver away from the microphone. A shrill whistle should now be heard. If no whistle is produced then the battery is probably faulty.

In a post aural aid you simply fit the battery, turn the volume control to maximum and hold the aid close to the ear canal, with the sound tube directed towards the canal. A clear shrill whistle should be heard. This check should be done daily with all post aural aids, to make sure that the battery is not in need of replacement.

It is bad practice to leave hearing aid batteries in an aid that is not in regular use. The batteries may leak and seriously damage the aid.

The battery can have a very significant effect on the amplification of a hearing aid, and this in turn can be critical to a young child. It is only by developing good habits of checking regularly and replacing the battery that parents can ensure that their child enjoys continual steady amplification.

The lead

The hearing aid lead runs from the output socket of the body worn aid to the receiver, and carries the electrical signals from the amplifier to the receiver. It is imperative to ensure that this lead is in first class working order. You can check this by switching the aid to a comfortable volume setting, while holding the receiver to the ear. The lead on the body aid does have well known weak spots at the points where stress is the greatest: at the connector junction of the lead and receiver, and at the output socket of the hearing aid. So wiggle the lead at the weak spots (see Plate 31) and listen for intermittent noises, or distortions of sound, either of which would be indications of a faulty lead.

One reason why faults develop in the lead is that people coil the lead in the wrong way during periods of non use. The photographs (Plates 32, 33) show the correct and incorrect ways to coil a hearing aid lead. Two sizes of lead are available, and parents should obtain short leads for young children: to conceal long lengths of lead beneath children's clothing is difficult, and often causes discomfort or distraction to the child.

The lead in a post aural aid is simply a tiny length of wire situated in the aid casing. It does not therefore present a problem to the user.

The receiver

The final unit of the wearable hearing aid is the receiver. This unit is situated internally in the post aural aid and is not accessible to the user.

In the body aid, the receiver is a button-shaped unit with a small nipple on one side that clips into the earmould. Its job is to convert the electrical signals from the amplifier back into sound to be passed through the earmould to the eardrum. It is therefore known as a *transducer*.

A child will be fitted with a particular model of body aid, and a particular type of receiver: any make and model of body aid may be used with a range of receivers, and the receiver will be chosen according to the child's individual hearing loss. For example, one receiver may produce a very high power output signal, while another receiver may produce a lower output, covering a wider or narrower range of frequencies. Thus choice from a range enables people with different degrees of hearing loss to be fitted with the same model of hearing aid.

It is very important for parents to be aware of the particular receiver chosen for their child, as an unsuitable or incorrect receiver will result in unsuitable amplication for the child. All receivers are coded, as may be seen in the photograph (Plate 29). *Parents should therefore check that their child has the correct receiver at all times.* It is particularly important to keep checking once children begin school, because they sometimes swop receivers with their classmates!

The vast majority of modern body worn hearing aids are used with *subminiature (small) receivers*. These receivers have replaced the conventional sized receivers (see Plate28) that are generally used with adults. The authors regard this as a very desirable move, because young children's ears are unable to support the relatively large receivers, which then often cause the earmould to tilt in the ear resulting in acoustic feedback. Alternatively, the moulds may fall continually out of the ear during everyday use. This clearly limits the effectiveness of the hearing aid and causes frustration and worry to the parents. All parents should therefore insist that their children are issued with subminiature receivers, which are freely available, so there is no reason why they should not be provided.

Steps to follow to make sure that the child derives maximum benefit from the hearing aids
Fitting
Once the child has settled down to consistent use of hearing aids, it is vital for the parents to ensure that efficient amplification is enjoyed at all times. The aids should be fitted as part of the dressing of the child every morning.

When fitting the body aid it is advisable to use a clean, well fitting harness. There is a wide range of these harnesses designed for children, and parents can either make them themselves, or buy them from one of the suppliers listed at the end of this book. It is important to ensure that the microphone of the hearing aid is not covered by the cloth of the harness, as this will muffle the sound; and that the aid is held securely so that it does not move about during everyday movements. Such movements cause clothes rub, which is distracting for the child and also reduces the efficiency of the hearing aid.

The ideal placing of twin body aids in a harness is shown in the photograph (Plate 43). The aids are positioned about six inches below the mouth so that the child is able to hear his own voice as well as the voices of other people. *It is vitally important for a child to be able to hear his own voice, because he is then able to hear himself practising sounds.*

NOTE that it is advisable to put the receiver in the ear on the same side of the body as the aid (see Plates 38, 39) so that the child is able to pick up clues as to the direction of sound.

Parents should check the aid and ensure that it is working properly before it is fitted to the child. Remember to listen through the hearing aid to test the battery power. On body aids, ensure that the lead is functioning by wiggling at the weak points.

Check the earmould before it is fitted; make sure that it is clean and that the sound tube is free from wax. When the aid has been fitted and the earmould placed in the ear, set the aid to the desired output level. Check that there is no acoustic feedback by getting the child to turn his head from side to side and up and down – these movements should not produce the feedback whistle. Once this procedure is complete the parent can feel confident that all is well with the hearing aid.

At the end of the day the aids will be removed when the child gets ready for bed. And as the child grows it is good practice to encourage him not only to clean his own teeth but also to clean his own earmoulds (Plate 40).

Our ears secrete wax. This is nature's way of keeping them clean. However, if the narrow sound tube running through the earmould becomes blocked up with wax, the result will be that little sound will get through, so it is therefore very important to clean the child's earmoulds with a little warm water and soap. A toothbrush is very useful for this purpose, as it can clear out any deposits of wax in the sound tube. The earmoulds are as important as the hearing aid itself, so it pays to look after them and keep them clean.

Once the aids have been removed from the child, they should be switched off and stored in a place of safety. The leads of the body aid should be coiled up as shown earlier.

Faults in hearing aids – curing and caring

Acoustic feedback whistle is one of the most common of day to day problems, and in children's aids it will have arisen because the child has outgrown an earmould. Children (including their ears), grow very quickly in the early years of life, so it is necessary to replace earmoulds frequently: generally at three monthly intervals, though individual variations are wide. A good guideline is: change the mould when it becomes difficult to obtain the desired volume setting without producing acoustic feedback.

Parents sometimes discover that their hearing impaired child has bitten the tips of his earmoulds, or generally damaged them. This is clearly an undesirable habit, and steps should be taken to stop it. If all else fails it is possible to buy a liquid (bitter aloes, which is also used to cure 'finger nail nibblers') that can be painted on to the mould. The liquid has an awful taste but is quite harmless. It is also useful to have a spare set of earmoulds in the home, in case of loss or damage. This will mean that the child will not be deprived of a hearing aid when awaiting a new earmould.

Hearing aids are also almost bound to develop faults, and more so with child than with adult usage. It is therefore advisable for parents to have a 'spare parts kit' in the home so that running repairs can be carried out.

Such a kit should include batteries, leads, harnesses and receiver, and possibly a spare hearing aid – or if not, access to one immediately should the child's aid develop a fault that you cannot cure.

If a child's aid does develop a fault, it will often be due to a minor problem – such as a broken lead – which most parents, with the spare parts kit, could solve without having to travel to see the hearing aid technician. The most common faults are: the aid is completely dead; sound is intermittent; output is low. It is therefore useful to adopt a fault finding procedure which you can follow before setting out to see the technician.

a) Examine the earmould and ensure that the sound tube is not blocked with wax.

b) Check that none of the controls – such as the M, MT, T control – have been altered.

c) Replace the battery – recheck the aid.

d) Replace the lead for the body aid – recheck the aid.

e) Replace the receiver for the body aid – recheck the aid.

As you move through the stages c to e, leave the new component in the aid even if the fault remains. Dual faults do occur and could otherwise be missed.

If none of these steps rectifies the problem, it will clearly be necessary to seek the urgent help of the technician.

It can be seen from this list that there is a higher probability of minor faults developing on body aids, where more units are exposed to everyday interference, than on post aural aids where it is possible to check only earmoulds and battery. It is therefore more likely that technical help will be needed to repair faulty post aural aids.

Calibration of hearing aids

The centres which supply hearing aids should have (though in many cases they do not) specialised equipment to check that the hearing aids are working to their design specifications. During continual use certain components, particularly on children's aids, may begin to perform poorly. Such a drop in performance may not be revealed by the simple routine checking procedures we have described, so it is imperative for parents to have their child's aids professionally tested regularly. Three-monthly checks on specialised equipment at the hearing aid centre would seem to be both practical and adequate.

Summary of guidelines for effective amplification

If a hearing impaired child is going to make use of his residual hearing, he will rely very heavily on good long term amplification. It will help greatly if parents adopt certain routine procedures. We would suggest the following guidelines:

a) Always use a clean well fitting harness with body aids. Leads should be tucked under the clothes so that they are kept out of the way and do not irritate the child.

b) Check the whole system – aid, lead, receiver, battery, earmould – before fitting each day.

c) Clean the earmould every night.

d) Change the batteries regularly. Store them in a safe place away from children.

e) Adopt a procedure of aid fitting that is part of dressing the child in the morning – removal being part of getting ready for bed at night.

f) Ensure that the aids are well maintained and protected from everyday enemies such as food and sand. Get the aids checked on the calibrated specialised testing equipment at three-monthly intervals.

g) Provide the child with a rewarding experience of sound, and hence help him to appreciate how valuable the hearing aids are to his everyday life. Value gradually brings respect and care for the aid.

Other types of hearing aid systems

One factor that does limit the effectiveness of conventional hearing aids relates to the nature of sound. The energy generated by a sound source, such as the vocal organs, becomes smaller and weaker as it travels through the air. The further away we are from the source, the quieter the sound is perceived. But a hearing aid microphone cannot discriminate between sounds. It converts background noise, for instance, as well as speech. As a result, the difference between background noise and the speech signals will become smaller (i.e. noise may become as loud as speech) as the speaker moves away from the hearing aid. Thus, hearing aid users can have great difficulty in understanding speech at a distance. The distance between the hearer and the speaker may cause the energy of the signal being picked up by the microphones to become so weak that the amplifier cannot increase it sufficiently for it to be perceived. Alternatively, the signal may be totally swamped by the noise in the vicinity of the microphone.

Steps have been taken to try to overcome this basic problem. Systems have been developed to try to render the level of the signal delivered to the hearing aid user constant, regardless of the relative positions of speaker and listener. Such systems also help to improve the listening experience in noisy conditions, thus making speech more meaningful.

These systems will now be discussed.

Alternative mode of operating a conventional hearing aid: the Loop Induction System

A conventional hearing aid may be used in one of three ways, according to the setting of the M, T, MT control switch described earlier. For normal everyday use this control should be set to the M position, when the microphone of the aid will pick up all environmental sound and convert it into electrical signals ready for amplification by the amplifier.

If this control is switched to the T setting, however, the aid will no longer amplify the sound that is impinging on the microphone. It will pick up signals only from a loop induction system, which may be installed in the home or in the school.

The loop induction system involves a wire placed around the room in which the system is to function. This wire can be situated at any convenient height (e.g. around a skirting board or under carpets), and may be run around door and window frames without causing any problems to the system. It is then connected to the source of sound which will drive the loop: a TV set, or record player, or a microphone and amplifier as is used in some schools. The basic arrangement of a loop induction system is shown in the diagram (figure 22).

If, for example, the loop is being driven by a teacher's microphone and amplifier, then whenever the teacher speaks, an electric current will run from the amplifier through the wire loop around the classroom. This current sets up a magnetic field, which floods the room and varies with the speech signal.

TYPICAL LOOP INDUCTION SYSTEM

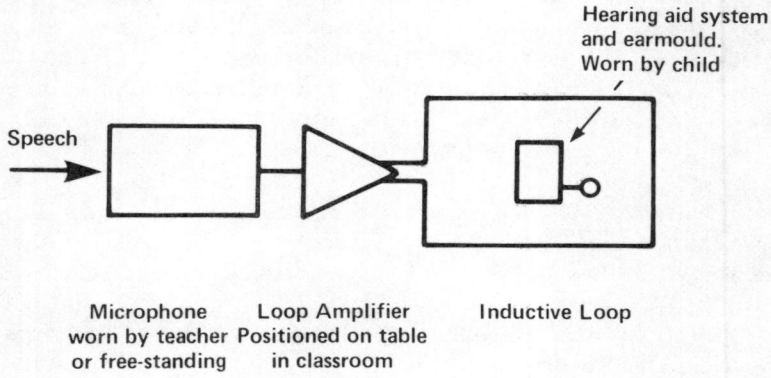

Fig. 22   The loop induction system.

Most conventional hearing aids have a coil of wire incorporated into the aid, which is able to sense the magnetic fields produced by the loop and convert them back into electricity. The electric signals are in turn amplified, converted back into sound at a louder level and delivered to the hearing aid user. Thus the teacher's speech will be converted into an electric signal by her microphone, then into a magnetic signal by the loop, then back into electricity by the tiny coil of wire in the hearing aid, then amplified and converted back into sound by the hearing aid: the coil of wire in other words replaces the microphone in the T mode of operation. It is important to remember that a hearing aid will not pick up any information other than via loop when the T mode is selected.

A loop induction system is designed to overcome the problem of distance between speaker and hearing aid user discussed earlier. The strength of the signal picked up by the hearing aid should be effectively constant, regardless of the child's position within the loop. Hence, in a classroom the teacher's voice level through a particular hearing aid should be the same regardless of whether the aid is at the front or back of the classroom. Furthermore, because the teacher has the microphone close to her mouth, her voice will be much stronger than the background noise picked up by the microphone. The problem of information being swamped by noise will therefore effectively be overcome.

A loop induction system may quite easily be installed and used in the home. The advantages are that it enables children to listen to television or radio together with other members of the family without having to have the volume at a high level; the child is able to concentrate on a programme without distraction from background noise in the room; and he is also able to move around the room and still receive the signals at a fairly constant level. (This is much more convenient than earphones or ear inserts connected to the set, which make mobility very restricted.) It is useful to remember that the child may also receive loop information and family conversation at the same time on the MT mode of the body hearing aid.

Fitting a loop induction system in the home
The fitting of a loop induction system in the home is illustrated in the diagram (figure 23). All that is required is a length of bell wire, which is run around the room, so the costs involved are very small. Remember that the wire can be laid under carpets and, if necessary, can go around window or door frames without impairing its efficiency. If a television set is to be used to drive the loop it is imperative to seek the advice of an electrical engineer, electrician or radio technician before proceeding.

The authors recommend that parents who are contemplating fitting an inductive loop system in the home obtain a copy of *Installing a loop system*, available free from the R.N.I.D. (see Appendix 3).

Using the loop in the home
Once a loop induction system has been installed and

connected – for example, to a television set – it is necessary to adjust the hearing aid for comfortable listening. This is best done by first setting the volume of the television to a level comfortable for the normally hearing members of the family. Switch on the aid and set to T or MT mode. Turn the aid's volume control slowly up until you get a satisfactory level of sound. Once the setting has been achieved it should be possible for the child to move around the room without a significant change in loop signal level, though some adjustment of the aid's volume control may be necessary if you change over from T to MT or vice-versa.

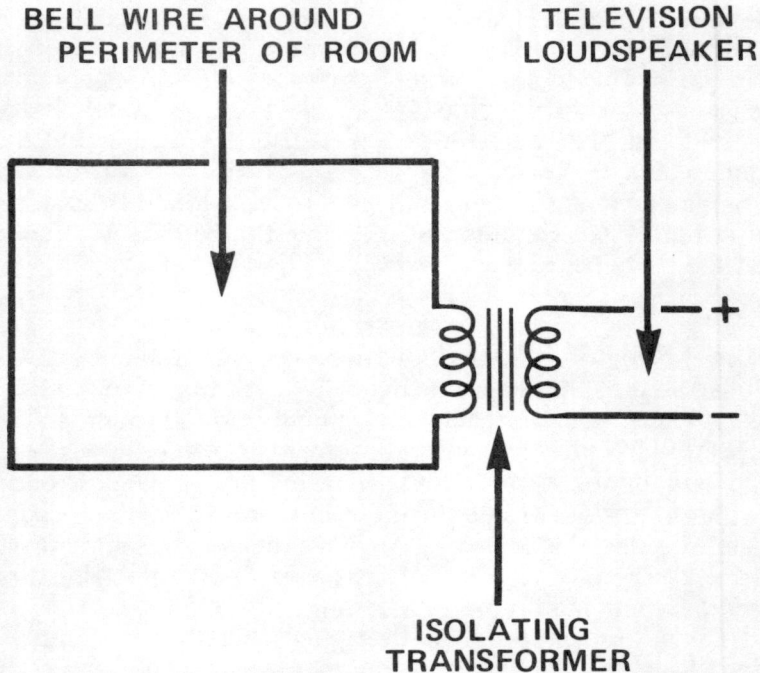

BELL WIRE AROUND PERIMETER OF ROOM

TELEVISION LOUDSPEAKER

ISOLATING TRANSFORMER

Fig. 23   Fitting a loop induction system in the home.

Although the loop induction system should not present too many problems in the home, it is important to realise that such a system has limitations. Dead spots can and do sometimes occur in spots within a loop induction system where the strength of the magnetic field generated by the loop is very weak. The information picked up by the hearing aid is therefore drastically reduced, and it is important to realise this and check the system out with a 'flux meter', which measures the magnetic field strength, or simply by listening through the aid. Clearly, if a child is sufficiently mature to indicate such dead spots himself, the problem will easily be managed.

The effectiveness of a loop induction system may also be limited because the frequencies of speech amplified by many conventional hearing aids in T mode are restricted, relative to the same aid's performance in the normal M mode. So the linguistic information that young hearing impaired users enjoy may be reduced in the T mode. It is also important to note that many post aural hearing aids do not have an MT setting. This means that the microphone of the hearing aid will be inoperative if information on the loop mode (T) is being received. This can be disadvantageous in situations where a child may wish to receive loop signals and also hear his own voice via the aid's microphone. However, despite such limitations, loop systems are valuable additions in the home, particularly in helping a child to be more fully integrated into family life. A matter as simple as using television at a volume tolerable to all members of the family is important, particularly when there are other children in the home.

It is not necessary to have a licence to operate an inductive loop system in the home.

Radio Microphones and the Loop Induction System
IT IS IMPORTANT TO REMEMBER THAT USERS OF RADIO HEARING AID SYSTEMS MUST OBTAIN A HOME OFFICE RADIO MICROPHONE SYSTEM LICENCE. (See end of chapter for details).

Radio microphones and radio receivers have been introduced in an attempt to improve the listening experience of the hearing impaired, particularly children, and a system which is particularly relevant in education is the radio microphone-loop induction system. The basic arrangement of such a system is shown in the diagram (figure 24). The child's own conventional hearing aids are used, together with a portable loop induction system which is contained in a small briefcase and can be carried around the school by the child; and a radio microphone-transmitter worn by the teacher (see Plate 56). In the classroom, the teacher's speech is sensed by the microphone, converted into electricity and then transmitted on radio waves by the radio transmitter to a radio receiver contained in the briefcase, which is positioned under the child's desk. The radio receiver in turn feeds the electrical signals to a power amplifier also in the small briefcase, which drives electric current around the loop around the inside of the case. The child is in fact situated in a loop induction field, just as in the case of the conventional home installed loop system already described.

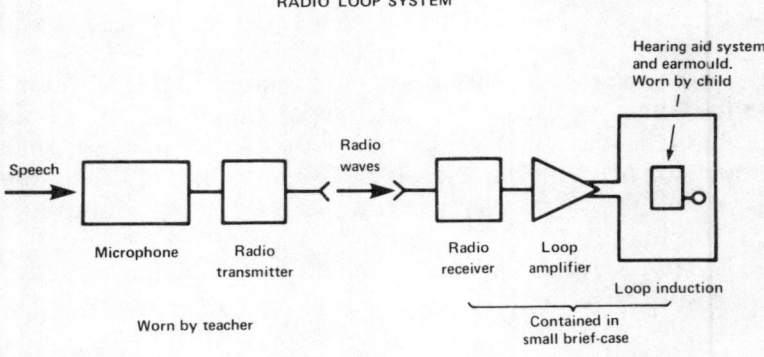

RADIO LOOP SYSTEM

Fig. 24   Layout of a typical radio loop system.

The only difference between the two loops is that one is a fixture in a room and serves all the children using the T mode in the room, while the other is a portable loop serving one child. In both cases the child operates the hearing aid on the T or MT mode (noting post aural limitation)

Assessment of Hearing in Children

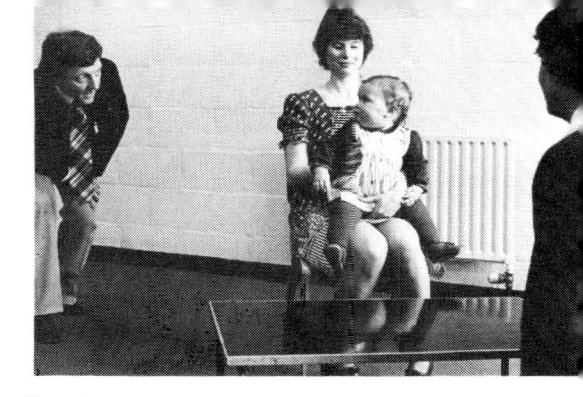

The distraction test of hearing—normal response to the vowel 'oo'.

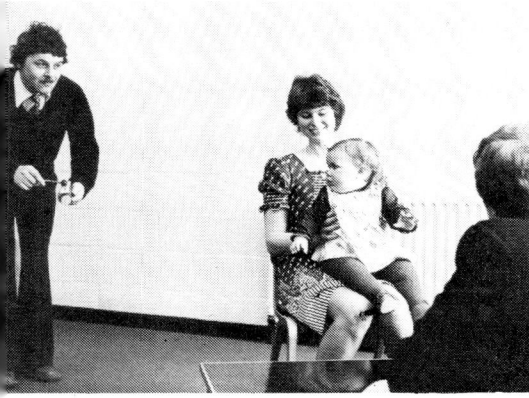

2 The distraction test of hearing—normal response to 'G' chime bar.

3 The distraction test of hearing—normal response to high frequency rattle.

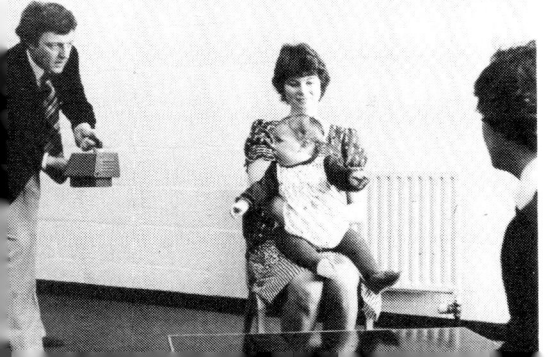

4 The distraction test of hearing—normal response to a warble tone.

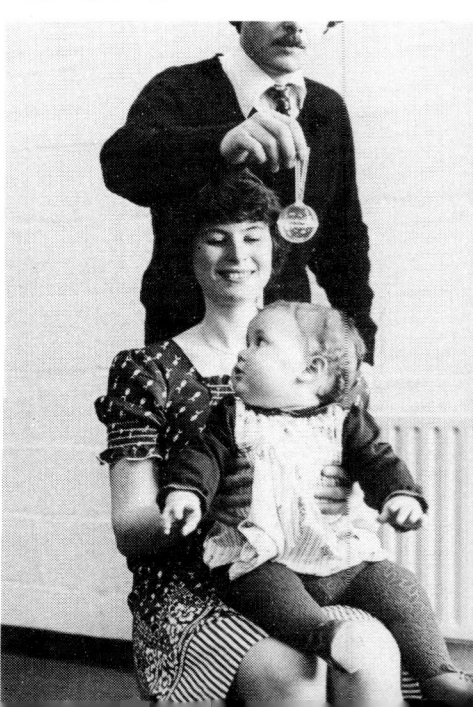

5 A four-month old baby showing developmental level—unable to sit without considerable support, poor head control, not suitable for distraction testing.

6 An eight-month old baby showing developmental level—sitting unsupported, good head control, suitable for distraction testing.

7 The localisation difficulty of an eight-month old baby when the stimulus is presented above the head.

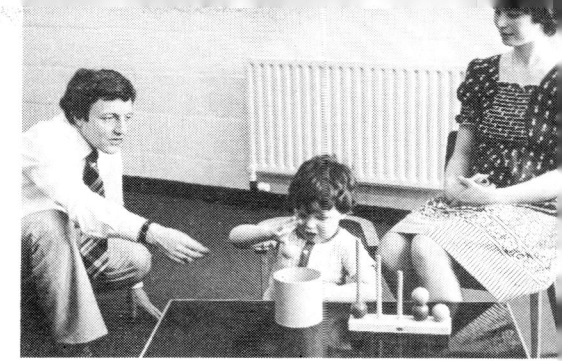

8 The cooperative test of hearing—the two-year old child has been asked to 'put the ball in the box!'

9 The cooperative test of hearing—the two-year old child has been asked to 'put the ball on the stick'.

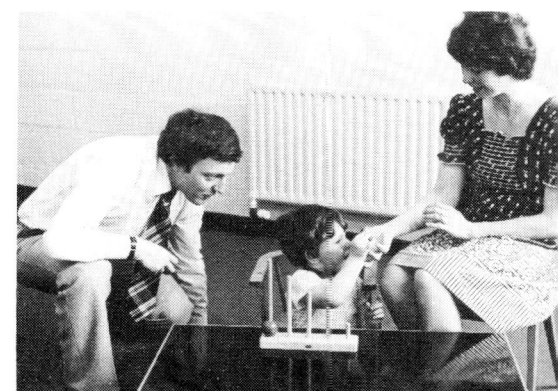

10 The cooperative test of hearing—the two-year old child has been asked to 'give it to mummy'.

11 The performance test of hearing. The child (two years eight months) places a little man in the boat when the tester says 'go'. A similar procedure is adopted using the stimulus 's'.

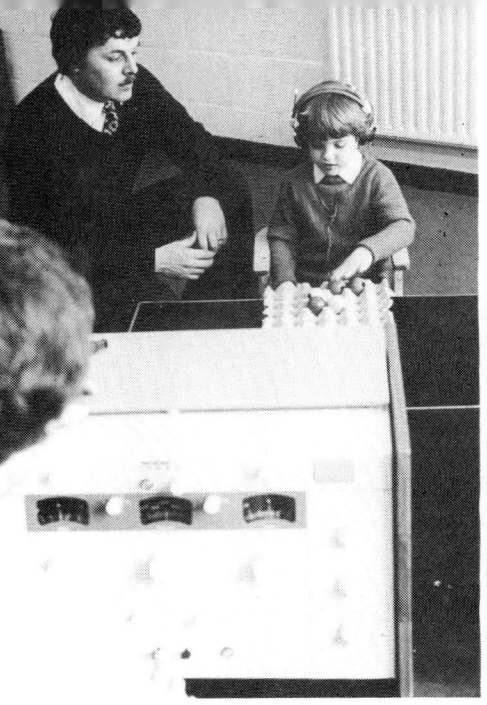

12 Application of pure tone audiometry for air conduction using headphones.

13 Measurement of the sound pressure level of a stimulus by means of a sound level meter.

14 The pure tone audiometric test of hearing for bone conduction.

15 The bone vibrator and head band as used in pure tone audiometry for bone conduction.

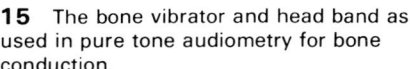

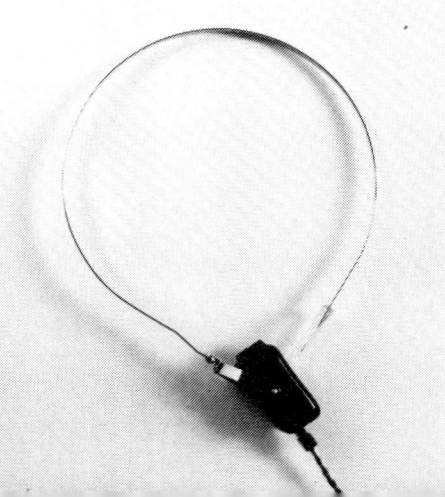

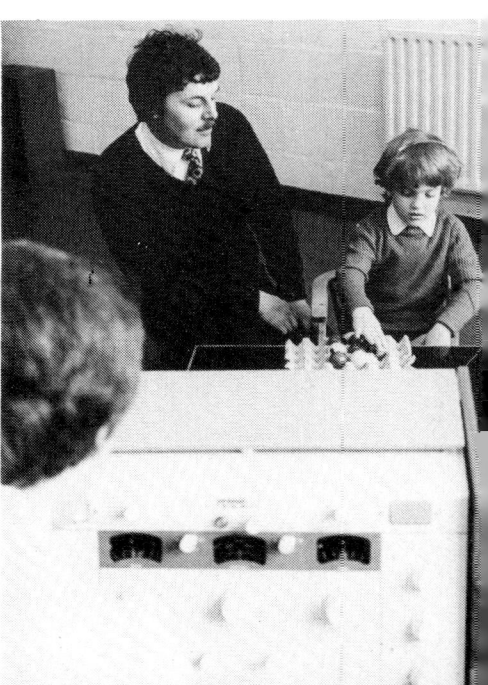

16 Measurement of middle ear function using a conventional electroacoustic impedance bridge.

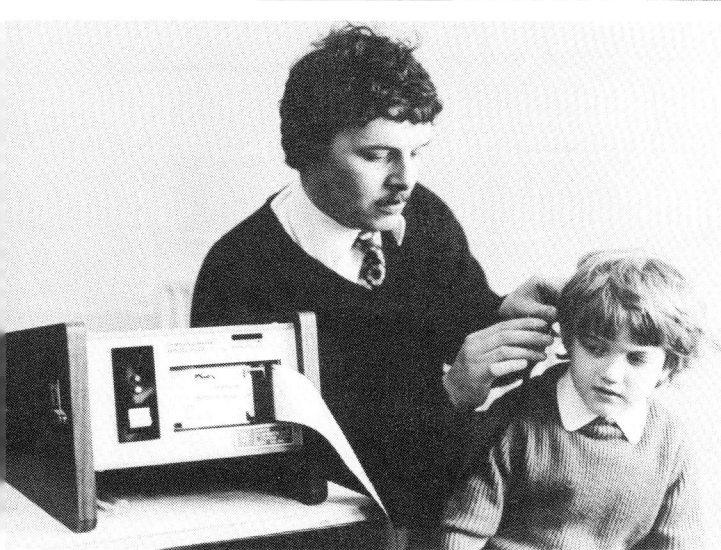

17 Measurement of middle ear function using the hand held probe of a tympanometer.

18 Application of the K.T. test.

19 An example of a test card of the Manchester Picture Test.

20 Application of the Manchester Picture Test.

21 Below: Example of a four-month old baby prepared for Brain Stem Electric Response Audiometry—electrodes attached to the head.

22 Below: The equipment and procedure involved in the Brain Stem hearing test.

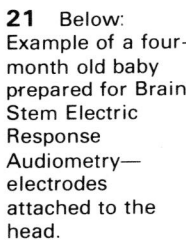
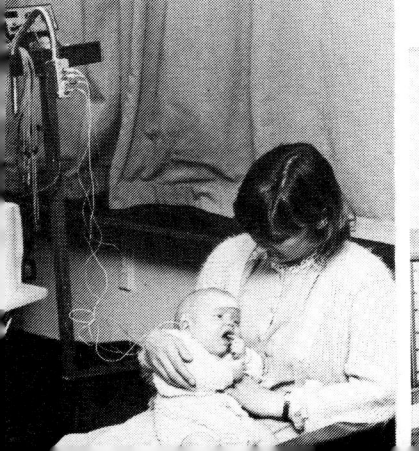
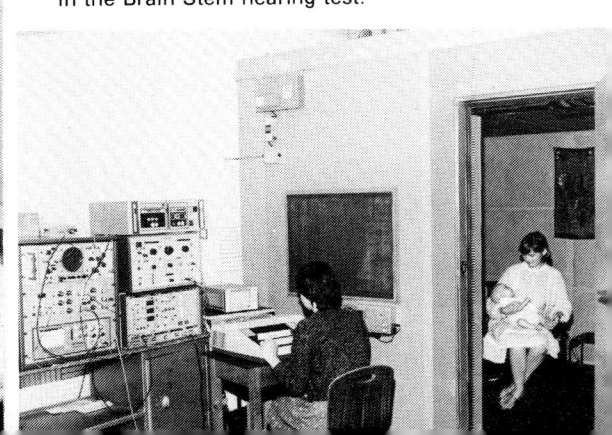

The Hearing Aid: How to Get The Most Out of It

23 Right: A receiver with 'blutac' in place of the sealing washer—this helps to reduce the problem of acoustic feedback.
24 Below: Manual impression taking technique.

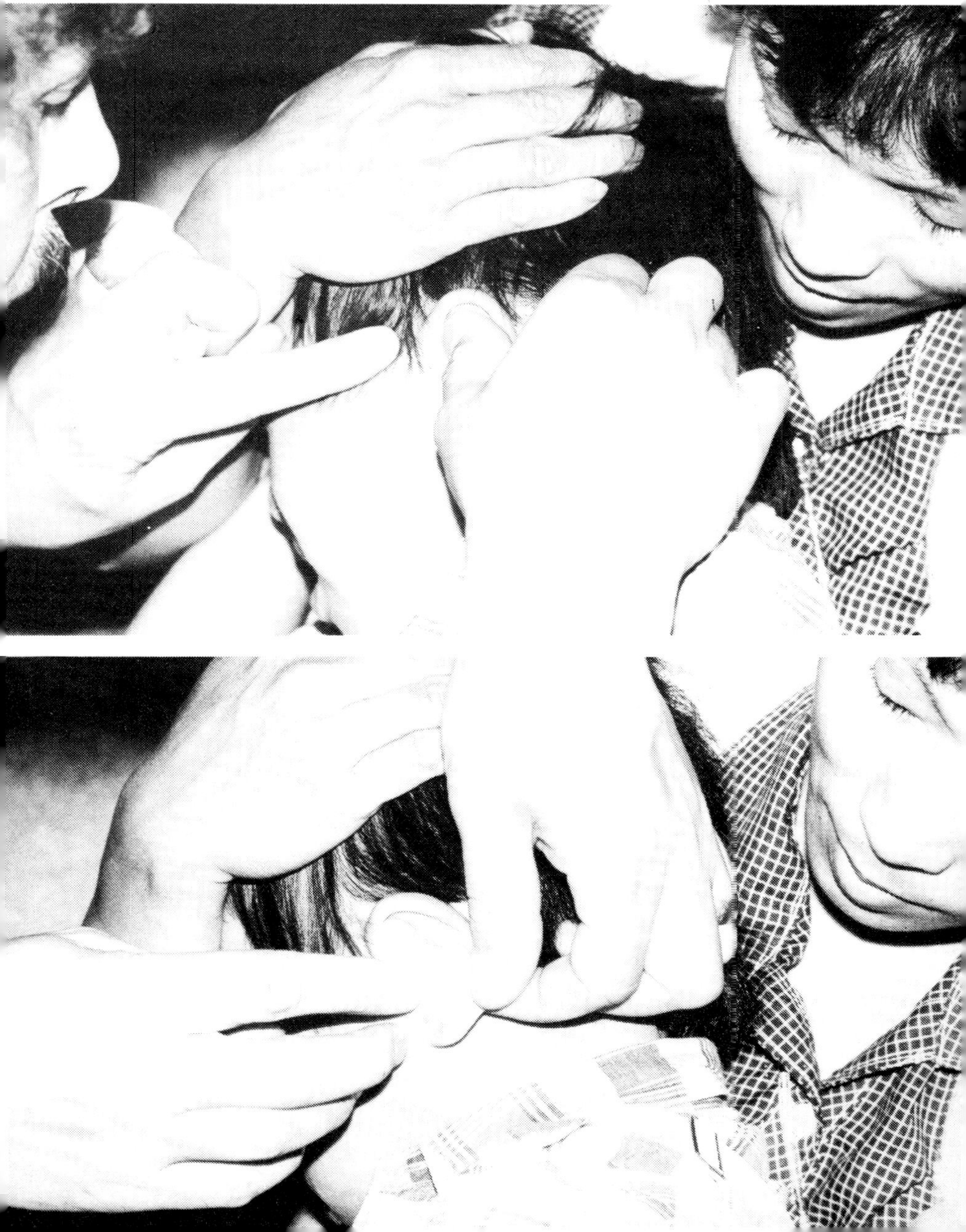

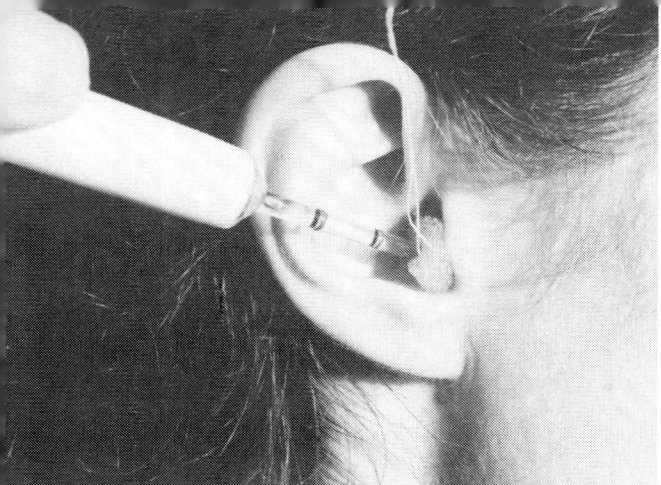

25 & 26 (Above and right)
The ear impression technique
using a syringe method. A
foam tamp is being placed in
the ear canal prior to
introduction of the impression
material. This tamp prevents
material from travelling too
deep into the ear canal.

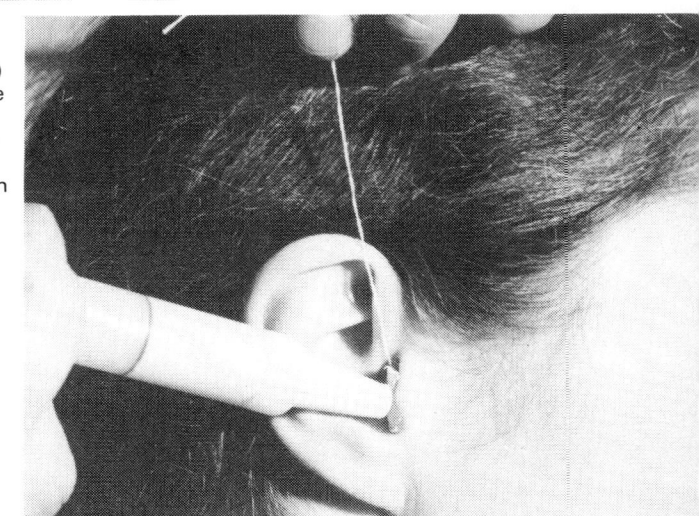

27 Examples of ear moulds
as used in body worn (left) and
post aural (right) hearing aids.

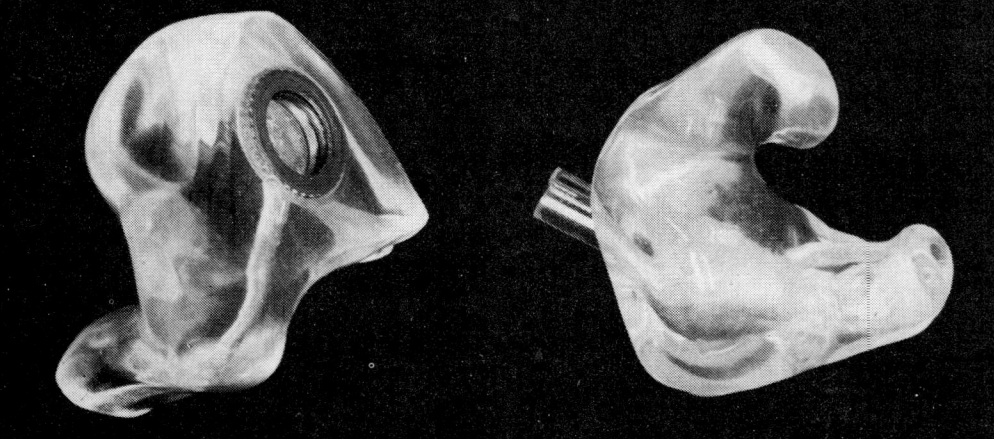

28 An example of a post aural hearing aid.

29 A conventional size receiver (left), together with a subminiature receiver (right) for comparison.

30 Examples of hearing aid receivers showing the identifying coding.

31 Above left: An example of a body worn hearing aid incorporating a protective baby cover.
32 Above right: The hearing aid lead—the weak spots are located at the two cable-connector joints.
33 Below left: The body worn hearing aid showing the correct way to coil the lead.
34 Below right: The body worn hearing aid showing incorrect lead coiling.

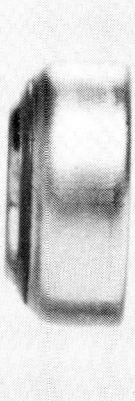

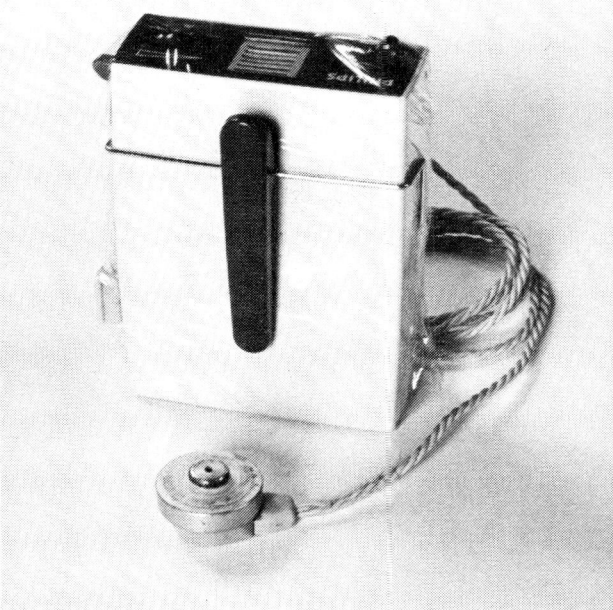

35 Above left: The pellet type battery as used in post aural hearing aids
36 Above right: A body worn hearing aid 'child proofed' by wrapping in cling film.
37 Below left: The cylindrical battery as used in the body worn hearing aid.
38 Below right: An example of a body worn hearing aid that has been affected by everyday enemies such as drink, food and sand, because of lack of protection with cling film or a baby cover.

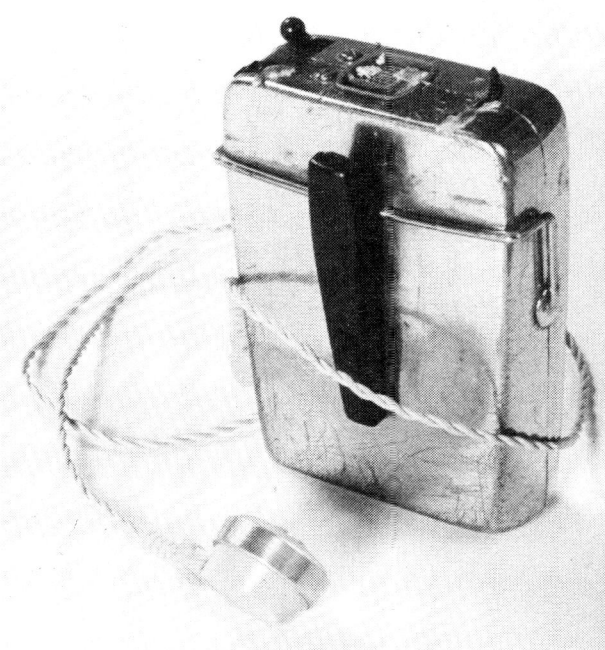

39 Above left: Twin body worn hearing aids with no crossover of leads—correct format.
40 Above right: Twin body worn hearing aids with crossover of leads—not recommended.

41 Below: A young child being encouraged to clean her earmoulds as well as her teeth.

42, 43 Examples of home activity encouraging sound making.

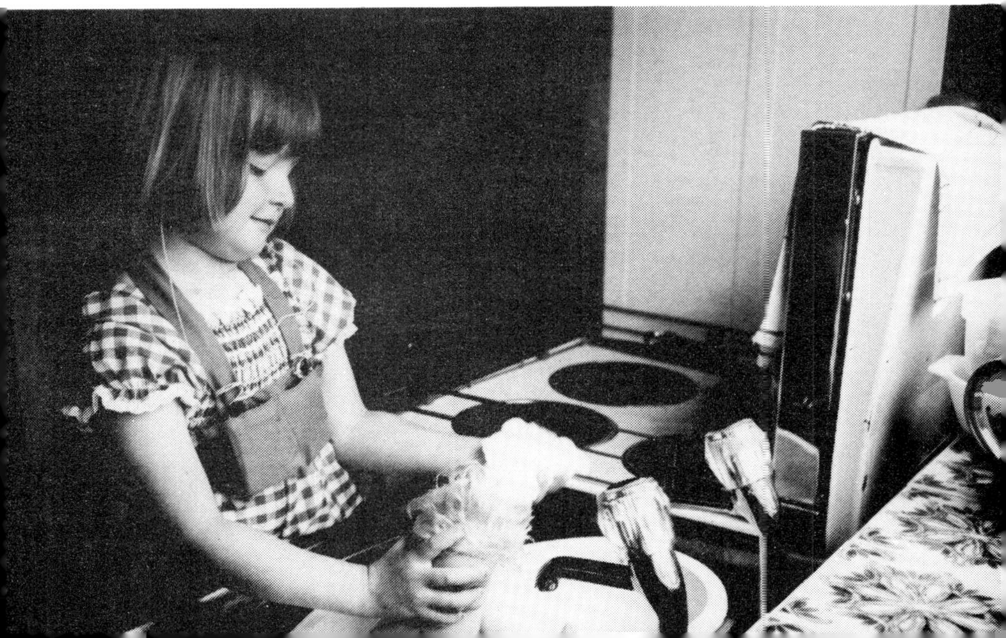

44 An example of
a young hearing
impaired child using
twin body worn
hearing aids in an
attractive harness.

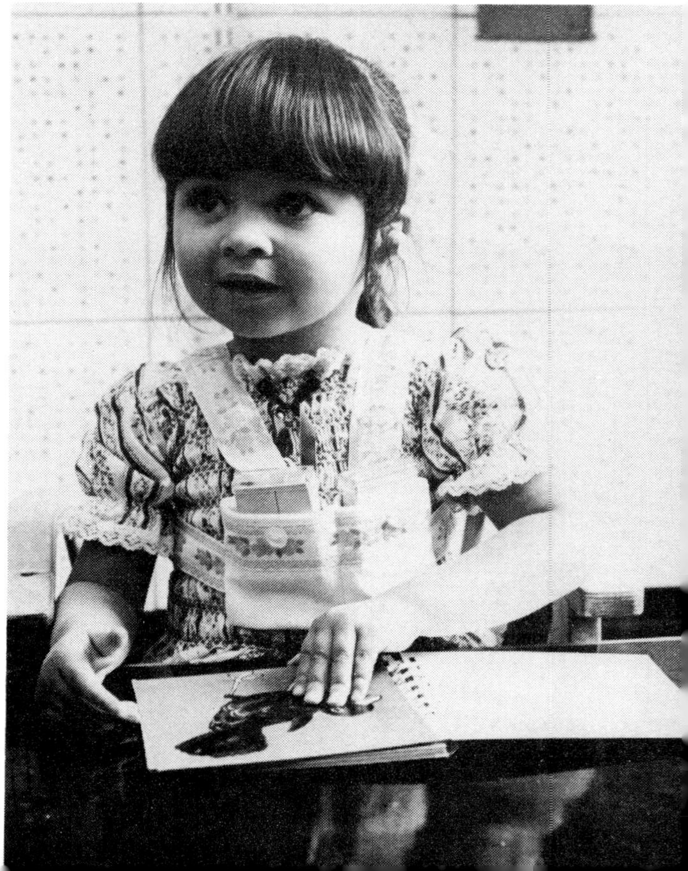

45 Ideal format for
twin body worn
hearing aids on a
young child.

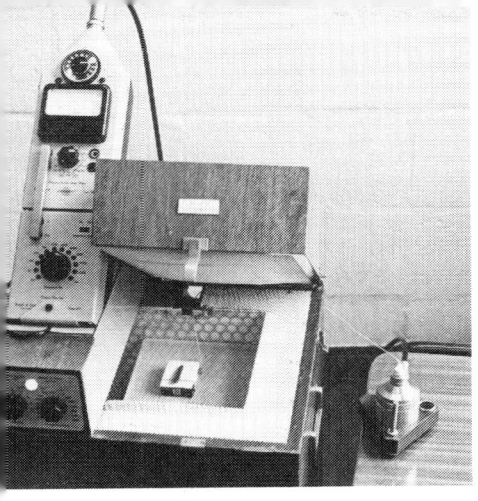

46 Above left: Hearing aid test box as used to test and calibrate body worn hearing aids.

47 Above right: Application of the hearing aid testing facility.

48 Right: Hearing aid test box as used to test and calibrate a post aural hearing aid.

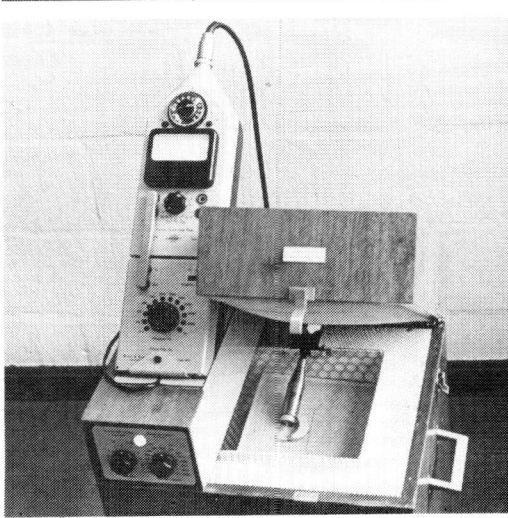

49 Above left: A post aural hearing aid with audio input facility showing the audio input connector.

50 Below: An example of a post aural hearing aid with audio input facility connected directly to a satellite microphone.

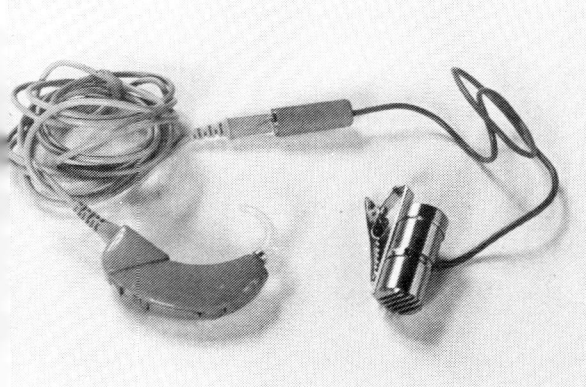

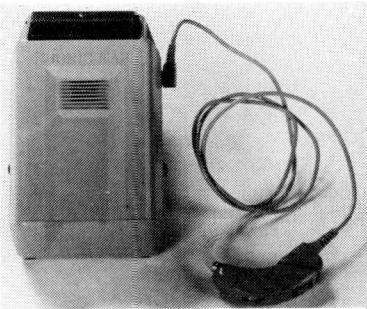

51 Above: An example of a post aural hearing aid with audio input facility connected to a radio receiver.

52 Above; A teacher and child using an auditory training unit.

53 Right: A parent and child using an auditory training unit.

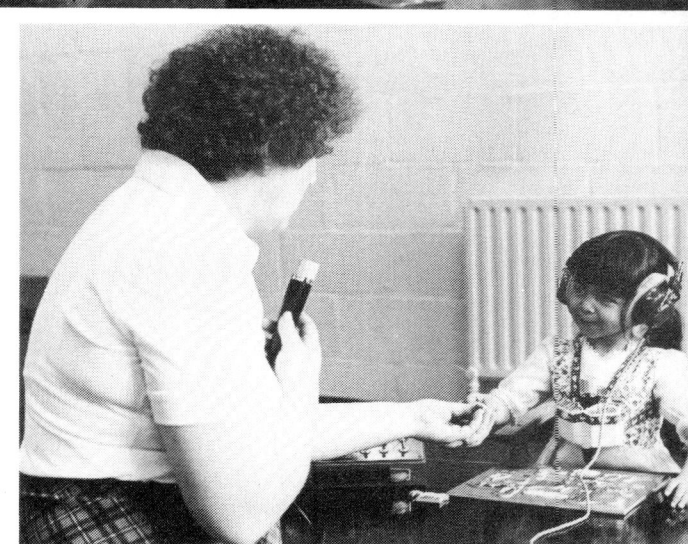

54 Below left: The Phonic Ear 441–445 radio microphone system connected to a post aural hearing aid with an audio input facility. The parents' transmitter is on the right, the child's radio receiver on the left of the photograph. This system is an updated version of that shown in plate 51.

55 Below right: An example of a radio microphone system employing a neck loop. The parent's transmitter is on the right of the photograph. The child's receiver is shown connected to the neck loop. This loop would normally be worn under the child's clothing.

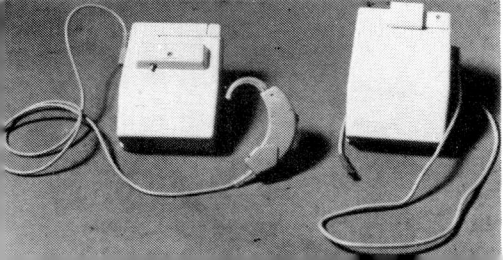

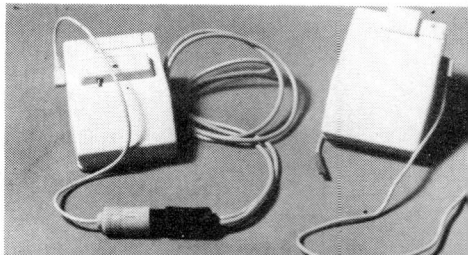

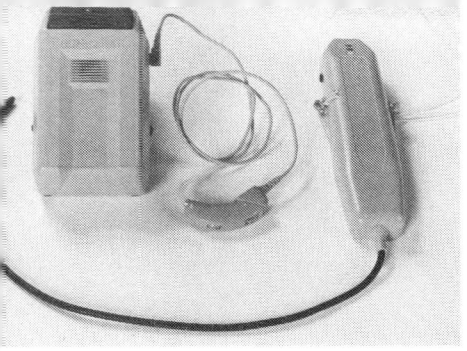
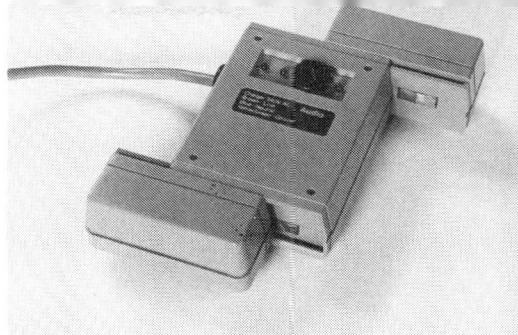

56 Above left: The equipment required to operate a post aural hearing aid with audio input facility on a radio transmission system. (left to right: radio receiver, hearing aid, radio transmitter).
57 Above right: Slideable battery packs being placed on the battery charger. (Cubex Radio Link Mk 111).

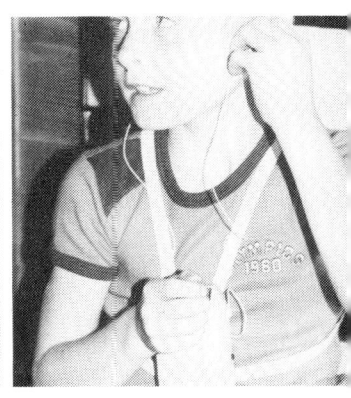

58 Above left: A radio transmitter being worn by a parent. (Cubex Radio Link Mk 111 system).
59 Above centre: A radio transmitter being worn by a parent. (Phonic Ear 421 system).
60 Above right: A radio hearing aid being fitted by a child. (Phonic Ear 421 system).

61 Below: A radio hearing aid in use in the home. (Mother wearing transmitter, child wearing radio hearing aid).

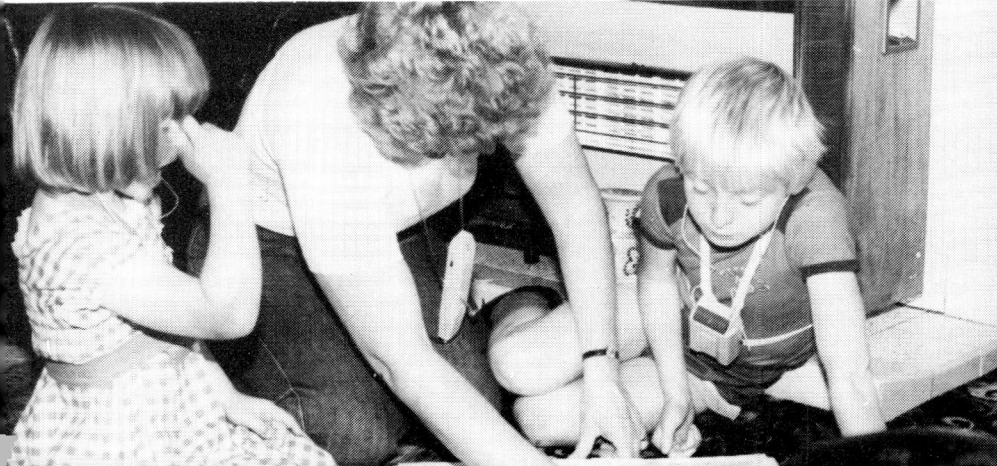

62 Above left: A radio hearing aid system incorporating slideable battery packs. Parent's transmitter is on the left, the child's radio aid on the right. The battery packs have been partly removed. (Cubex Radio Link Mk 111).
63 Above right: The battery charger and mated battery packs as used in the Cubex system.

64 Right: Example of a home sound making activity when a parent would be advised to switch her transmitter off.

65 Below: The battery charger as used in the Phonic Ear radio hearing aid. Both child's aid and parent's transmitter are connected to the charger. The battery packs are not detachable (421 system).

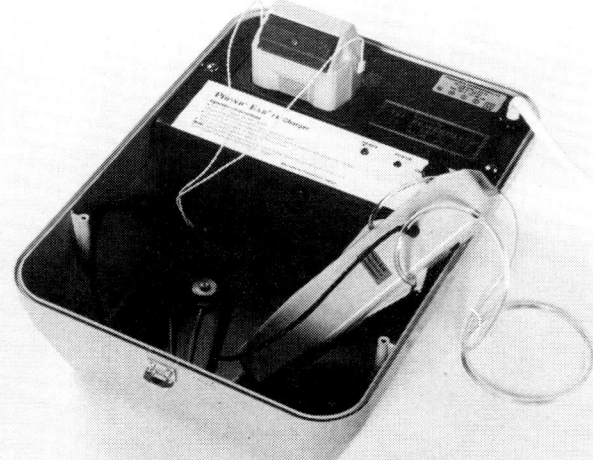

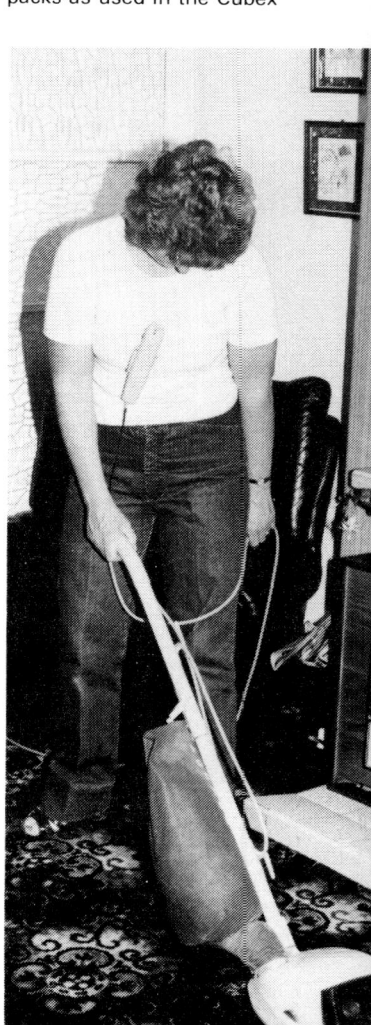

Stimulating
Language Development

66 & 67 Washing Dolly—an example of play as imitation of mother's household tasks.

68-72 Playing with dough—
another imitative game.

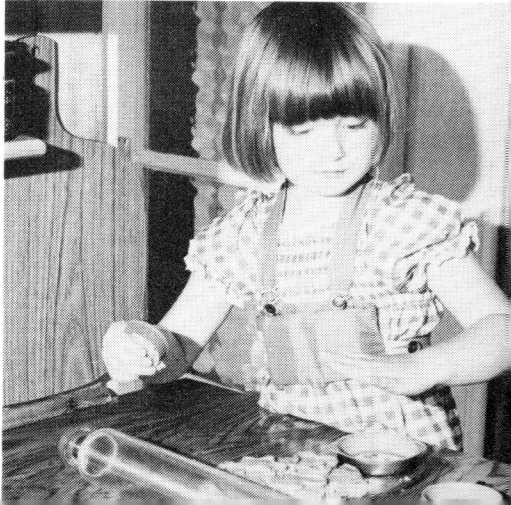

73-75 Playing with jigsaws—here the adult actually involves the child in play, in order to stimulate the desire to communicate.

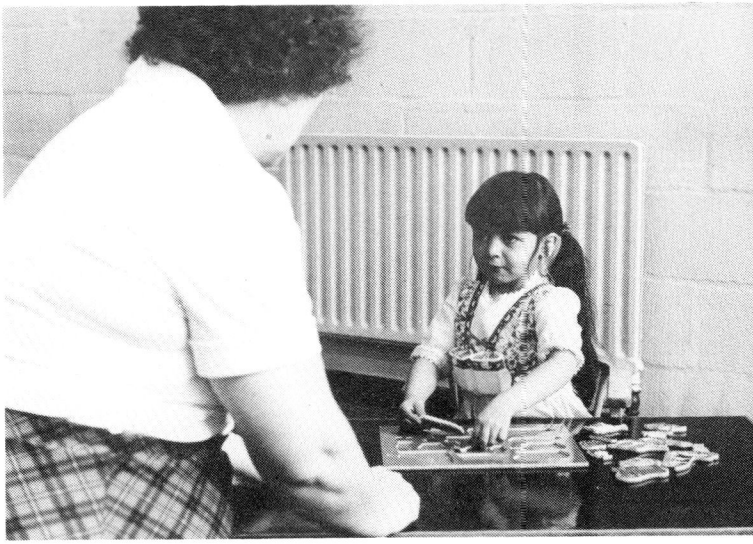

76-77 Playing with picture lotto—now more than one child is involved.

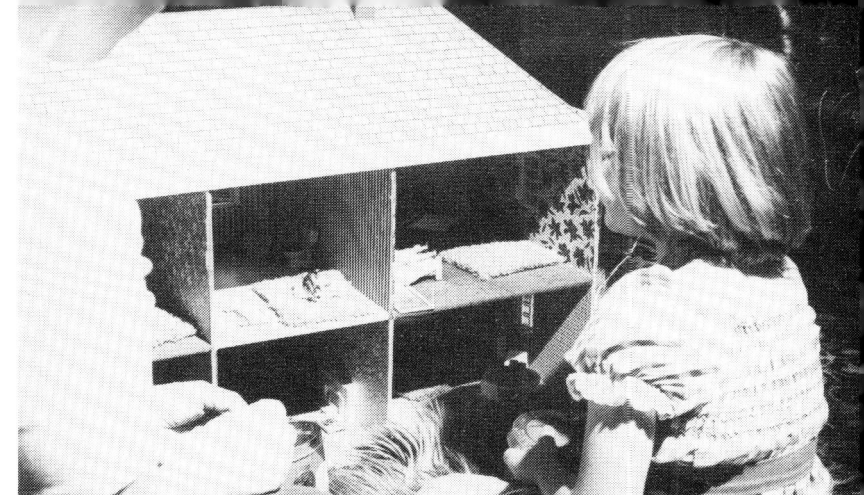

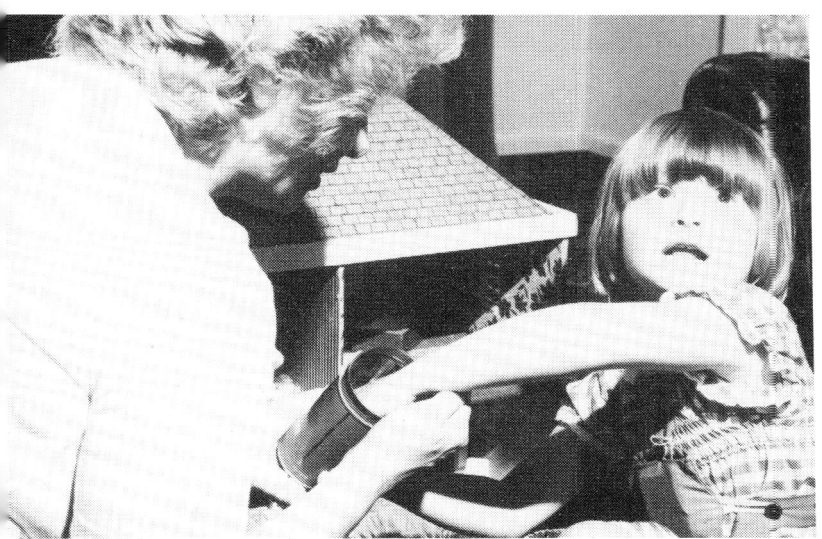

78-79 Above and centre: Playing with the dolls' house—'let's pretend' play.

80 Right: Playing with the roundabout—again, the game is 'let's pretend'.

81-83 Playing with sand. Here hearing impaired and normally hearing children are playing together without adult supervision.

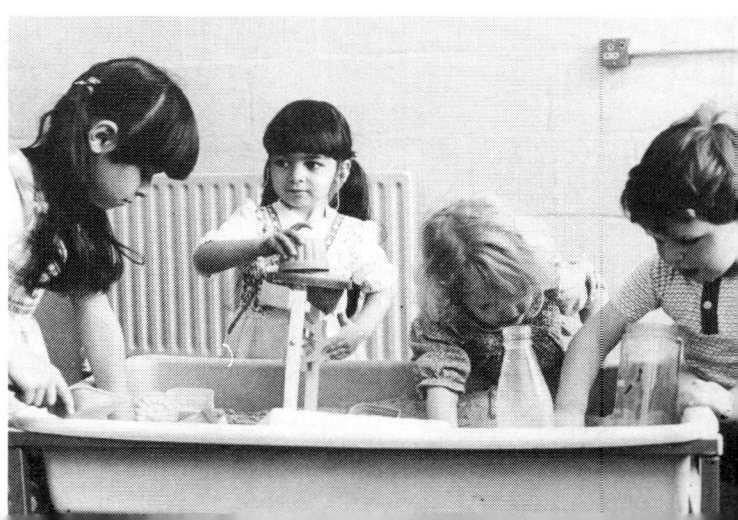

Briefcase systems are particularly useful when a hearing impaired child is being placed in a normal educational setting. The child uses the same hearing aids at all times as sounds are received normally on M mode, while lessons are received with the aid on T or MT. The effectiveness of the system is limited only by the loop performance of the hearing aid.

The use of radio transmission in hearing aids is an extremely important development, because it overcomes the problem of distance between speaker and listener. Most radio systems have a range of approximately one hundred metres, and signal strength remains effectively constant regardless of the relative positions of speaker and listener.

Radio Microphone with the child's own hearing aid
One factor, as we have already said, that does limit the effectiveness of a loop induction system is the performance of a particular hearing aid on the T mode. This problem may be overcome using the child's own hearing aids, with a radio microphone-transmitter-receiver system – if the hearing aid has an 'audio input socket'. **Not all hearing aids have this facility**. The arrangement of the system is shown in figure 25.

RADIO MICROPHONE – RECEIVER
WITH CONVENTIONAL AID

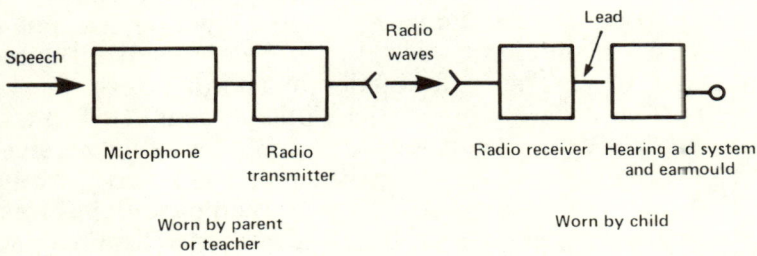

Fig. 25   The audio input system.

The radio microphone-transmitter is worn by parent or teacher, as in the previous system. The radio receiver is contained in a small box (the size of a body worn aid), which the child wears on a belt or in a pocket under the clothes, and is connected via a lead to the audio input socket of the child's hearing aid. The parent's voice is transmitted via radio waves, as in the previous example; the radio receiver worn by the child picks up the signals and feeds them along a lead to the hearing aid amplifier, the sound is then processed in the conventional manner and delivered at an amplified level to the ear.

The hearing aid's own microphone also remains sensitive to sound while this system is in use (if the user so wishes), so the child continues to receive information from the environment, including the sound of his own voice; and the radio receiver may be disconnected, leaving the aid solely a conventional hearing aid.

Hearing aids with audio input sockets may also be used with a wire link to a television set, tape recorder or radio. Clearly mobility would be restricted in such situations, but this should not preclude its use with children. It is likely to appeal to older children in particular, where mobility is not a significant consideration. One of the advantages of this system is that the change in frequency response from M to T mode that takes place on a loop system, when a significant change in the amplification pattern may occur, is avoided.

It is possible for a child to use this type of system with a conventional hearing aid without audio input facility, but in this case the child must use his own hearing aids set to the T or MT mode. The child would wear a portable loop (placed around the neck and under the clothes), connected to and driven by the radio receiver. That is, instead of the receiver driving the child's aids via audio input, the receiver would drive the portable loop and the aid would pick up information in the T mode – or, if the child wished to hear his own voice as well, the MT mode. The limitations of such a system are similar to those of the loop system carried in a small briefcase which were discussed earlier. Clearly the child's aid could be used normally without the loop when this optional system was not required.

It is of interest to note that it is now possible to overcome the problem of an inoperative microphone on a post aural hearing aid (which does not have an MT setting) when loop information is being received (i.e. aid set to T). To do this one uses a radio receiver such as Phonic Ear 445R shown in Plate 54 which has a built in environmental microphone. This allows a child to monitor his own voice whilst receiving radio transmitted signals.

Fitting and checking procedure with the Radio Microphone Transmitter Receiver System.
It is obviously important for parents to check that the optional facility of a radio microphone transmitter–receiver used with conventional hearing aids is functioning correctly. They must obviously first check that the child's personal hearing aids are functioning, using the guidelines described earlier. Once this has been done the optional radio facility may be checked.

In the case of a radio–microphone induction loop employing a briefcase, the following procedure should be followed.
1) Place the briefcase under a chair in the home and switch on.
2) Place the radio transmitter by a source of sound, say a radio, in another room, and switch it on.
3) Sit on the chair with the aid set to T position and check for sound reception.

As a rule this system is only used in school. However, the batteries in the teacher's transmitter and child's receiver must be recharged overnight for the next days use. If the child brings this system home each evening it is relatively easy for parents to keep a check on it and ensure that the batteries are recharged. If the system is left in school the teacher will have the responsibility of ensuring all is well.

In cases where an audio input connection to the child's aid is employed the following procedure should be followed.
1) Connect the child's radio receiver to the hearing aid by

means of the audio input cable. Switch receiver on and set to mid volume level.

2) Place the transmitter by a source of sound (e.g. a radio) in another room. Switch on.

3) Switch on the child's aid and set to a mid volume level with the function selector set to receive signals via *audio input only*. (Recently such aids have been coded O, A, AM. In such cases select A – audio input. If unsure ask your local technician).

4) Listen to the signal received, check the quality.

5) If there is no reception replace the battery (if possible) in the transmitter. Listen again.

6) Replace the battery in the child's receiver (if possible). Listen again.

7) Replace the audio input cord. Listen again.

If this fails to cure the problem, seek the advice of the local services.

In cases where a neck loop is used with a radio microphone-transmitter-receiver system, one simply follows the steps:

1) Place transmitter in another room by a source of sound (e.g. radio). Switch on.

2) Secure the receiver to your body. Attach the loop to the receiver and place around the neck. Switch on.

3) Switch the aid on and set to mid volume.

4) Hold the aid within the loop and select the T mode.

5) Listen to sound quality.

If there is no reception, replace the batteries as in the last example. If this fails to cure the problem seek help from your local services.

It is vitally important for parents to ensure that the batteries in the radio transmitter and radio receiver are fully charged. As a rule of thumb it is advisable always to use rechargable, rather than disposable batteries in such units, and remember to place them on overnight charge each evening. The batteries in the latest radio transmitter-receiver system (i.e. Phonic Ear 441T-445R) which is used with conventional hearing aids will last a full day without loss of output. The same cannot always be said of the *Radio Microphone hearing aid systems* which will now be described. Battery life in these systems may vary from as little as 8 hours to a maximum of about 12 hours.

The Radio Microphone Hearing Aid
This system is a logical development of the previous system. In this case the child wears one unit that is both a radio receiver and a conventional hearing aid. The unit is therefore of a body worn design. The arrangement of the system is shown in the illustration (figure 26). It works on the principle that the parent (as in the earlier systems) is fitted with a radio microphone-transmitter worn around the neck as shown in the photograph (Plate 56). The child's hearing aid is in fact two units in one box: a radio receiver which picks up the radio waves generated by the parent's transmitter, and passes them on to the amplifier; a microphone, and an entirely conventional hearing aid system which enables the child to hear sounds in the vicinity of the aid, including the sound of his own voice. The child therefore receives information from both the radio side and the conventional side of the system.

RADIO MICROPHONE HEARING AID

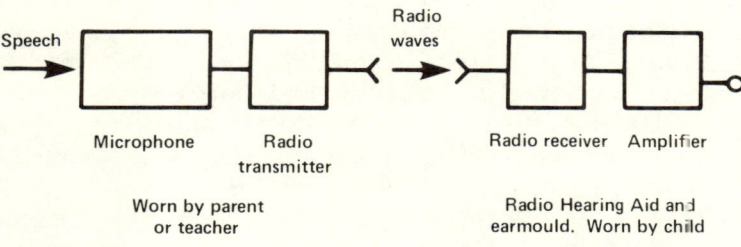

Fig. 26 Layout of a typical radio microphone hearing aid.

The child's microphone may be switched off so that radio transmitted signals only are received, to reduce the environmental background noise picked up by the microphone; but since it is so important to language development for the young child to hear his own voice as much as possible, it is not good practice to use this type of system on radio alone for any length of time.

The system may also be used solely as a conventional hearing aid when the radio facility is switched off.

See Plates 54-63 for photographs of commercial radio hearing aids in use with children.

To get the best out of radio transmission systems, it may be useful to think of them in the following way. Imagine the parent (wearing the radio transmitter) as a person compering a radio programme in a BBC studio, and the child's receiver as the radio in the home. The radio station transmits the programme (just as the parent's transmitter would transmit his or her voice), and the radio receives and reproduces the programme (just as the child's unit receives and reproduces the parent's voice). It should be noted however, that the power of the parent's transmitter will be much weaker than that of a radio station, for its range is only about one hundred metres.

Conventional hearing aid users encounter problems because sound becomes weaker as it travels through the air – as illustrated in the diagram (figure 27). The top picture shows how a hearing aid user relatively close to the speaker hears the message despite background noise, and turns to reply. The person further away, however, receives a very weak signal which, despite amplification, is unheard because it is swamped in the background noise.

The lower picture shows the same situation with a radio-microphone hearing aid system. The speaker's message is transmitted on radio waves and is received by both hearing aid users at the same intensity. No loss in strength of signal occurs, and both subjects turn in response to the message. The message to the listener furthest away from the speaker is not swamped by the background noise.

It is fair to say that radio hearing aid systems have gone a long way towards overcoming the basic problems they were designed to overcome, and they can provide great benefits to a hearing impaired child. A number of such

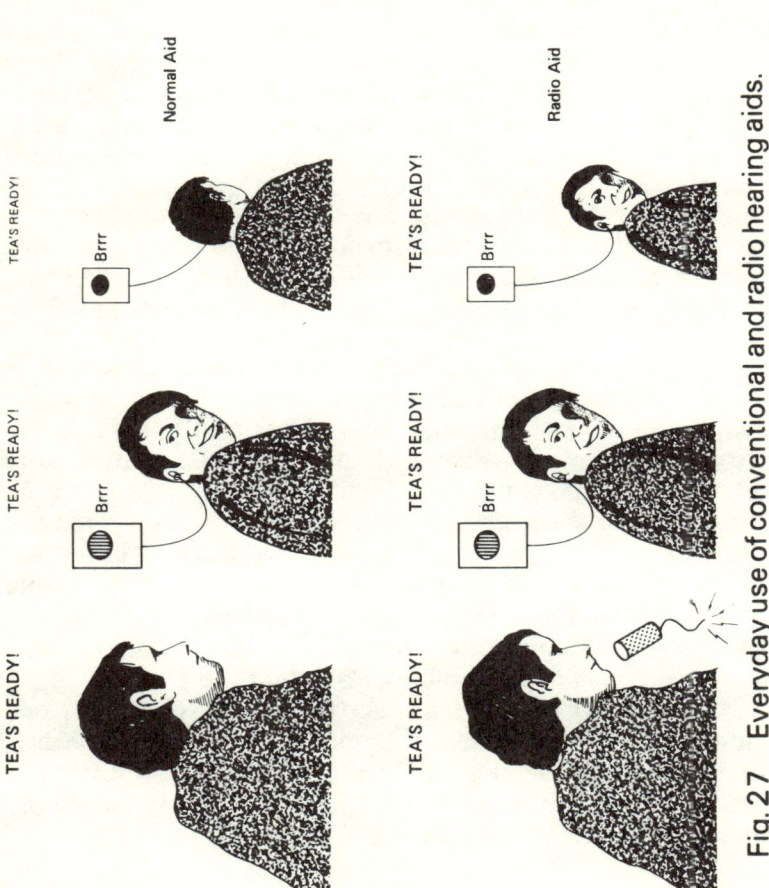

Fig. 27   Everyday use of conventional and radio hearing aids.

systems are available in the United Kingdom, and are used for example with hearing impaired children in normal schools, thus aiding the integration of such children into a normal educational environment.

The radio microphone hearing aid, and systems involving radio microphones in general, also have a number of what may be loosely summarised as disadvantages relative to conventional aids, and parents should be aware of these before buying them for their children – radio hearing aid systems are not provided free of charge under the National Health Service, though they are sometimes purchased by schools or local authorities. They are also relatively expensive both to purchase and to maintain, so it is important for parents to ensure that the local authority, for instance, agrees to maintaining the aid even if it does not purchase it.

The radio microphone hearing aid systems presently in use are all powered by rechargeable batteries, which have a daily life of approximately 10 – 12 hours, though this can vary depending on usage and some batteries may require recharging after only 8 hours. Since many hearing impaired children use their hearing aids throughout the day, it may be necessary to change a radio hearing aid during the latter part of the day and fit conventional hearing aids to make sure that the output from the radio aid does not fall to an unacceptable level. Rechargeable batteries require a full overnight charge to restore them to full potential for the following day.

It is not however good practice to change a child from one model of hearing aid to another during the course of the day, since the child is then exposed to different amplification patterns that may influence linguistic development – continual steady amplification from one particular hearing aid is desirable.

Certain manufacturers have recently begun to introduce an interchangeable battery pack, which slides on to the hearing aid, making it possible to remove one battery pack for charging and replace it with another. This ensures that the child's radio aids can be used at all times throughout the day without loss of output.

The radio hearing aid is a relatively bulky object, mainly

because of the battery pack. It is therefore important to examine the various systems carefully before selecting a particular one. While the child is small, and again in the teenage years, very bulky hearing aids may cause problems: physical fitting may be a problem on a very young child, and to a teenager the cosmetic aspects may become important so parents should discuss the situation with the professional workers who are guiding and supporting them.

NOTE: The radio microphone also uses a rechargeable battery, so do not forget to place this unit on overnight charge when recharging the child's hearing aid.

Also, remember that each radio hearing aid is designed to receive radio signals on one of a limited range of frequencies specified by the Home Office, and will be colour coded or letter coded accordingly. The parent's radio transmitter will have the same code, so its transmissions will be picked up by the child's radio receiver. If a child is in school, it is likely that each class will operate on a separate radio frequency, to ensure that no child picks up the signals of another teacher elsewhere in the school. The child will simply change his radio receiver frequency as he moves from class to class; the principle here is much the same as changing the stations on a transistor radio: if the radio is tuned to channel 1, we do not hear channel 2.

Fitting and checking procedures with Radio Hearing Aid Systems

Similar fitting and checking procedures apply to radio hearing aid systems as to conventional hearing aids. But clearly radio systems are more complex and problems may prove more difficult to resolve, so it is particularly advisable for parents to have standby conventional aids. If a radio aid has to be returned to the manufacturer rather than be repaired by the local technician, there will be a period of at least 48 hours during which it will be out of commission.

Routine checking of a radio aid can be done fairly quickly:

1) Switch on the hearing aid microphone, with radio facility switched off, i.e. transmitter off.

2) Hold receiver away from aid and turn up to full volume. Whistle should occur.
3) Listen through the aid receiver held to the ear at mid volume setting, and speak into microphone. Check for voice quality and lead faults, i.e. wiggle leads at known weak spots.
4) Switch off microphone.
5) Switch on transmitter. If only one adult is available, place transmitter by a source of sound e.g. radio. Take child's aid into another room, hold receiver to ear at a mid volume setting and listen to sound level. Get used to the power of the aid.

Such checks will ensure that there are no faults in either the conventional or the radio facility.

If problems arise try:
1) New lead – listen again;
2) New button receiver – listen again;
3) New battery pack, in aids where slidable pack is used.

On aids where it is not possible to gain access to batteries it will be necessary to seek the advice of the hearing aid technician should steps 1 and 2 not prove effective.

If the aid is functional on the radio facility but not on the conventional microphone facility, then the aid will have to be returned to the technician because the trouble is clearly not in the lead, receiver or battery.

Some parents may have neighbours with hearing impaired children using the same radio hearing aid system, in which case it may be possible with their help to isolate a more serious fault, and thus reduce the time in repair. If for example the radio facility does not function, but normal conventional microphone facility does, a problem in the radio transmitter or radio receiver is indicated, so it would be useful to borrow the neighbour's transmitter (checking of course that the frequency used in this transmitter is the same as that used in the suspect transmitter – i.e. that colour codes are the same. If not take the receiver crystal out of your aid and replace it with your neighbour's) and test the system again. If the child's aid now functions on radio facility, this would confirm that the parent's transmitter was faulty. If the aid is still non functional, the indication is a fault in the radio receiver. Confirm that the parent's transmitter is functional, as a cross-check, by using it with the neighbour's radio hearing aid receiver.

It is only by careful checking on a daily basis that parents can ensure that the hearing aids work steadily and satisfactorily.

For instance, they should listen through the radio hearing aid early every evening, if the child has worn it throughout the day. Listen to the power of the signal in comparison to that obtained first thing in the morning. If the signal is weak, this indicates that the battery resources have been drained and the battery requires recharging, so you should fit conventional aids on the child for the remainder of the day; or, if the aid has a detachable battery pack, replace the pack with a newly charged battery. It is vital to remember that both radio hearing aid and radio microphone batteries must be placed on nightly recharge.

As with normal aids, regular routine calibration is necessary at the audiology centre or hearing aid clinic.

It is good practice for parents to switch off their radio transmitter when they and the child are apart for a significant length of time in the home. Children need to be able to spend time listening to their own voice, and to the sounds they generate from play activities. We are all required to do some tasks in the home when it is best to leave the child in another room, such as vacuum cleaning, and if the parent's transmitter in such circumstances is left on, the child will receive the sounds of these activities at the same loudness as if they were in the same room – the parent's transmitter conveys the sounds to the child without loss in energy, so that any sound-making attempts by the child picked up by the hearing aid microphone would be drowned out.

Remember that the child's hearing aid microphone will in any case pick up some sounds from other rooms in the home, though at a relatively quieter level than from the radio transmitter. In the example above, if the radio transmitter were turned off the child would be likely still to hear the noise of the vacuum cleaner, but not to have his own noise making activities masked out. It is therefore suggested that a parent should bear this point in mind and switch off the radio transmitter, particularly when away from the child and engaged in a noisy home activity. This will also increase battery life in the hearing aid.

The Auditory Training Unit

One of the problems facing parents of hearing impaired children is that of ensuring that the child derives full benefit from amplification, and therefore makes full use of her residual hearing. The problem of maintaining the required output level from a hearing aid, particularly where the child is severely or profoundly impaired, is made more difficult by the problem of acoustic feedback, that often limits the amplification enjoyed by a child.

An auditory training unit, as shown in the photograph (Plate 49), is a very useful and important facility that can be used most effectively in encouraging the development of language. The system is best used in short (ten-minute) sessions during the day, when the child is not very active. A session with mum around a table is an ideal situation, playing perhaps with an animal farm, picture lotto, a jigsaw or a story book.

The basic advantages of an auditory training unit, particularly for a severely hearing impaired child, stem from the high fidelity design and the freedom from acoustic feeback. The system has a wide frequency response that can be shaped to a particular child's needs. High quality earphone receivers in the headphones and excellent quality microphones for both parent and child ensure a good listening experience.

The auditory training unit is clearly not practical as a personal hearing aid, because it is too bulky, but it is able to amplify a wider range of speech sounds than a conventional aid, particularly in the high frequencies where much consonant sound information is contained. The system should generally be used in a quiet room where the signal quality of parent's and child's voice (each has their own microphone) will not be impaired by background noise. The majority of severely hearing impaired preschool children will have an auditory training unit in the home, and parents should be instructed in the use and setting of the system by the professional worker who is advising them.

Summary

The general day to day use of hearing aids with children presents parents with wide and varied problems, but problems which if overcome make an enormous contribution to the child's subsequent language development. In the early years of life the child is totally dependent upon the parents for fitting, setting and maintaining the aids. The parents in turn require support and guidance from the visiting teacher of the deaf, the audiologist and the hearing aid technician.

The selection of a particular hearing aid for a child will depend upon the degree of loss and the age of the child. There is however no doubt that hearing aid selection does vary between clinics, and we do see cases of children who have been issued with inappropriate amplification, so parents should see the provision and maintenance of hearing aids as a team effort and persist in discussing their observations of their child's response to the aids with the professional workers.

One of the most common and frustrating problems facing a large number of parents with hearing impaired children, is that of obtaining satisfactory earmoulds. This is a world wide problem; although great advances have been made in hearing aid design and provision over the past few years, little if any progress has been made in earmould provision. The problem is basically two-fold: use of unsuitable materials that are unable to handle high output levels of amplification without causing acoustic feedback; and lack of experienced, well trained personnel to prescribe, make and fit them.

The authors have spent considerable time in earmould research, and concluded that soft acrylic, silicone and vinyl earmould materials are desirable for young children. These materials, when used by trained personnel, can and do to a large extent overcome the problems of feedback. However, of these materials only soft acrylic is presently available under National Health Service provision. The authors feel strongly that future research should be aimed at developing one-stage 'on the spot' earmoulds for children. This policy could overcome the feedback problem while at the same time ensuring the child was not deprived of the aids during the waiting period involved in two-stage processes. However, even with an 'ideal' material the problem will not be overcome until it is realised that mould making is a highly skilful job, requiring the services of a well trained technician. So advanced training courses for earmould technicians are essential.

Parents must therefore persevere in their attempts to obtain satisfactory earmoulds. Sometimes the problems can be overcome by obtaining private earmoulds from specialist companies, and the authors would be pleased to advise parents who have difficulties with earmould provision. We feel strongly that the best possible moulds *should* be available on the NHS.

Parents who develop routines in the care, maintenance and fitting of hearing aids greatly help their child to derive full benefit from the aids. However, it is important too for parents to realise that the benefits in terms of linguistic skills will take time. Linguistic development does not happen overnight, and parents who spend time playing with the child and making use of everyday home activities as language activities, will best facilitate the child's own language development. Remember, the normally hearing child listens for a year or more before he says his first words; and the hearing impaired child may have been completely unstimulated by language prior to being issued with aids.

NOTE: The Home Office Radio Microphone System Licence is obtainable by requesting form BR9 from the Home Office, Radio Regulatory Divivsion, Waterloo Bridge House, Waterloo Road, London SE1 8UA. A fee will be payable. Parents who purchase radio systems privately should seek the advice of their local hearing aid technician, if in any doubt. Systems provided by Education Authorities will be licenced and in such cases no further steps need to be taken.

6 : Stimulating Language Development

In the early part of this chapter we plan to put forward our views about how hearing-impaired children develop language. We feel this theoretical understanding is vital, and that basic attitudes are more important than any individual practical decision. Your basic philosophy determines the whole of the language environment you provide for your child, so that individual language activities – involving the child in household tasks, for instance, or playing with toys – will fit into an overall strategy.

First it goes without saying that you want your child to develop language. But he will not learn language because you want him to – he will learn it *because he wants to*. This fact we believe to be fundamental to our understanding of *how* he will learn: he will learn language through an interaction between the efforts of his own brain, and events in the outside world.

There is now a great deal of evidence to support the claim that normally hearing children, as they learn their language, take what information they need from the environment and construct their own language system from the data they receive. They do not passively imitate adult language – we shall demonstrate this later. For the moment we suggest only that we provide the environment, but the child must organise the sensory inputs and construct his own language system for himself. So in this sense language may be learned, but not taught.

We believe that the language learning facility possessed by normally hearing children is also possessed by hearing impaired children, and that, with the exception of some with severe secondary handicaps, hearing impaired children learn the mother tongue naturally. Of course there will be variations in the level of functioning, as there are with normally hearing children, but we know that oral language can be their tool of thought and communication.

Many parents tell us that what they want for their child is for him to fit into society, to be acceptable socially; and paramount in their minds is that he should talk. For the great majority of hearing impaired children this is possible, given that they are provided with an environment where at the early stages the only form of communication is through spoken language, and later through spoken and written language. Success depends further on emphasising normal standards in behaviour (as we describe in this book), work and play, as well as normal standards of communication; and it also depends on the fullest and most efficient use of what remaining hearing the child has.

We would argue that the language of hearing impaired children suffers delays related to an absence of early stimulation, but that once started, and provided sufficient stimulation is given, it follows a pattern very similar to the language development of normally hearing children.

Children begin to acquire language because they realise very early on that speech is a way of operating in the world, of controlling and manipulating it. From the language input she receives, the child starts to abstract the acoustic features – such as stress, rhythm and intonation. Normal users of the same language may process these speech sounds differently, but this will be of no consequence to the child as long as she devises a method enabling her to recognise all the distinctions which the language 'English' demands. Hearing impaired children can use their remaining hearing to make these distinctions just as colour blind people can learn to accommodate the inability to distinguish between the colours of the traffic lights.

It is very important for parents to understand that, in language acquisition, reception takes place before production: the child understands more than he can say. What the child learns is then applied to his production of language. However, parents should also be aware that reception and production are interactive, so the child will be providing himself with auditory feedback – talking to himself, if you like – in order to build up the appropriate patterns in his brain. Thus a child's microphone is every bit as useful in enabling him to hear himself talking as it is in enabling him to hear others.

As your child starts to recognise sounds you will feel rewarded for your early efforts, particularly when the first words start to flow. However, children learn words because the things they represent are appealing to them at that time, so do not over-emphasise the *teaching* of words at this stage. Even if you are successful in getting a child to say a particular word, it is unlikely to appear again spontaneously in his vocabulary, at least until he has heard it many more times and he decides the time is right to transfer it from his passive to his active vocabulary. You should concentrate on giving the child the opportunity to receive your language, and leave him to organise his own production.

When he reaches the stage of seeing that words can be strung together, he has reached a very important milestone: he has started to understand the *structure* of language. He will begin to make statements of two elements, which have a syntactic connection, such as **All-gone cup.** What is interesting is that such two-word sentences are not used in adult speech in the same way: the child has constructed his own unit of language from his own experience. The two words are personal to him, they encompass a 'meaning' for that child at that time.

At this point your child will be greatly encouraged by feedback to him. If he says **Bye-bye Teddy** you may say **Where's Teddy gone?** Thus you repeat part of his utterance (to reinforce it) and offer new information for his brain to work on.

At the next stage, the child uses what some people have called telegraphic speech, such as **Mummy rabbit garden**. These sentences are not only like telegrams, they are just as susceptible to confusion. Key words carry the message. So we often need clues about the situation in order to understand what is meant.

Another interesting stage is that when children perceive general rules, such as those for tense changes, and apply them universally. We hear sentences like **Iain waked up, The house is saled**, although the child has certainly heard 'woke up' and 'sold'. He has perceived the rule that to change to past tense we usually add 'ed', and is applying it – the rule takes precedence over his aural perception of 'woke', 'sold' etc. He does the same with saying **mouses** instead of 'mice'. So a fascinating feature of language development in normally hearing children is that, although the children are not exposed to a uniform presentation of language, they rapidly generate rules and start to learn their own language. What is of great interest to us is that researchers are reporting *the same phenomenon* among hearing impaired children, thus providing further support for the notion that hearing impaired children too act positively on the language input in constructing their own grammar.

Parents of young children learning language speak to them in a particular way – naturally, and without anyone telling them how to do it, they adopt a specific style of speech. This style is adopted by adults other than parents as well, and even by older children when they are talking to one– two– and three–year-olds. And it does not consist simply in baby talk ('horsey' and 'piggy') since some parents deliberately avoid this. The language we all use to young children has shorter, simpler sentences, a smaller vocabulary and is somewhat slower in delivery than adult/adult speech, and is more repetitive. It would seem to have been specially designed to help children recognise the important features in sentences. As the child's language develops, so the language spoken to him becomes more complex. In other words, the adult speaker is *accommodating to the language level of the child*.

As far as hearing impaired children are concerned, we would want to provide a stimulating environment similar to the one which seems to be so successful for hearing children. The normally hearing child receives most of his linguistic information auditorily, with a little support from vision – information carried by non-verbal aspects such as facial expression, lip movements, gesture and so on. In the past, a great deal of stress in the teaching of hearing impaired children has been on these non-verbal, visual elements, particularly on lip-reading, and undoubtedly skills are developed in this direction. But there is no doubt that, if treated as the major component of reception, lip-reading is unreliable and imprecise. Two thirds of the sounds that make up the English language are either invisible or visually ambiguous. Many are for instance greatly dependent on voicing and nasality for their intelligibility, features which are not visible, so that groups of sounds such as /p,b,m; t,d,n; s,z/ are liable to frequent confusion. Other consonants, /k,g,j/ are made far back in the mouth and are totally invisible. In any case, normal speech is too rapid and impermanent to be easily lip-read, even by the most skilful.

Lip-reading will thus support a child in his attempts to build a communication system *at a level which he prescribes*; but our newest evidence suggests that there is a less central role for it with hearing impaired children than was formerly thought to be the case. We are noticing that young hearing impaired children fitted with modern high powered hearing aids pay much less visual attention to their mothers than we might expect. And we believe that this is because they are building language auditorily, and using vision only for the same purposes as normally hearing children – that is, to maintain contact in the interaction situation, to signal to mum that she should say something, to make sure she is paying attention, and so on. In our view there is no point in insisting on visual attention before speaking, but there is every point in speaking if the child looks at you, and your interpretation is that he requires information. There is even some evidence to suggest that continually attempting to draw the child's visual attention to the speaker actually results in the breakdown of interaction. We are convinced, and our experience supports us, that the auditory mode can be *the* mode of information transmission for hearing impaired children.

The prime requirement is that you forget the language (it will take care of itself) and focus on the needs of the communication. If your language is governed by the child's communication needs, it will be appropriate. People may try to encourage you to talk – talk – talk, and of course some extra input is required to start to offset the child's deficit of language stimulation; but to concentrate solely on talk leads to the real danger that your child's offerings will be ignored (remember what we have said about how *he* constructs his own language), and that talk will then become merely background noise. When you focus what you say on the communication act, your language will be more appropriate and meaningful to the child. An example will illustrate what we mean. If you and the child are playing with a doll and the child is attempting to feed the doll, but you say **Here's dolly's pillow**, ignoring what he is actually doing, you are missing a real act of communication. You must learn to interpret and predict your child's interests and language needs.

The first step that the child takes in learning language is to learn that it is a turn taking game. He makes a sound, someone imitates it, he makes it again, and so on. So going for communication means giving the child his turn. This gives him the opportunity to practise control over his vocal organs, and to feed back his growing knowledge of the sounds, and later the words, of speech to his ears and brain.

It is important for talk to be at a normal rate, with normal structures, intonation and stress. This will make available to the child the clues of timing, pitch, rhythm etc. that are important if he is to learn to speak naturally. If speech is too slow, emphatic or over articulated it will reduce rather than increase the amount of information available to the child.

Work at Manchester University has confirmed the hypothesis that distortions of the time elements in hearing impaired children's speech contribute significantly to its poor intelligibility: duration of vowels and monosyllables, number and length of pauses, and overall speech rate all correlate highly with intelligibility. In the Manchester study the most intelligible children spoke more than three times faster than the least intelligible.

We have seen many parents move through stages of wondering whether it was worth talking at all because the child was deaf, through over-articulating and distorting their speech, and finally back to talking to him in the same way they did before he was found to be hearing impaired.

As speech starts to develop, our advice is to do nothing about 'correction' or 'speech improvement' except auditorily by demonstration. Articulation teaching is a teacher's job. With many children it need never be undertaken and with others it will be undertaken only when fluent communication is established.

At this point we propose to comment a little about play and language, and to list some suggestions for activities broadly appropriate to the various age ranges. (In the information section we list excellent sources on activities with children which you can consult – remember again that the attitude to communication is more important than the activities themselves).

Let us consider three categories of interaction, each of which may be brought under the broad heading of play, and all bound up with the development of communication skills.

1 (Plates 64, 65) Household and everyday activities, in which the child can be involved and which offer much in the way of stimulation to communicate. (Mothers call this area work, children regard it as part of play.)

2 (Plates 66-69) Play with toys: we actively involve the child in play for the purpose of stimulating a desire to communicate.

3 (Plate 70) Free play where the child is left to himself to indulge in play of his own choice, whether it be building a tower, carrying out an operation, or pretending to be mum getting in the shopping. In this play the adults are not intervening.

In play related to household activities, the important fact to remember is that almost any activity can have communication potential for a child, but that this does not mean that every household activity must be used for that purpose every time. Nor is there any need for a running commentary on every activity you undertake: we do not think the major components of language can be drip-fed in this way. Communication is meaningful when you have something you must get over to the child, or he has something to tell you, and this will happen most often when you are involved in activities together. Suppose for instance that you are washing the dishes. You might comment as follows: **'I'm putting some washing up liquid in the bowl, now the hot water.**

Oh look, lots of lovely suds.' On the other hand, you might get a stool for the child to stand on, and another bowl for him to put some dishes in, and make conversation along the following lines: **'Put some washing up liquid in the bowl'** (hand the child the container); **'Careful, not too much. Can you turn on the tap? Come on, let's put some hot water in. Turn it on.'** In the second example, each time you say something to the child there is a meaning for him to grasp. When you say 'turn on the tap,' you are expecting the child to do it, so you will persevere until he grasps what you mean. In the first example the child may attend or not, because he is not really involved, and as like as not he will continue playing with his cars on the kitchen floor. Trying to provide experiences in household activities and shopping trips etc. gives opportunities for a shared 'meaning' or 'understanding' between you and the child.

As far as play with toys and other materials is concerned, we would encourage you to put aside a few short periods each day when you can give your undivided attention to play. Here are some general hints for these play periods.

Physical aspects of the play situation
An ideal arrangement is a low table with your child sitting on a suitably sized stool or chair – the chairs we use in our clinic have arms, which make the child secure and comfortable. With very young children it is a good idea to use the 'baby relax' type of chair, which has a wide range of adjustment. It is useful for you to be opposite the child so that you can show him things easily, but also so that you can be seen easily by him – crouched on your knees is a good position. If you have an auditory training unit, this is a good time to use it; but in any case you are likely to be providing a good auditory signal for the child in the relatively good acoustic conditions of a quiet room.

Limit of the choice of play material
One of the problems frequently encountered in directed play is overstimulation and distraction because too many toys have been set in front of the child. Either choose something yourself which you feel will interest him or allow him to

choose a toy, but once the choice is made remove what is not being played with.

Gain the child's attention
There are clearly many ways of gaining the child's attention. You can call his name frequently or touch him, but if his interest is not only to be gained but sustained you will need to mind the following points:

1 Try to develop vivid facial expressions, these are likely both to arouse and retain the child's interest: show surprise, pleasure, anger and other strong emotions.

2 The element of surprise is always intriguing to young children. On occasions you can hide a toy (under the table or under another object), and offer clues to its position such as a quick peep (without letting the child see), or a face full of expression, and **what's under there?**, pointing at the object. You can doubtless think of many ways of building the element of surprise into other activities.

3 In many cases the attention of the child will be best maintained by the simple expedient of doing what he indicates he'd like to do. If you have a toy with a variety of possible uses, observe the child and develop the play in the way that interests him.

Remember that with all young children you have to work at getting and keeping attention.

Pace the activity
An activity too easily completed offers limited opportunity for communication – an example that springs to mind is the child who can complete the inset jigsaw so quickly that he has put in all the parts without giving you any opportunity to develop the interaction. So you have to pace the activity. You can perhaps put all the parts in an envelope and allow the child to select the pieces one at a time, and use the occasion to teach concepts such as **just one at a time,** and **reach in,** as well as to discuss the individual jigsaw pieces. Another possibility is to introduce models or examples of the picture in the jigsaw, and then get the child to match the two.

You will think of many more developments for this and other games.

Flexible use of toys

When looking at the following activities and comments about child development, remember that some toys suggested as useful early on can be used profitably throughout the pre-school years, though the child will be using them in different ways at different ages. Thus the bricks may be sucked at three months, will probably be built into a little tower (and knocked down) in the second year, and will later be counted, sorted for different colours, and built into more elaborate formations such as a castle, the airport or the zoo. These latter uses can be allied to play with other toys, such as knights, model aeroplanes and animals. The major point to absorb is that toys may be used very flexibly by the child. His interests should constantly be anticipated and the appropriate toys provided, but this does not necessarily mean buying new toys, so much as bringing out again toys which he has not used for some time, but which might now be put to a different use.

In what follows you will notice only meagre reference to the use of books. We regard books as entering the child's life at a few months, and gradually taking a more and more important position in his life. A sectionalised list of books suitable for pre-school hearing impaired children appears in Appendix 1. This is only a small selection of the thousands which are available. Publications useful to you are listed in Appendix 2, and in Appendix 3 are addresses which you may find useful.

Play in the first year of life

This is a year of rapid development of many skills, and the toys you use and games you play will reflect your interest in helping your child to develop.

In terms of movement, or motor skills, he progresses in a single year from largely uncontrolled and reflexive actions, with no ability to sit up or hold the head up, to sitting firmly in one position on the carpet, his back now straight and head erect. He can turn while sitting and reach for toys; he can stand; is likely to be walking with one hand held or possibly even without. He will also have been developing his visual perception, following shapes, recognising them, positioning them in space and learning to reach them, and to explore them when he has them in his hands.

In terms of sound the normally hearing child will have had experience of all sorts of sounds arriving at his ears from different directions: above his head, from side to side, in front. And by the time he is one year old he will be vocalising quite deliberately as a means of communication, expressing friendliness or annoyance. He will shout for attention, listen to check on your response and then shout again. He will probably be babbling in a tuneful way strings of syllables such as **dad-dad, mam-mam, adaba, agaga**. It is likely that by the time he is one he will understand several simple instructions, such as **Give it to mummy, Where are your shoes?**; and in his own expressions several word forms may be recognised.

It may have been distortions of this very early language development which pin-pointed for you the possibility that your child might have a hearing problem. The hearing impaired child does babble, but the babble remains at a primitive level and usually does not develop into the tuneful, repetitive speech-like babble of the normally hearing child – at least not without the stimulation of a hearing aid. We therefore need to create similar experiences for the hearing impaired children to those which have been provided for normally hearing children. He will need to hear sounds in all planes and see sound makers of many different types. Many useful items are listed below; but it may take quite some time for your child to associate sounds with their source.

The child initially enjoys exploring toys with his mouth; but from around six months he will like being involved in give and take games with balls and other toys. He should be encouraged in this natural development of turn-taking – roll a ball to him, for instance, and hold your hands ready to receive it back.

The child from the first year will delight in rhythmical activities, and you can do no better than start with action nursery rhymes – the ones where some action is synchronised with the lines of the rhyme: e.g. I'm a little teapot, Incy Wincy Spider or Pat-a-Cake. Your child will be able to follow the actions even before he can make a lot of use of his auditory discrimination, and if the activities are done often he will soon progress. Probably the best way is for you to sing the rhyme whilst guiding the child in the actions, but for those who have forgotten all their rhymes there are records and cassette tapes available commercially.

Toys to stimulate the child in the first year may include the following:

Toys to hold and suck
Rattles	Soft balls
Teething rings	Cotton reels
Cubes	Most plastic toys

To rattle and bang etc.
Rattles	Drums
Clacker	Clothes pegs
Bells	Bricks
Xylophone or chime bars	Squeaky toys

To feel/look at
Picture books in card or cloth	Cellophane, velvet, silk
Soft toys	Wooden spoons
Baby mirror	Pans and pan lids
Mobiles	(Tins filled with pebbles,
Colourful alphabet and nursery rhymes frieze	dried peas, rice or sand make very good shakers.
Pebbles and stones	Tin foil bottle tops nailed
Rough and smooth wood	loosely to a dowel stick
Toys to be recognised by feel	make a lovely sound.)

An essential requirement at this age is the safety of the child. The toys must have no toxic paint on them, and no sharp edges, and they must not be so small that they can be swallowed. However as the child's manipulative skills advance (towards the end of the first year), provided he is under supervision a child can be given smaller items: pieces of wood or plastic with holes in them, and small containers with one or two sweets in them to encourage him to explore inside. It must be remembered though that for much of the first eight to twelve months he will still explore items in the mouth. When he is twelve months he should be able to hold an object in each hand, pick up small objects, crumbs, sweets etc., and drop and throw toys deliberately, so a whole new series of games will suggest themselves. You will be able to think of many items to add to the above list, to help develop and extend the child's language skills.

Year two
As year two progresses, the child becomes more mobile. By fifteen months he is walking and may even be running. He likes to climb, though sometimes finds 'retreat' difficult. He will reverse into a small chair, or slide in sideways to sit down. In an adult's chair, he will probably climb in forward and then turn round to sit. As the year progresses the child is more keen to explore and your play with him should reflect this new curiosity: you can hide things for him to find, encourage him to post shapes in posting boxes, put on lids, and place small objects in and take them out of containers, pour water, sink ships and so on.

The child will by now play alone with his toys, but he is still very dependent on familiar adults and will enjoy you joining in with his play. He may not be too keen on strangers at this stage, particularly if they do not give him time to get used to them. He will no longer be taking toys to his mouth, and knows where many of the objects around the house belong. (With such a keen explorer, it is vital that dangerous substances such as bleach and powerful disinfectants are locked securely away.) If you introduce picture books to the child early, he should enjoy looking at them and recognise many of his favourite pictures.

The second year is a good time to introduce the child to drawing and painting. He will enjoy scribbling, and though initially he will grasp the pencil in his whole hand he will gradually develop the pincer grip, and his movements, and therefore his drawing, will become more controlled. He should be given the opportunity to use paints, perhaps finger paints at first, or ordinary powder paint with a paste such as Polycell added to thicken the mix (choose a paste *without* fungicide.) A child-size easel (we use the regular school-type easel and extend the boards almost to the ground for pre-schoolers) is a real boon, and some kind of plastic apron for the child (and probably for the floor) is essential.

A child's increasing co-ordination between hand and eye will be reflected in his greater ability to build towers, stack rings, pour water carefully from one container to another, make constructions with bricks, such as Lego, use posting boxes etc.

Various researchers have reported observing swings in the child's mood between clinginess and resistance, or 'negativism', at some point in the second year. This is a period when the child seems to oppose you out of sheer wilfulness, and this seems to happen whether or not the child is hearing-impaired. It may reflect his growing independence, and also perhaps an underlying desire for boundaries to be defined for him. He is mobile and wants to explore his environment; you want this, but quite naturally you want also to protect him from things which may be dangerous (and your home from damage). There is clearly an area of potential conflict here, and it may help you in handling it if you look more carefully at the issues. Are you attaching more intent to a child's actions than is actually warranted? Is it vandalism for an eighteen-month-old old baby to draw with crayons on the television screen, or to throw bricks near that expensive piece of equipment? We think not. We are not suggesting that a child should not be taught that throwing bricks is likely to damage things, but we are suggesting that at this age he will not know that doing so will damage the set. Try to look at it from his point of view. Until this point in his development you have always been encouraging, smiling when he threw his toys from the pram, or at his first attempts to scribble. Now you show another side of your personality – the angry face, the wagging finger. If you are now to guide him through this difficult stage you will need to be *positive*. For example, if the child is starting to scribble on the wall with his crayons, you may conclude more of your attention is demanded. For a while, give him crayons only when you are with him, and make sure that you have ready a good supply of the paper you want him to draw on. He will soon realise the way to do it, and come to you for paper and crayons. In this way you will be dealing positively, teaching what is acceptable.

There is no way to remove all temptations from the child, but it is in everyone's interest to remove as many as possible. If you do not want your expensive ornaments 'played with', put them in a safe place! Keep the number of things you need to be negative about to the child to a minimum, and be firm about the few remaining ones. Convey your disapproval by shaking your head and saying **no** firmly. Be consistent about things, and don't say **no** one day and **yes** the next. You are defining the boundaries for your child. We shall say more about this later in the problems section, but when tempers run high, one of your most trusted methods can be distraction. Try to get the child's attention off the things about which you disapprove and on to some enjoyable but acceptable behaviour.

You will notice that somewhere between 18 and 24 months voluntary bladder control starts to develop. At first the child wets his pants, and only afterwards indicates this to you, too late for the use of the potty. Then, restlessness and vocalisations precede the wetting, and become indications that he requires his potty – there will usually be a great urgency at this stage, as the child just cannot wait. Gradually the urgency disappears and the child is able to wait a little longer as control of the bladder begins to develop. Soon after the child is two years old he has fairly good bladder control. Many children are also dry at night a few months later.

Towards the end of the second year, the normally hearing child will have moved through babble and jargon (tuneful strings of utterances which are not intelligible, but have some of the features – rhythm, intonation and pitch – of normal speech) to using clear single words, perhaps fifty or more, and later combinations of words to make himself understood. He will talk to himself in long monologues as he plays, but much of this speech is still incomprehensible to others.

With hearing impaired children development will clearly be slower. Indeed, if the child is severely impaired and has been diagnosed only at one year you will do well if you maintain the child babbling into the second year. Remember to try to think of him as being as old as his hearing aids, and to build expectations of language on this fact. You will be using toys and materials appropriate to his general development, but his discrimination of sounds and his vocalisations will be at a more primitive level.

Mothers of normally hearing and hearing impaired children at this age need to remember that their children's attention span will still be relatively short, and that short sharp sessions frequently are better than infrequent long sessions. They will also be more enjoyable for both.

Toys for exploration
Posting boxes
Different shaped boxes
   with a variety of lids
Construction toys
   (preferably wooden or
   plastic, with large pieces)
Containers and water
Pegs and holes (different
   sizes)
First formboards (you may
   know these as inset
   jigsaws)
Bricks

Finger paints
Safe scissors
Bit box (this should be
   filled with all sorts of
   'goodies', such as paper,
   egg boxes, containers of
   all types, pieces of wood,
   cloth and old clothes: in
   fact anything which you
   think may be useful for
   exploratory play,
   including 'making
   things.')

General toys and materials.
Hammer and pegs set
Men in the boat
Balls on sticks
Wooden blocks and shapes
Laundry set
Rocking horse
Telephone

'Feely' box (Mum puts
   small toys, or materials
   of different textures,
   sizes and shapes, into a
   black bag so that the
   child feels them before
   seeing them.)

Screw rods   Horse roundabout
Wind up toys   Construction toy

Keep up the work with the nursery rhymes and songs, and
the outdoor activities such as running, jumping, playing with
balls of different sizes or with large play equipment such as
the slide, swings, outdoor train etc.

Year three
Negative and tantrum behaviour may continue to be a
feature of the first half of this year, but as your child nears
three years we would expect him to become more amenable
and possibly more affectionate.

The two-year-old will constantly demand your attention
and may well show jealousy of attention given to other
children. However, though he is still emotionally very
dependent on you, you will notice increasing signs of
independence and a growing desire to do things for himself,
even to the point of wanting to do things alone that he cannot
manage without assistance. This is a very interesting period
and we always recommend parents not to do things for him
that he *can* do himself. We have noticed rapid fluctuations
in mood during this period and a liking for rituals. This is part
of boundary setting and pattern organisation, which perhaps
occasionally is taken too far! He may demand a ritual pattern
at bedtime, which he insists you follow however much you
try to speed up the process. He may have become very
possessive of his toys (including not being willing to go
anywhere without 'teddy' or another favourite toy), though
towards three years we would hope that your early work on
'sharing' such things as toys and sweets will be beginning to
pay dividends. The social standards you are to set for your
hearing-impaired child are the same as those we would set
for any child – no more, no less. There is no more reason
why a hearing impaired child should be rude, snatch, be
selfish or unkind than a normally hearing child. His
behaviour will depend on what you expect and demand of
him, and upon his behaviour to a large measure will depend
his level of acceptability to others.

During this year your child's ability to run around the

house avoiding obstacles will gradually increase. He will start to enjoy jumping, climbing on to things just to practice this skill. When children start walking upstairs they use two feet per step, but later they start to use alternate feet. (Coming downstairs using alternate steps is learnt later still.)

Along with this progress in gross motor development he is progressing in manipulative skills. He will during this year be able to thread large beads on a string, build a tower of six or seven bricks, post the shapes into a posting box, unscrew lids and turn the door knob. He should now be progressing with more difficult formboards (tray and inset jigsaws), and later large-size floor interlocking jigsaws. Good quality jigsaws tend to be expensive, so do not hesitate to borrow them from a toy library if there is one near you. At about two-and-a-half years you will notice that your child's drawings are starting to take more shape, perhaps a head and legs are present. Capitalise on this and encourage him to do drawings of mummy, daddy, brother Simon and so on, with you occasionally doing drawings to act as a stimulus and show him that you enjoy it too. He will be really starting to enjoy his play with paints, perhaps doing hand and foot-prints, potato prints, making shapes with modelling clay or dough made from flour, salt and water. Water play will take on new dimensions of pouring, squirting, bubbling, whisking, floating and sinking.

We would anticipate that by the time he is three you will have noted progress in his reception of speech, shown by what he understands of your speech and in his own expression, which may by now contain some intelligible words, or may simply be becoming more like the rhythmic babble of the normally hearing child at an earlier age. When these factors are reached depends on a number of factors, including the severity of your child's hearing loss, so it would be unwise for us to offer any time scale. But rest assured that when the child's vocalisations do start, they will be much like those of normally hearing children if you have provided experience of the natural patterns of language as we have recommended from an early age, and have ensured the continuity of his amplification.

Toys and play materials

Clock (with moveable
  hands)
Jigsaws
Teasets
Dolls house
Garage
Zoo
Farm
Cars and aeroplanes
  (preferably several of the
  same, so that you can
start colour and type
  matching)
Balls (including use for
  colour matching)
Nuts and bolts game
Hammer and nails set
Scrap-book (worth starting
  now with postcards and
  familiar pictures)
Colouring books
Finger puppets
Picture story books (a wide
  variety are available, see
  Appendix 1.)

Games to play

More nursery rhymes
  (encourage the child to
  lead in ring-a-ring-a-roses
  and other familiar ones)
Blow bubbles
Pretend games (I'm a plane,
  a dog, a police car)

Discrimination tapes (these
tapes can be bought from
an educational supplier,
or sometimes borrowed
from the specialist
teacher of the
deaf – they are
recordings of familiar
sounds, and the child can
listen to the sounds, for
example, and then play
the game of picking up a
corresponding object,
e.g. fire-engine, lion, dog
etc.)

You should be starting to move into all sorts of matching
games: arranging sets of the same colour, the same category
e.g. all the cars as distinct from the planes and animals.
These games will be helping auditory and visual discrimination, and also provide the very early baselines of an
important aspect of mathematical development – classifica-
tion. You must not rush this work if the child is not ready
for it. Its further development will take place when the child

is in school. There should be plenty of rough and tumble 'roly poly' type games as well.

Years four and five

In his fourth and fifth year your child will have much more confidence in his mobility. He can walk in all directions, forwards, backwards and to either side. He runs confidently and is able to stop and start at will. He will also enjoy playing on climbing frames and other large apparatus in the park. Mothers may notice a marginal improvement in shoe wear as the child becomes able to pedal rather than scoot his tricycle, although this could be more than offset by his increased desire to climb and kick his football.

Again his drawing ability is improving, so that by about four years most of the parts of the human figure are present. He should be able to draw a house with doors, windows and a chimney. He should also be developing his ability to copy shapes as you demonstrate them, such as a square and later a triangle. Perhaps as he nears five you could start a little practice at writing patterns.

Be careful, because children do find this difficult and if your child is not keen, or not able to do it, do not press the issue. The teacher will follow it up in the reception class. However if he wants to try, start by drawing the lines on a large sheet of paper and then get him to draw on your lines. While he is doing this you can guide him by saying **Up and down, up and down, round and round** as appropriate. After this, encourage him to do it underneath your lines. Finally ask him to make some patterns of his own.

During these years there is not a lot to add to the sort of play materials already made available: perhaps more books, with information about animals, ships, aeroplanes, insects, plants, dinosaurs. More sophisticated construction material can be offered, and more emphasis placed on games. Here the selection can be left to you, from the masses that are available in toyshops. The main thing is to offer as many experiences as possible.

Toys and games

Ludo

Snakes and ladders

The 'Feely' bag

Magnetic fishing

Picture lotto

Picture dominoes

Snap

Happy families

Playpeople (roadworkers, firemen, nurses etc.)

Zoo, farm, garage, airport, railway station etc.

Any games where the child has to match shape, size, colour.

We wish to draw your attention to games such as picture lotto, which are ideal for developing many skills. Lotto, played like bingo with pictures in places of numbers, is a game of turns, so the hearing impaired child can learn to wait and take his turn. A card is turned over, showing a picture. The parent says **Who has got the tea-pot?** The child has to check if this picture matches with any of the pictures on his board. This will aid his visual discrimination. Further, throughout the whole game the participants are talking – about what they have on their boards and what they have left to get, and whose turn it is next – and this will help his language.

Play with a 'pretend' model such as the garage becomes more complex as the child's language progresses, which it undoubtedly will be doing by now. **Where are the petrol pumps? Are you going to put some petrol in that sports car? He needs some oil too. Where is the oil? That car has broken down, can you bring the breakdown truck?**

Encourage your child to mix with other children, and encourage them all in pretend play by providing a suitable box of dressing up materials. If you have talked about doctors and policemen and had books on them from the library, you will find your child engaging in role play, perhaps carrying out an 'operation' on Teddy or arresting one of your neighbour's children.

Alongside this your child will be talking more and more, and it will be becoming less of a strain for you to get him to understand. His talking will encourage you, make you less tense and show you that all the effort that any family (but

yours in particular), puts into its children is really worth-
while.

7 : Preparing for School

As parents, we all hope that our children will fit happily into school when the time comes for them to attend full-time. The following comments are aimed at helping you to prepare your hearing impaired child for school.

Much time in the early part of the child's school life is spent 'playing', but you should never assume that this time is 'wasted', for play is children's 'work', and it is through play that they learn. Building with bricks of different shapes and sizes, play with water and sand, classifying and sorting objects, weighing nuts and beads and playing 'shops' all help a child to learn, for instance, important relationships relevant to their understanding of mathematics. For mathematics is not just a question of 'sums'. Similarly, imaginative and creative play is important in developing language and communication skills; and playing 'mummies' and 'daddies' and 'doctors' and 'nurses' in the Wendy House is a vital activity all children should be encouraged to pursue, developing their ideas about roles in society, and co-operation with others. Fine physical skills too are developed through play, with construction toys, jigsaw puzzles, clay modelling, painting and crayoning. These activities also help the further development of language, and co-operation with others.

Singing and saying rhymes, and listening to stories are important in encouraging verbal and other communication skills. They also act as transmitters of our culture; and to help the child feel he is really a member of a class, and that he can interact with his classmates, for story times and singing times are usually class activities whereas many other activities are done individually or in small groups.

These are all among the many things the child will do in his classroom, so it will be very useful if he can already play constructively both on his own and with other children as he nears school age. The best way to achieve these abilities is for him to be introduced gradually to them, so play a lot with him and as he nears school age, encourage him to go out to play with other children and encourage other children to come in and play with him. If he is to move towards separation from you, it is important to encourage him to spend time away from you, with friends and relatives, so that he gets the idea that you can leave but that you always return. (From the point of view of the parents too, it is important that the child accepts separation. There are no stars for the parents who claim they have never been out together because they cannot leave the children!)

It is not our intention to discuss at length the development of play in young children, since there are already many books on the topic. But we shall point to the uses of play in developing the skills and attitudes that are so important when the child goes to school. We shall do this under several headings.

Sharing and taking turns

A few examples will serve to illustrate what we mean. It is important that children are trained to share: to share their sweets and toys and to take turns in games and activities with others. You cannot start early enough to encourage children to do this. So, instead of giving children their sweets individually, make a point of getting out the quota and sharing them out in front of the children so that *share* becomes a part of their vocabulary as soon as possible. The same with toys – our children should be trained to share toys and to take turns very early in their lives. Remember that it is much easier to start early than later to re-educate a child who snatches and will not let other children have a turn. Being accepted by other children will depend far more on these social factors than on whether the child is handicapped by deafness.

There are many games you can use to encourage this skill. Follow-my-leader games, where the children follow the activity of the parent or another child, are a good example. Snakes and ladders, ludo, picture lotto, picture and colour dominoes are but a few games that can be introduced later, but basic turn taking should be started before children are old enough to be able to play them. Try to start with games with as few rules as possible, and gradually build up to the full game when you feel the child is capable. Do not let the child win all the time, or always take first turn. This is wrong for any child, and therefore it is wrong for a hearing impaired child. Learning to take turns and to lose gracefully is something we must all learn to do. However, you should try to manipulate enough success to keep his interest and motivation.

'Manners' matter

We believe that it is important to encourage a child to say *'please'* and *'thank you'* and not to snatch when handed things. A useful anti-snatching ploy in the early stages is to make a child sit down when he is receiving something. This is obviously practical and useful with food and or drink, but it can be extended to other things. Children find it much more difficult to 'snatch' if they are sitting. However you decide to tackle this problem, *be consistent*: from the very start, never allow snatching – if the child does snatch, remove the item from him. Whenever the child takes things from you properly, give him a big smile – **That's a good boy**. You can show pleasure or displeasure visually even before your hearing impaired child has much command of the language. **Please** and **thank you** are early words in the vocabulary of most normally hearing children, and for hearing impaired children they can be too if they are trained carefully.

Children like stories

When the child goes to school, story time and reading will occupy an important place in the school day. This is so in schools for hearing impaired children as well as in normal schools, and it will be very valuable if your child is used to books: if he knows how to handle them with care, is aware of stories and knows some of the traditional tales himself.

A child's love for books and stories can start with his first picture story books. Your enthusiasm will encourage him to look at, point to and eventually name pictures. You will use the same books over and over again, because your child will demand this. You should try to let your child see that you enjoy reading your own books; and, even better, to make a weekly trip for the whole family to the library to change the books. Teach him to carry books carefully and not to damage or write in them. In our experience librarians are very helpful and will obtain library books which parents recommend, as well as recommend books to you. The good local library is often much more than a 'book lending shop', more a focal point for information on local events and activities. Reading will ultimately be one of the hearing impaired child's main sources of knowledge and you should therefore nurture it early.

When you move on to 'proper' stories, use the ones which have visual content and are repetitive. 'The Three Little Pigs' is a good example – **I'll huff and I'll puff**, with you and the child actually 'huffing' and 'puffing'. Another one is the story of 'The Three Billy Goats Gruff,' but there are very many to choose from and there should be no difficulty in finding ones to interest your child. Tell the story, referring to the pictures in the book. Use your own words and have a very lively expression – make your face talk! A good time to tell stories is after a child's bath, when he is relaxed and usually receptive. Remember to refit the child's hearing aids or put on the auditory training unit headphones so that sound is loud and clear. As the child becomes familiar with the story, it is a good idea to get him to act it out. And the time will eventually arrive when he will want to tell you the story, so be ready to listen. Parents, in their efforts to stimulate a child with natural language, sometimes forget that the child wants to communicate with *them*. We can be so keen to push our language to the child that we ignore, or do not see, his attempts to reciprocate. Watch for these attempts and listen to what he has to say. *Listening* is important in *both* directions. Many teachers of normally hearing children are saying that there are today many youngsters who seem unable to sit quietly and listen either to stories or instructions, and some blame home backgrounds where the child is constantly bombarded with noise from the television or record player. It is of course even more a problem for the home to be continually noisy where there is a hearing impaired child in it. So try to have quiet times through the day, and to use television constructively when both you and he can take part in activities which interest him.

Many of the games you play with your child will be encouraging his visual development and/or fine control of fingers. This is all necessary ground work for developing reading and writing skills.

Developing reading skills
The child's growing ability to communicate is the vital baseline for the development of reading skills. Teachers talk of pre-reading skills, and language development is the first stage of pre-reading, so the right early emphasis is on the training of listening skills and talking skills. As far as listening activities are concerned, you might add some of the following to your repertoire:

1) Copying clapped patterns, as in some nursery rhymes.
2) Making a noise with an object the child cannot see, and asking him to identify it.
3) Making pictures or stories in sound: some of these can be obtained on tapes, ranging from the simple noise of a fire engine to quite complicated sound stories. Sound stories also help the child to think in sequence.
4) Playing with puppets, mime and drama encourage the child to be more relaxed and outgoing.

Allied to the above, there is always the need to give the child opportunity to tell you things. Encourage him to tell stories as soon as he is able. Encourage any interest in nature, science or one topic which will enable valuable conversation to spring forth.

Activities which would have the benefit of extending his vocabulary are limitless. Nouns are easy, so do not give them too much emphasis. Try to offer words in as many contexts as possible, so that the child sees that the same word can be used in many ways.

Encourage your child to look carefully and in detail at objects and pictures. Ask questions that require this careful looking. The idea of sequence, which is important in encouraging the child to read from left to right for instance, can be further stressed by use of picture stories (some comics are good for this). It is possible to obtain picture sequence cards which the child has to put into the correct order. And encourage the child to think: do not ask him just what **is**, ask him what **is not**, what **is missing**, what **is different?**

Encourage your child to match pictures. Build up a collection of your own with lots of duplicates, so you can say **Find me another cat, Is there another tree?** and so on. Play games such as picture lotto, picture dominoes, snap, happy families, lost and found, all of which encourage this skill. This can be linked with the development of one-to-one correspondence in mathematics, where one item, say a picture of one saucer, is matched to a picture of one cup.

As far as the actual reading of words and sentences is concerned, we shall outline our general view and make some suggestions to follow. Teachers talk of 'reading readiness', and if this concept is to have meaning then we would take it to be the point where the child has matured sufficiently, or has enough previous learning, to enable him to proceed easily with learning the skills of reading. There is indeed plenty of evidence to show that activities such as we have described, which improve a child's visual and auditory discrimination, help him towards readiness to read. In the early years we often limit the child's language experience to the experience of spoken words, but there is good evidence that the same early period should be used for the mastery of visual language symbols.

But in saying this we are not advocating early formal instruction. We do not in fact believe that parents should be using a formal reading scheme at all – not because we believe that only the teacher can use this, but because this is not where reading should start. Reading should start from the child himself and his own experiences, and not from the second-hand experiences in printed books. In other words, we must devise an environment in which they learn to read as they do to talk, naturally.

Where better to start than with the child's own name? You could for example make a large book, draw a picture of the child on the cover, and write (in a balloon coming from his mouth) **I am Peter.** Then ask the child to read it with you. On the next page draw a picture of yourself, and write **I am Mummy**, or **I am Daddy**, and so on for the rest of the family. Later you can work on **I can . . . . . I have . . . . .** etc. and gradually encourage the child to do his own drawings, and to ask for the words. Whatever you write for the child should be in lower case letters, as follows:

a b c d e f g h i j k l m n o p q r s t u v w x y z

This is most important because this is what the teacher will use in school, and what the child will see in any printed book. It is also helpful if in the early stages you write clear large letters.

Alongside this, you might encourage the child to read labels, such as **television, chair, door,** by sticking labels on these items around the house, and then getting him to match further labels to them, and to read the words. Encourage him to attempt to read the many labels in everyday life and make a collection: **cornflakes, honey, butter, no entry, stop, wait, car park, bus stop,** and so on.

As the child's interests extend outwards, he may be encouraged to produce his own scrapbook of **the living room, the kitchen, the garage, the zoo, the park, the seaside**, using pictures from old magazines, catalogues, and postcards. You write in the appropriate words for him. Use these home made books as his first reading books. You can even make flash cards which he can use to match to words in the books. This works best if you make the books fairly big, with large print. You will soon see that this method gives you the opportunity to develop quite a large reading vocabulary without resorting to a reading scheme. You should be guided by the child, however, since if you push too hard and reading becomes a chore, he will react adversely. If you are sensitive, he will come to you for more words, to demonstrate his growing skill at reading them.

As far as his writing is concerned you will be able to encourage by drawing various shapes and wavy lines and allowing him to copy them. These are known as writing patterns. If he attempts to draw over these and then to copy them, encourage this and compliment his efforts, but if he is not interested, leave him to do his own drawings and paintings. Make sure he has large pieces of paper and fat crayons and thick paint brushes.

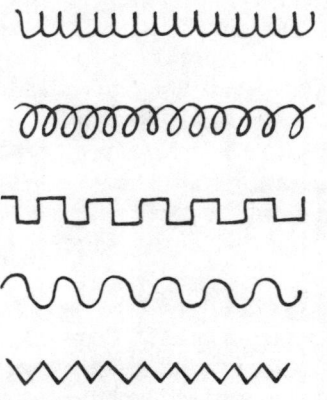

Fig. 28   Examples of writing patterns.

So far, the tactics we have suggested are those to encourage *word recognition*. This stage in reading is the easiest one, and many children will appear to read before they are actually able to do so in the true sense. Your task, as it is the task of the teacher later, is to ensure that the reading of words goes hand in hand with the child's understanding of them. Forget any thoughts you may have that your child is learning reading only when he is being instructed on a reading scheme, and encourage him to see the words which are all around him.

If the child is going to a residential school
If your child is to attend a residential school, make sure he will have special places for his personal possessions, both at school and at home, for he will be very distressed if he comes home and finds that there is no longer a special place for him. Give him photographs to take to school, and show him that you always have his photographs on display at home.

Anyone who has taught in a residential school will know the atmosphere of expectancy as the letters are being distributed at morning assembly or in the classroom, and the delight of the child who realises that there is one for him. Write just as often as you can, and include simple sentences, *clearly written* so that your child can start to read them himself. We are pressing this point because teachers sometimes find parents' letters difficult to read, never mind the child himself.

Try to give the child a method of working out how long he will be away and when he will come home. This could be a little calendar which you make, with a picture of home and one of school, so the child can tick off the days as they go by.

Families with handicapped children often become rather isolated, so that they do not make use of baby-sitter groups or let neighbours look after their child. It is very important, and we stress this at other points in the book, that you train your child gradually to become used to being away from you, especially if he is to go to residential school. He should be ready to take separation, and to understand that he will be coming home after his week at school.

School visits
Parents on the guidance programme at Manchester University are encouraged to visit a variety of educational establishments before any decisions about placement are made.

Parental choice is not as free as we or some parents would wish, but in the Manchester area there is a good range of provision available, which is not the case in all parts of the country, especially in some rural areas. Manchester is able to provide the full range of services for hearing impaired children, from schools for profoundly deaf children, to schools for partially-hearing, to partially hearing units in normal schools, to a range of support services for children in normal classes.

We give parents the opportunity to visit a range of educational environments and it is our experience that they are usually clear in their judgment of what sort of provision is most suitable for their child. If you have the opportunity to make such visits, take it, and make the most of it in terms of influencing subsequent school placement in the light of your child's handicap. If you are not offered such visits, ask for them.

What to look for when you visit a school

1) Get to know what your child's audiogram looks like and compare it with those of the children in the school or class. This will allow a comparison of degree of deafness, but *not* degree of handicap, since the amount of handicap depends on many other things as well as the deafness: age of diagnosis, your effort in the early years, your child's intelligence, personality and motivation.

2) Look at children at both ends of the school if possible, new entrants and school leavers. Observe the communication skills at both these ages, and you will have at least a rough idea of the general level of communication skills attained in the school.

3) If the school is residential, ask to see the dormitories, and see if it looks as if attempts are made to provide a homely atmosphere. Ask about the child care supervision in the evenings: who looks after the children and what sort of things they do. You are looking for a school that is well staffed and lively in terms of activities. However, trust your eyes as well as your ears. If you are told that the school has a photography club, then ask to see the darkroom and some of the children's work if it is available.

4) It may be difficult for you to evaluate the academic aspects of the school or unit, but you can ask for information about the average achievements of pupils. Look at the children's written work at different stages in the school. Try to see uncorrected work, since this is the best guide to the child's skills. Also look at any text books in use, to get some idea of how they relate to books used with normally hearing children of the same age.

5) Note the number of pupils in the school, and try to gain an assessment of whether there are sufficient to allow careful grading and planning of courses; and whether, particularly at the secondary stage, there are

sufficient pupils to allow for specialist subject teaching. This is particularly important in view of the falling rolls in many of the special schools. Ask to look at the specialist facilities, such as science, domestic science, art and craft rooms.

6) Look at the use of hearing aids in the playground, as well as in the classrooms. Ask whether group aids, radio aids, individual aids etc. are used for classroom teaching.

7) When you get home, discuss with your partner how you feel your child would fit into such an establishment. Try to do this under the headings of your child's handicap and capabilities in relation to what the educational establishment has to offer. Remember, whether the establishment is a school or a partially hearing unit, to think what happens at the secondary stage.

8) Finally, above all: do not pass too many comments, but treat the opportunity as one to look, listen and question.

Summary

Have a checklist by which you can assess your child's readiness to start school successfully.

CAN HE ... ?

1) Do his laces and buckles up?
2) Do his buttons up? (Make him a button practice doll with cloth)
3) Put on his gloves and outdoor clothes?
4) Let us know when he wishes to use the toilet?
5) When he gets there ... can he manage?
6) Drink through a straw?
7) Handle scissors, crayons, paints?
8) Use a handkerchief?
9) Share with other children?
10) Treat books and property with respect?
11) Adapt to new situations without fear?

HAVE YOU ...?
1) Played 'counting' games with him?
2) Sung rhymes and told stories?
3) Helped him to recognise his own name?
4) Marked his clothing clearly in the same script as his name?
5) Encouraged him to be curious?
6) Encouraged him to listen?
7) Given him plenty of opportunities to copy *good* behaviour?
8) Encouraged him to play with all sorts of objects and toys?
9) Encouraged him to play with toys and materials which will further his development of visual perception and hand-eye co-ordination?
10) Had a planned programme of 'separation' so that he can readily leave you at home while he goes to school?
11) Shown him what is involved in travelling on public transport?

DOES HE KNOW HOW TO ...?
1) Put in his moulds?
2) Switch on his aid to correct volume setting?
3) Put on his harness? (try Velcro)
4) Indicate his toilet needs?
5) Handle potentially dangerous things, such as knives?
6) Share?
7) Take responsibility for the care of a younger child, or the care of a pet on a regular basis, or care for his own section of the garden?

When the decision about placement has been made, arrangements will often be made for you and your child to visit the school with increasing regularity until the important day arrives when he stays for the full day with his new friends. Going to school is a new adventure both for your child and for you. We hope the suggestions and comments we have made help you in the preparation for what should be a joyful and rewarding event in your child's life.

You should not believe that once your child goes to school you will cease to be important to his development. He will still spend much more time at home than he will at school, and if you keep closely in touch with the school and in particular with your child's teachers, you will see how you can complement and extend the work they are doing with him.

8 : Problems Frequently Encountered by Parents

In this chapter we propose to consider some of the common problems encountered by parents of hearing impaired children – common, that is, in the sense that they arise for many of the parents who attend the clinics at the Department of Audiology at Manchester University. What we report here will be a mixture of our own suggestions, based on our experience with hearing impaired children over quite a long period, and the opinions of the parents themselves about the problems and their solution.

You need not fear that all, or even most, of these problems will come your way; but we hope that our suggestions help in some small way, with those that do. Remember also that there are very few problems in this world that have only one solution, so if your experience leads you to a better one than ours, have the confidence to use it: there is one thing that we are sure about, and that is that we have a monopoly neither of problems nor of the solutions. You have also in your peripatetic teacher a source of much skill and understanding, so do not be afraid to broach problems with her or him.

Hearing aid problems
Many common problems are related to the fitting and use of hearing aids, the quality of the child's earmoulds etc. We have considered this subject of sufficient importance to warrant a separate chapter (Chapter 4), so we hope that you will look there for information on all technical problems involving the aid.

Early problems
Around the time of diagnosis, you may find difficulty in getting the diagnosis in the first place, in gaining information about possible causes and future prospects, and in coping

with your own reactions to having a hearing impaired child.

Parents often ask why it has taken so long to gain a diagnosis for their child? Of course there can be many reasons, some more defensible than others. Testing may have been inefficient, so the child passed a screening test of hearing when he clearly should have failed. Even if you were concerned about his hearing prior to testing, it is possible that after testing your natural fears were allayed ('They say he's okay so he must be – they are the experts'). Or there could have been delay in gaining a referral to a specialist centre. This is more likely to have arisen from the local services' uncertainty about whether to refer or not, than any inability of the specialist centre to see patients in a reasonable time. And there are also factors in the child's hearing condition which can cause clinicians difficulties: moderate hearing losses, particularly sensori-neural losses with middle ear conditions in addition, can cause confusion, especially to local services. One major cause of delay seems to be the situation where the assessment is not made by a team made up of all the relevant disciplines, so the child is shunted from one to the other to get his problems sorted out. Passing from one specialist to another is frustrating and confusing to all concerned. In addition, hearing problems which are linked with other physical or developmental problems do make testing of young children extremely difficult.

Some parents who are positive from early on that their child is hearing-impaired naturally feel bitter when diagnosis is delayed. Questions such as 'Can we sue for negligence?' are not uncommon. In our experience only rarely is it possible to pinpoint direct negligence, and of course it is one thing to identify negligence and another to prove it in a court of law. The problems often seem to be a compound of errors or delays with no single agent at which to point the finger. However we would suggest, if you feel very strongly about a grievance, that you consult a solicitor to see if your grievance would have substance in law. On the other hand, also ask yourself the question 'Am I delaying doing something positive to help my child in order to fight what may be a long and difficult battle, with only a symbolic victory to be gained?' When the child is diagnosed there are many things to do, and all of us, parents and professionals, need to pull together to help the child make up for lost time.

Professionals who are involved with the families of handicapped children understand very well the wide variety of reactions at or around the time of diagnosis. 'Is it normal for me to feel so depressed and alone?', 'Is it normal for me to feel angry and hostile?' These and many others are quite normal reactions. All your hopes for the future are centred on your baby, and it may seem that these have all been dashed to the ground with the diagnosis of deafness. You may want to hit out, be angry with your husband/wife, blame the doctor who delivered the baby, blame yourself for the baby's problem. *All of these are common and natural feelings.*

At the time of diagnosis it is helpful if you have a trusted confidant, so that you can give these feelings an airing. This person may well be the peripatetic teacher, who will have met many families in a similar situation. It is certainly useful if you can develop a good rapport with one or more knowledgeable persons, because even if they are not initially teaching you very much – it may take you some time to be ready to consider, in detail, the practicalities of how to help your child – they will be able to dispel a lot of the myths about deafness. Such a person will also be able to gather information about the cause of the deafness and/or point you to other professionals who can do so, in case you are considering another addition to your family.

Remember that your hearing impaired child has already been deprived, although it may not seem so to you if he is diagnosed before one year. He has been deprived when he was in his cot and could not see you, of the sounds of your voice, and the noises from other parts of the house; and if he is severely impaired, he has been deprived of hearing your voice in all situations. This deprivation can show itself in extra anxiety when he is left alone, and, as we mention elsewhere, in the quality of his own vocalisations. So here we have a starting point for you: handle him more than usual, do activities with him on your knee, sing close to his ears and show your love for him in your face as well as in your voice. We can promise you that you will enjoy your child if you treat him primarily as a normal child, and only second as a child who needs help with his hearing.

As far as causation is concerned, we hope you have found our chapter on this subject informative. We would only suggest here the importance of searching for causation as soon as possible. This is not an academic exercise, since certain tests, such as the one for rubella antibodies, are useful only if carried out early. If you wish to add to your family, this is a strong argument for attempting to identify the cause; but perhaps the most powerful reason is related to the child himself. He will grow up, and if he wants to get married he will ask you 'What if we have children – will they be deaf too?' If no investigation was carried out when he was small, some tests will be impossible; and the chances of family investigation too may be severely reduced if family members are widely separated, or dead. It is also possible that the child's own medical records will no longer be available, or the doctor who compiled them no longer available for consultation. Causation imposed by recessive genetic deafness is in any case difficult to identify, and these further problems may make it impossible.

Family problems
Your child's handicap is bound to affect the way you handle and treat him, but we have already stressed the need to treat him as normally as possible in all aspects of socialisation and discipline. There is, further, a need for consistency of treatment between you and your spouse. Try also not to make discriminatory allowances for the child in family situations, or to treat him differently from your other children. However we do appreciate that these are areas of real difficulty, and perhaps some comment here may help.

If you are aware that you *are* treating your hearing impaired child differently from your other children, and you and your spouse are *not* being consistent, it is worth trying to look at some of the possible reasons for this. The chances are that only one parent – very often the mother – is receiving the information and advice from the teacher. Many parents have reported finding it a considerable strain to be the one who has to pass on this information, and thus in many ways become the family 'expert.' On the other hand, the other partner finds himself the one 'reported on'. The wife is also likely to be the one charged with the care of the child for most of the day, and to meet more of the problems of discipline and related issues than her husband. Husbands often admit to being more lax with the hearing impaired child than is the wife. This suggests that there is a real need for more evening 'guidance' so both partners can be fully involved in the guidance process. Both partners should appreciate that with hearing impaired children, even more than with normally hearing children, there is a need for consistency of treatment, so it is immensely important to sit down and discuss the problem together on a regular basis. Husbands should not let their wives down by allowing behaviour which the wife would not.

Do your best to treat all your children as alike as possible. They should respond to the same family rules and demand an equal share of your attention. In this way your normally hearing children can become sympathetic allies for helping the hearing impaired child, rather than resentful rivals who feel neglected and perhaps even wish that they had a hearing aid too if it means all these privileges! Your peripatetic teacher will involve your other children in sessions when he/she visits you, and may even do complete sessions with a normally hearing child present to stress the importance of involving him, and giving him a fair share of adult time. We are confident that one of the prices we have to pay for devoting more attention to the hearing impaired child is to do more with the normally hearing child to balance it.

It is certainly not uncommon for the normally hearing child to feel jealous. This is the same sort of jealousy that arises with the birth of a new baby who demands all of mum's attention. One mother reported to us for instance that her hearing daughter wished she could have a hearing aid, demanded a go on the auditory trainer, and hated to miss the visit of the peripatetic teacher.

It is not easy to be fair in this way. One family, who did

not normally allow the children to interrupt adult conversations, confessed that 'we were so pleased when Susan (the hearing impaired child) was trying to say things that we let her interrupt.' Another parent admitted that she did not always carry out threats to punish the hearing impaired child because she had had so much difficulty, early on, in getting the child to understand what the punishment was about. It would be totally unrealistic to insist that there should be no allowances for the impairment: you must work out the balance points for yourself, with the guiding thought that you need to carry with you the goodwill of all the family members.

Most parents spend a good deal of time with their children and the parents of handicapped children sometimes an inordinate amount. However, do remember that marriage relationships are not once-and-for-all situations, and that they too need to be worked at. Many parents have described spending so much time either with the hearing-impaired child, or, when the child was in bed, planning work with the child, that they gradually grew apart from each other, their whole lives a focus on the child. So spare time for each other, have a regular night out together, have periods where talking about deaf children is taboo, develop other interests. Occasionally, try to arrange for relatives to look after the child so that you can have a trip away together. This way you will be fresher, and more interesting, and your marriage will be more secure, to provide a stimulating and secure environment for your child.

Many parents worry about explaining the handicap to family and friends. The best way is to teach them gradually, as you learn yourself, and to allow them to learn as they play with and talk to your child. Answer questions carefully, and if you don't know the answer ask your peripatetic teacher. The best starting point is to tell other people to talk clearly but normally to the child, and to explain that if they keep fairly close to his hearing aid microphone he will receive a good signal. Try not to put your friends off by getting too technical: if you nurture their relationship with the child, they can become a real source of support and encouragement.

Problems with outsiders

As parents of hearing-impaired children you will all encounter attitudes that sadden you or make you angry. People
will spoil your child, patronise him, or make concessions
because he is deaf, and you will be put in a role you may not
enjoy (that of teacher or counsellor) in order to combat this.
You must be polite but firm in explaining to people how you
are trying to bring up your child. Parents have often
described, for example, being upset by strangers who
obviously disapprove of their disciplining their child in
public. No parent enjoys disciplining in public, but children
with language difficulties, more than any others, need the
training to take place *at the time the problem arises*. You
need to harden yourself and look to the future, to a
well-adjusted and socially acceptable child. We have nearly
all had at least one experience of our child throwing a
tantrum on being denied something in a shop. It is no use
giving in and then taking the child home to explain the errors
of making unreasonable demands in shops. You are the one
who has to live with your child, not the interested bystan-
ders.

Explaining to others how much your child can hear can be
very difficult. People often have a view of deafness as total
deafness, with no concept of a range of severity: when the
child turns on being shouted at, he cannot be deaf. Here
again you might enlist the aid of the peripatetic teacher, who
will have specially prepared materials to lay on demon-
strations that provide information for your friends and
neighbours. Perhaps as a preliminary measure you might
explain that whilst loud sounds from behind might attract
your child's attention, *instructions* from behind may not be
understood, particularly if the child has no aids on.

People involved with all types of handicapped children are
aware of the great lack of knowledge in the general public.
One thing we clearly need to do is to educate teenagers at
school, while they are still in the position of captive
audience, and we have noted a number of educational
programmes that now include aspects of handicap. But there
is still room for much more, and one very positive effect of
education could be the effective immunisation of teenage

girls against rubella, and thus the elimination of a major cause of congenital deafness.

Social and developmental problems
All sorts of questions and problems arise in this section: 'Can deaf people dance?' 'Do they appreciate music' 'Will his general development be different?' 'Is deafness the reason for his not sleeping? being bad tempered and aggressive? not sharing things? not being toilet trained?'

Deaf children have a range of abilities, like any group of children, and in some activities the severity of their loss will clearly affect the level of skill they attain. Dancing and music will be affected to some degree, but even very deaf children can appreciate natural rhythms, so dancing and enjoying music can be encouraged. They will enjoy music if you provide it for them frequently and allow them to become involved in it. We know of many hearing impaired children who enjoy dancing, or who are learning to play musical instruments. Start them off as we have suggested by using singing action – rhymes, so that they have to take an active role. The hearing impaired child, like any child, will have certain aptitudes, gifts, call them what you will, and one of these may be music. Aptitudes are there to be fostered.

Encouraging hearing impaired children to 'take turns' and 'share' are often cited as problems. We feel that one of the best answers to this problem is to start the education process early. To encourage turn-taking, start with games that have turns built in to them. Make sure that the child has a good view of you. The game can be as simple as taking turns dropping toys into a box, later introducing the more complex dice games such as lotto and snakes and ladders. At first the child needs a game where his turn comes quickly, or he will become bored with the game and lose interest altogether. But the best way of learning turn-taking is by imitation, copying other members of the family.

Toilet training
Sleep difficulties and toilet training problems are regarded

by some parents as the most serious problems they face, so we shall look at these in a little more detail.

As far as toilet training is concerned, it would seem to us, after speaking to many parents, that one of the most important reasons for difficulty is starting to train too soon. Many mothers have described starting early with the first child, and encountering problems that were difficult to overcome. With their second child they were able more accurately to gauge the child's developmental readiness, and so had a much easier time.

At around twenty months many children are ready to be trained, but this is by no means a rule. It is a relatively simple matter to check on readiness: in respect of bladder control, check whether the child urinates a good deal at any particular time or whether he is continuously wet. If your child stays dry for several hours, this is a good indicator of bladder control readiness, particularly if the child indicates or appears to know when he is about to urinate.

Whilst there are obvious exceptions, it is very helpful if at this stage the child also has the physical capacities to pick up objects easily, and to walk by himself from room to room.

If the child is to be trained he also needs to be able to follow instructions. Help him towards this by identifying body parts, and getting him to imitate simple actions such as 'Pat-a-cake' or 'Two Little Dicky Birds'. Ask him to bring a familiar object to you. It is clearly possible, even with the deafest of children, to train along these lines.

One contributor to training is imitation, which means providing a model for him to imitate. So it is helpful for the child to see other family members using the toilet, and modesty should not prevent parents from providing this model.

If your child tends to be generally stubborn, you will need to overcome this before you train him, for if he will not obey everyday requests he is unlikely to follow your toilet training instructions. It is helpful if you give only one instruction at a time, and do not move to another until the first has been obeyed. Do not allow a tantrum to deter you. Examples of such 'training' might include insisting on picking up toys after play, coming to you when asked, sitting down and so on.

An interesting method has been devised by Azarin and Fox in a book called *Toilet Training in a Day*, which is well worth reading. In their method, the mother checks that the child is ready to be trained and then sets aside a day or two when she can be absolutely free to concentrate her full attention on the training. The method involves providing the model of a doll that 'wets', then sitting the child regularly on the potty, inspecting the child's pants at regular intervals and rewarding him with a drink or a snack each time he performs in the pot. Initially, the child sits on the pot every fifteen minutes, and for the first few trials he should sit for a long time, say ten minutes. Remember that when a child is successful he needs the reward of at least a hand clap, **You did it**, a smile, a hug. When you are instructing the child regarding toileting, be brief, use gestures where necessary, be enthusiastic and use the same words and gestures each time. When the child fails, give verbal and visual disapproval, but remember that this method stresses the positive.

We know a number of parents who have found aspects of this method useful, particularly the one of concentrating on the training to the exclusion of almost all else for a few days. But do remember to check for readiness or all this effort will come to nought.

A few details from a national study of child development may interest and guide you in respect of toilet training. Of more than fourteen thousand children examined, mothers reported that one in nine (11%) were regularly wetting their beds after the age of five (boys 12% and girls 10%). And one in a hundred were soiling after four years of age. It is not possible here to examine all the possible reasons for this, but suffice it to say that there is, as a rule, no reason, other than communication difficulties, why the hearing impaired child should be any different from the average in this respect. After allowing for quite wide individual variations, we suggest that persistent enuresis during the day should be regarded as abnormal after the age of three, and persistent bed-wetting abnormal after four years.

Sleep difficulties

For parents who have children who do not sleep through the night, the problem is a real one: the parent really suffers, the whole family suffers. We have heard of children who spend several hours in the middle of the night shouting, playing, jumping on parental beds and generally creating havoc with the sleeping habits of the rest of the family. We thought it may be of interest to tell you of a survey of sleeping patterns of hearing impaired children compared with normally hearing children, which was carried out in the Department of Audiology and Education of the Deaf in Manchester in 1976.

Mothers were asked to give some details about the way they prepared the child for bed; and then for thirty nights they recorded on an inventory the time they put the child to bed each night, how long the child took to go to sleep, how many times he woke in the night and for how long, and what time the child woke in the morning. Fifty mothers of normally hearing children of the same sex, age and social class as our study group co-operated in carrying out the same task.

All the times recorded by the parents were processed and a computer was used to analyse the information. The results, based on averages for the whole comparison groups, were as follows:

1) On average hearing impaired children go to bed at the same time as normally hearing children;
2) Hearing impaired children take longer to go to sleep once in bed;
3) On average hearing impaired children do NOT wake in the night more frequently than normally hearing children, but there is evidence approaching significance that once awake they stay awake slightly longer;
4) On average the total time asleep is the same for hearing impaired children as normally hearing, i.e. hearing impaired children may go to sleep a little later, but they make up for it by sleeping a little later in the morning.

Indeed it was noted that many of the children who woke

very frequently, both hearing impaired and normally hearing, also slept very late in the morning. It would seem, again on average, that children of similar ages have similar sleep requirements and that whatever the pattern of their sleep they get the total amount required.

There is absolutely no doubt in our minds that some parents do have great difficulties – indeed how they survive is a matter of some concern to us. But the parents' comments quoted in this survey tend to point to similarity between the groups, rather than to differences. Comments such as 'This can't last – he slept through', on one night, followed by the next night's entry of 'It didn't,' from the mother of a hearing impaired child, is matched by the mothers of normally hearing children, one of whom said, 'I finally threatened her with the vicar and she went up to bed and stayed there', and another who said in the comments section, for one night's entry, 'Not good, but then not unusual either', and on another night when the child slept through, 'miraculous'.

The routines for putting children to bed are worthy of mention, since the vast majority of parents of both normally hearing and hearing impaired children had routines which were clearly defined. However, the routines varied, in both groups, from fairly loose sequences to complex routines with ritualistic elements. One fairly typical example might run as follows: the child is warned that in five minutes it will be bedtime, is asked to tidy up, and then told to go to the toilet, bath, clean teeth. The child is then dressed in pyjamas, chooses clothes for the next day, chooses story, has story and is put into bed. Mum kisses teddy, kisses child, child lies down, cuddling teddy and goes to sleep.

This area of routines was not a major part of our study, but we think that it is very likely that differences between children's sleeping behaviours lie both in their individual personalities (over which we have little *immediate* influence) and in the routines and procedures carried out by parents when they put the children to bed. A good number of children in both groups have night lights. This may be of particular value to the hearing impaired child, who when he is being put to bed is likely to feel very cut off, in darkness, with no hearing aid. This isolation is perhaps even more acute when he awakes in the middle of the night.

From general observation of what many parents have said, it seems to be generally useful to have a winding down period before bedtime, where quiet games are played or books are read or songs are sung. Children seem to react favourably to routine they can rely on, and also to attempts by parents to stress the continuity between today and tomorrow, for instance by choosing clothes today which they will wear tomorrow, or telling or showing them what they will do tomorrow. Many parents spoke about being firm without being rushed. Certainly allowing plenty of time for bedtime routine seems to be important.

When the child wakes

Even after a few months the child can recognise evening bedtime as the end of play and company; and also perceive that when you are woken in the middle of the night you are not at your most playful. But the fact is that many children are wakeful. What strategies can you use for coping?

Suppose when you leave your child he cries, when you return he stops, then when you leave him again he cries but louder. It has been suggested by some psychologists that, after checking pins, nappies etc, you leave and do not return. They say 'be decisive' and the child may cry for fifteen to twenty minutes for the first night, ten minutes the second night and probably not at all the next. They argue that the baby is not at all 'traumatized': he suffers no harm.

Others have suggested 'interim' alternatives of letting the child fall asleep downstairs and then carrying him up. The danger here is that you wake the child as you carry him up, and also that you will have to wait longer and longer as he gets older. Another suggestion is that you wait in the child's bedroom until he goes to sleep. This can tie you down for a long time.

We think you have to choose the method based on your knowledge of the child. You are the only one in a position to tell when the child is 'swinging the lead'.

Who gets up if the child does wake? We have good evidence from the study that fathers are heavily involved in the putting to bed routine, so we have no reason to believe that they are not taking their turn when the child wakes in the night. Perhaps someone can research this?

One doctor with a non-sleeping child reported to us a shift routine that worked as follows. If the child woke the husband or wife, whoever was on 'duty', went into the child's room and would play or do whatever else was necessary, so that the partner was not disturbed. This was done however many times he woke. The other partner was on 'duty' the next night. Each partner could count on the opportunity to sleep through on at least one night in two. Now his children are grown up, but he still gets nightmares about playing with Lego at 2.00 a.m.!

We hope that through the results of our research you can see that there is no reason to treat hearing impaired children very differently from normally hearing children as regards sleep, since their sleep patterns are similar.

If your child follows an erratic course of sleep through the night, it may not be your fault; it is probably not due to his hearing impairment; there are a good number of children like yours, both normally hearing as well as hearing impaired.

Finally, as your child gets older the chances are that sleep problems will recede into the increasingly distant past; though honesty does prompt us to add 'and new ones will spring up to take their place!'

Tantrums
Aggressiveness and tantrum behaviour around two years of age have frequently been cited by parents of hearing impaired children as among the problems linked to deafness; yet those of us who have normally hearing children of that age know that it happens with them too. It is a fact of life that, as children start to develop towards independence, our will and theirs will clash. They have to learn that they cannot always have what they want or do what they want. Yet one of the problems at this time is the unclear guidelines we as parents get from our culture, from society generally. We are warned against being 'overpermissive' on the one hand, and yet that we must be careful not to stifle 'individuality' or

'creativity' on the other, so we have to make up our own minds about the behaviour we will accept from our children, and then work towards getting it. If society is not offering clear guidelines then we must set our own.

If the child is to become acceptable socially, which is what you probably want most of all, the aggressive, demanding, snatching, bad-mannered child must be discouraged. But if your child reacts in a violent way to your attempts to correct his behaviour, above all do not react with fear or by having a tantrum yourself. In the former case you risk frequent repetitions of the behaviour, and in the latter you are almost certain to escalate the situation to a pitched battle (we are not saying that this must never happen but that it need not happen frequently).

What is clear is that we must approach these child rearing problems with much love and patience – for one of the biggest and most powerful advantages you have as a parent is that your child loves *you*. He will do things to please you because he loves you.

Calmness and decisiveness are the order of the day. Quickly analyse the possible causes of the tantrum: you may notice that the child is imitating the anger of those around him, that he is tired, or that he has got used to demanding and getting what he wants. Of course he may not understand what you want, and with the hearing impaired child misunderstandings can lead to tantrums, but you will find a steady improvement in this respect as you and he learn to communicate more easily.

Next take the decision as to how you are to respond. You may choose *deflection* '**no – I said you are not to pull on the curtains – come on** (take hand) **lets go and look for the jigsaw Grandma bought you for your birthday**.' On many occasions you can, without giving in on your point of discipline, direct or deflect the child towards something which is both acceptable to you and enjoyable for him. However, if he is to be trained you must be *consistent*. If some part of his behaviour is unacceptable today it must be unacceptable tomorrow also. Apply your disciplinary procedures con-sistently and you will have a much greater chance of success. If you intend to have a direct confrontation with your child, be sure that you can carry it through.

We might also suggest that you have an absolute minimum of rules and regulations, so it will be so much easier to enforce the ones you do have. Before you say **Don't touch that** or **Don't do that**, decide whether you could instead show him how to do it carefully and safely. In many cases we are sure that you will find you can.

Finally, let us tell you what happened to one of us in a well known store. We were out shopping with our two-year-old boy, and he demanded some sweets. We said he could not have sweets shortly before lunch. So he proceeded to kick up a terrible fuss and was marched out of the store by Daddy, firmly holding his hand. Mum, who was following some yards behind, overheard a man saying to his wife 'That chap will damage that little boy's spine.' That little boy calmed down immediately on leaving the store, and we concluded two minutes later that he could not even remember what he'd kicked up such a fuss about. This experience provided us with some insight into the comments made by so many parents about fear of what other people will think. It *does* hurt. But we have to live with our children, others do not. If we let the child have exactly what he wants in every shop, then we will soon have a monster to live with.

In concluding this section we would suggest to you that, except in the areas of speech and language, you should assume that your child's development will be the same as that of a normally hearing child, and then work to rear him and socialise him in the normal way. If you do meet problems (in some rare cases for example a sleep problem can be organically based, as can some problems with toilet training), consult with your advisers who will do their best to help you.

9 : Educational Provision for Hearing Impaired Children

The home and the nursery school
Educational provision for sensori-neurally hearing-impaired children starts with the diagnosis of the child. It must start right away. As far as the child and his language development is concerned, we could call him zero age at this point and then age him by the length of time since he has had his hearing aids. Since you are obviously looking for language, probably expressive language, to start, we can in this way put a reasonable time scale on your expectations of the child. If your child has had no, or next to no, stimulation from auditory input then we cannot expect him to start to talk immediately. We need to give him consistent amplification over a considerable period before this can begin.

The services which provide support for families of hearing-impaired children at home and in normal schools are called ancillary services, and it is impressive to note the enormous growth of this area of service over the past twenty years or so. In 1959 there were four special teachers (now called peripatetic, visiting or advisory teachers), whilst in the late 1970s there were more than 500. (The detailed work of the peripatetic teacher was described earlier, in Chapter 4). This growth in numbers reflects both demands for help from parents, and professional realisation that the earlier help is provided, the narrower the gap between the achievements of normally hearing children and those of the hearing impaired. It also points to the fact that educators have placed a growing emphasis on the skills of parents, instead of on very early placement in special nurseries for the hearing impaired. It is, in fact, policy of the British Association of Teachers of the Deaf that, when hearing impaired children are placed in nurseries, wherever possible they be placed in local normal nursery schools: provided, that is, that appropriate and adequate support can be given to the nursery school and concurrently to the child and his family. This provision in turn depends on recognition by the Education Authority that the children have 'support needs', so that the authority is committed to provide what is still special educational treatment.

So placement in the normal nursery environment does not mean that the child does not need help. He needs the specialised support of the peripatetic teacher of the deaf. What we are saying is that if your child is hearing impaired he is best stimulated at home by you, his normally talking parents, and in a normal nursery by normally talking children and teachers.

We appreciate that on occasions there will be inadequate local facilities, or that in a few cases the child's level of handicap may be so great that there is a need to place him in the nursery of a special school; but this in our view should be a rare situation.

We believe that people, both parents and professionals, need to have clear aims in view when they place a hearing impaired child in any educational situation. Initially, we are strongly of the opinion that it is sound policy to 'place' the child in the educational environment of the home, and we do not recommend, as a general rule, early nursery placement. The young child plays much of the time alone or with mother, not co-operatively with other children for any length of time; and the child's mother can provide a good speech model in generally quiet acoustic conditions. She can also provide much one-to-one attention, certainly more than is possible in any classroom, where the teacher's attention must be shared. On the other hand, a nursery (for nursery read also playschool, or mums and toddlers playgroup) can provide contact for the child with other children, normal children, of similar age; so later on, when the child is three plus perhaps, a few mornings or afternoons in a nursery or playgroup will be educationally sound. This will gradually develop his willingness to be separated from you, practice for the full day at school. It will also offer opportunities for interaction with other children, encouraging social play and the development of useful skills such as turn-taking and sharing. (It is to be hoped that you will also have started teaching these skills earlier in the home on the advice of the peripatetic teacher.)

An important point to bear in mind is that very often normal nurseries with large numbers of noisy, active children playing in areas which have not been specially sound treated, are acoustically far from ideal for the hearing impaired child. The floors are often hard and bare, and many of the toys used are of solid wood. All this is ideal for play, but may be very poor for communication. Our aim in using the nursery is not as a *major* source of language stimulation for the child, but to encourage him to mix with normal children and to play socially. The question of hearing-aid use in these circumstances requires further research, but undoubtedly the child will receive a better signal from the adults in the nursery if he is wearing a radio receiver than if he has a conventional one. However since much time will still be spent in solitary play or early contact play with other children, the benefit at this stage is probably not a crucial one.

The peripatetic teacher will visit and advise the teacher in the nursery on the use of aids, including ways of achieving the most acoustically from them. In all dealings with the nursery the parents, who may feel quite expert by now, and the teacher of the deaf should keep their briefing of the nursery teacher as simple as possible. It is far better to give a little information on each visit than a whole course on the first, and too much technical information may make the nursery teacher feel that the child is really so special that she cannot possibly cope, when nothing could be further from the truth. On the use of the hearing aids, it is useful to start with only such information as the nursery teacher asks for. The first query may be how to switch the aid on and off. Then the teacher may notice that it is difficult to get the earmould back in the ear when it falls out in play, and you can show her how to do it; she hears the characteristic whistle of acoustic feedback, and you can show her what to check and how to eliminate it. Gradually the nursery teacher, who may never have seen a hearing impaired child before, will feel more confident and you or the peripatetic teacher will be able to explain things in a little more detail.

If the peripatetic teacher has a few such interested teachers, she may choose to provide a day or afternoon course to demonstrate some effects of hearing loss on how a child perceives speech, explain the common causes and site of damage to hearing, and offer more detail on the use and function of the aids.

This sort of information will give the nursery teacher clearer guidelines on what steps to take in the classroom to ensure that the child gets the most benefit from his aids. Choosing a quiet corner to do individual work, and holding the aid in the hand like an ordinary microphone, or at least getting close to the microphone when trying to communicate with the child, are steps whose purpose will become clearer. The peripatetic teacher may also visit the nursery for speech encouragement sessions with the hearing imparied child, or with small groups including the hearing impaired child.

Before we move on to consider the educational provision available to the hearing impaired child of statutory school age, we would like to consider some ideas surrounding the term 'integration', a word which must be familiar to parents of all handicapped children who hope for as normal an educational environment as possible for their child.

Ideas behind the term 'integration'
Section 10 of the 1976 *Education Act* states that 'handicapped pupils are to be educated in county and voluntary schools in preference to special schools, unless this would be impracticable.'

The 1978 *Report of the Committee of Enquiry into the Education of Handicapped Children and Young People Cmnd No 7212 Special Educational Needs* (The Warnock Report) also recommends that, wherever possible and practical, handicapped children should be educated in a normal setting.

Being educated with our normal children is for many people involved with handicapped children, synonymous with the term integration. If this is what integration is about, then for hearing-impaired children the trends have been in this direction since the formation of the first partially hearing units in the late 1940s, and the appointments of the first peripatetic teachers in the late fifties. These factors involved with the physical integration of hearing impaired children into the normal educational system are illustrated in Tables IV and V.

Table IV. Number of Peripatetic Teachers

Year	1959	1969	1971	1972	1973	1975	1976	1977
Peripatetic Teachers	4	200	212	259	283	363	461	469

Table V. Number of Partially Hearing Units

Year	1966	1967	1968	1971	1976	1977
Number of Partially Hearing Units	162	173	191	212	454	463

The rapid development of these forms of educational provision through the 1960s and 1970s is clear. It can also be seen that placement of hearing impaired children in special schools has changed correspondingly. There has been a decline in the number of children placed in schools for the deaf, and an increase in numbers placed in schools for partially hearing children and in partially hearing units.

Along with the trends shown in figure 29 however, is a growing tendency for more multiply handicapped children to be placed in schools for the deaf, which is to some extent disguising the rapid fall in numbers of deaf children in special schools.

This trend in the direction of educating more children in ordinary schools has resulted from many factors, including the political climate, improvements in diagnostic services and improvements in the educational provision for the pre-school hearing impaired. These factors, together with improved amplification, have all contributed to better standards of oral skills (understanding and talking) among children of school age, so that educationalists can more seriously consider the hearing impaired child for normal educational palcement, or for placement in a special class in a normal school (in a Partially Hearing Unit or P.H.U.). We feel that this trend will continue in the forseeable future.

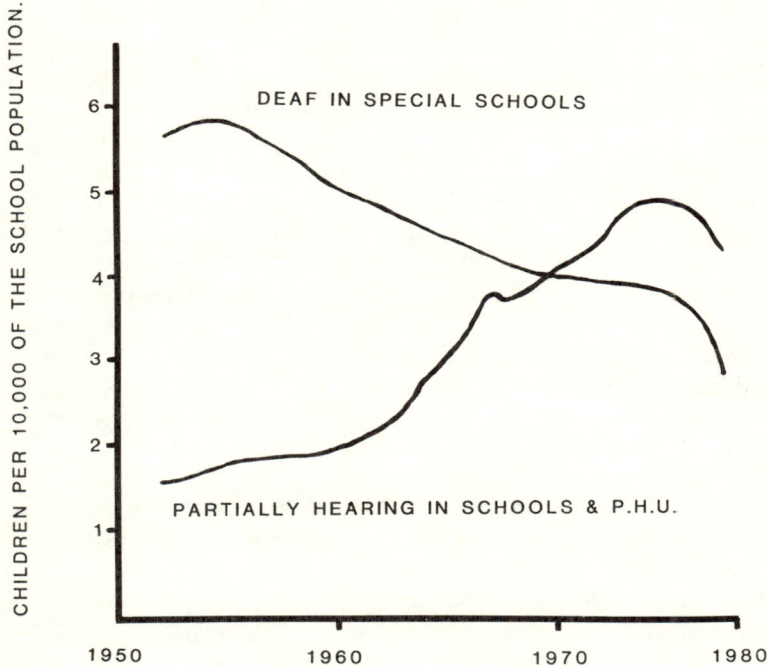

Fig. 29 Trends in school placement of hearing impaired children.

The movement in the direction of more normal environments for the hearing impaired is not a uniform movement, however, since some authorities are still placing children rigidly in special schools. But it is gaining momentum. It is based on the assumption that hearing impaired children can learn to talk, and that they will do it best where the environment is naturally oral and the motivation to achieve good oral standards is high. It also rests on another very important assumption, and that is that normal social relationships develop best if they are started early. We can start hearing impaired children off with normally hearing children far more easily than we can implant them at a later stage. However, in noting a trend, and indeed supporting it, we do wish to draw to your attention some of the principles of integration and some of the practical problems involved in implementing it for your child.

Integration first implies differences between individuals, since if there were no differences there would be no need to integrate: and then it also implies bringing together or unifying these different individuals. Differences as far as hearing-impaired children are concerned are not once-and-for-all differences, they lie on a continuum and may have differing impacts on the child's life at different stages. For example, if your school age child has a minor hearing loss only, it may not even be detected, or if it is it may be regarded as insignificant. Yet at the language learning stage even a minor loss can have a marked impact on the rate of language development. Those professionally involved in the education of hearing impaired children have a responsibility to assess what effects the handicap is likely to have on the child, and thus the best sort of provision to offset these effects.

There is no doubt also that the terms in common usage, such as partially-hearing and severely and profoundly deaf, mean different things to different people, and that the ambiguities do on occasions lead to confusion in the minds of parents. Certainly more and more professionals are classifying children on a functional basis, according to what the child can do: the absolute level of any child's hearing loss is being seen as not so important as how he is using his remaining hearing to aid his development. So we may see one child with a 90dB hearing loss responding as a partially-hearing child while another behaves as a severely or profoundly deaf child. These responses will depend on many things, including the age at which he was diagnosed, whether or not he has additional handicaps, his intelligence and personality, the fitting and use made of amplification, the support and stimulation from his family and the quality and effectiveness of early counselling and guidance.

We hope thus that you will see that there is more to integration than putting hearing impaired children in a school or class with normally hearing children. The children are, in these situations, physically integrated: but they may not be integrated socially or educationally. For example, there are partially hearing units in normal schools where the hearing impaired children spend most of their day with the normally hearing children, only returning to the unit for individual sessions with a specialist teacher. But there are also units where the children spend their whole day segregated from the normally hearing children, although in the same school. Some even have separate playtimes, so the children do not have a chance even of social contact.

It has been suggested that, in order eventually to be integrated into normal society, deaf children need to be separated educationally and given special attention, so that they can be raised to a level where they can integrate ultimately. We think that this is rarely true. Training for integration by segregation leads to lowered expectations, reduction of opportunities for social contact and ultimately to greater difficulty in integration. The dangers of institutionalisation, though less now than formerly, are nevertheless real. We believe that there are some severely and profoundly hearing impaired children for whom the above applies and where the special school is the most appropriate placement, but that the large majority of hearing impaired children can and should be educated in environments closely approximating to the normal one, in normal schools with the support of the peripatetic teacher, or in partially hearing units in normal schools. We are not presenting an argument for a reduction of special help for your children, more an argument about where and how that help should be given, and we shall say more when we consider the learning experiences in specific educational environments. Progress will certainly need to be closely monitored, and this can only be done with adequate specialist support. We are arguing for positive discrimination in as normal an environment as possible.

Research has shown that substantial educational gains are made when the child is placed in a normal school with suitable support. In one experiement, six children in normal classes were supported by a specialist teacher of the deaf who co-ordinated and provided the speech work, and three support teachers. The hearing impaired children made positive reading and speech gains with this advantageous provision, and the ordinary classroom teachers appreciated the assistance of another professional, who also involved normally hearing children in small group work. This sounds a very expensive provision, and it is, but the education of one child in a special school, particularly if it is a residential school, is also very expensive. We cannot get by without spending money on the hearing impaired child, but in the normal school, that spending can be very productive indeed.

As the Snowdon Report (1976) reminded us, 'Integration does not mean treating everybody exactly as they would treat everyone else. It should go without saying that to compensate for their disadvantage in order that their lives may most closely approach "normality" the disabled must have deliberately favoured treatment in every aspect. Discrimination in fact must be positive.'

It is necessary that, before making decisions about educational placement, the educationalists and psychologists involved with your child assess his abilities, speech and language skills and his level of social competence. You should ask them what they have found out. You have the right to know professional opinions about your child.

Placement in the ordinary school

There are many advantages that are believed to spring from placement in an ordinary school, and we would like you to be acquainted with some of these.

1) The major advantage of allowing the child to live at home: in many areas, because of relatively small numbers of hearing impaired children, special placement cannot be provided locally so it means travelling thirty, fifty or even a hundred miles to the nearest special school. Placement must then be residential, with the resultant dislocation of the child's social life. Children need to develop friendships in their home

locality, and this is most easily achieved if the child goes to a local school.

2) It is claimed that the normal school provides a more stimulating learning environment and a wider curriculum than is usually available in a special school. This would seem to be particularly true at the secondary stage, where subject specialist teaching facilities are often lacking in the special school.

3) Normal placement tends to lead to normal (therefore higher) expectations of the child.

4) A normal school is a normal oral language environment as a matter of course. In special schools, greater efforts have to be made to approach anything like a normal language environment.

5) The normal school is argued as the best training ground for encouraging hearing impaired children to adjust to life with normally hearing people.

The child starts to find ways of coping in a normal situation very early on, and his resultant ability to cope in a hearing world is consequently higher.

Any major arguments against the above would have to be based on an analysis of whether or not a particular child is in fact coping, being successful, being put under too much stress, and so on. Having high aspirations and pushing for them can indeed result in a stressful situation for the child; but low aspirations are more problematic still. In our view this conflict can only be resolved by a careful analysis of the problems of the individual child. Clearly by far the majority of hearing impaired children now receive some or all of their education in ordinary schools, but we still have the responsibility of deciding whether the child's ultimate achievements are being helped or hindered by his current placement. Such a decision must be based on a careful monitoring of his progress by the specialist teacher. We think that parents should do their best to ensure that decisions about their child's educational placement are based on *facts* about the child: on results from specialised tests of reading, language and other skills, and on careful professional observation of various lesson situations. They should not be based on mere opinions as to how it is 'felt' the child is progressing. Parents should also themselves give some thought to the following points, and discuss them with their advisers:

1) Is the child achieving as well as he possibly can, not only for this environment but for any environment? (*Not* Is he achieving what a normally hearing child is achieving?) Children are sometimes moved because they are not achieving at the same level as their hearing peers, with no evidence that the new placement will aid more rapid achievement.

2) Would removing him and placing him elsewhere foster his development in any specific areas? If so, which areas?

3) Would removal to a new environment raise new problem areas? If so, what areas? (We can think of the examples of losing friendships with neighbourhood children and making family relationships more difficult.)

4) Achievement apart, is the strain of competing with normally hearing children really proving too much of a strain for the child, or is the child not seriously affected by his lower level of achievement?

Child factors affecting educational placement
There are clearly many factors regarding your child which will affect decisions as to his placement. We propose to outline only some of the major ones.

1 Degree of deafness
By the time we are seriously considering placement we will have the information of the pure tone audiogram which was described earlier. However, as we have already mentioned, children with very similar audiograms may have very different educational needs. One child may be very severely handicapped by his 80dB hearing loss, another may be progressing very closely along normal lines. How the child is functioning educationally and socially with his hearing loss is more important than the loss itself. Nowadays it is entirely feasible for one child with an 80dB hearing loss to be in a school for the deaf, another with the same hearing

loss in a partially hearing unit, and yet another child in an ordinary class in his local school, all dependent on their level of educational functioning.

2 Intelligence

Your child's intelligence affects his ability to cope with his handicap, and the educational psychologist will usually undertake investigations of intelligence around the time that he is assessed for special educational requirements. Hearing impaired children are almost always linguistically retarded, so they would clearly be disadvantaged by intelligence tests presented verbally, so psychologists tend to use non-verbal or performance tests. By far the most frequently used is the Weschler Intelligence Scale for Children (W.I.S.C.). We feel however that the verbal measure too should be administered where possible, so that we can gain a picture of the effects of the linguistic retardation. Parents and professionals should however be aware that psychologists rarely have special training in the education of hearing impaired children, and in our view the opinion of an advisory teacher of the deaf should always be sought before placement decisions are made.

3 Linguistic development

We need to know the level of your child's understanding of spoken language and his ability to express himself verbally. There is no completely satisfactory test battery, but the Reynell Developmental Language Scale, which has both Comprehension and Expression Scales, is commonly used, as are tests of receptive and expressive vocabulary.

4 Social and emotional development

It is very useful if information is available about the child's social and emotional development, and the psychologist will be able to provide information on this level of adjustment. Factors such as his ability to share, to accept frustration, to respond appropriately in social situations (e.g. table manners, personal social skills including dressing etc.) will have a bearing on the type of placement most appropriate to his needs. So will aspects of his personality, such as his resilience, competitiveness, self-control and whether he is outgoing or withdrawn. We shall mention these areas in more detail elsewhere, because you can have a marked influence on your child's development if you tackle the problems appropriately.

5 Use of hearing aids

An assessment of the child's use of hearing aids needs to be made at this stage. This will include his attitude to his aids, as well as his ability to perceive speech through them. Even with very young children, speech tests can be carried out which will indicate the effectiveness of his use of hearing aids (e.g. the Kendal Toy Test which we discussed in Chapter 2).

All the above information will affect the professionals' judgements in respect of school placement, though the weight attached to each aspect will depend to some extent on the educational philosophies of individuals, or the practices of a particular educational service.

The final decisions rest with the local authority, but, as we have mentioned, there are particular points in the assessment procedures where you, the parents, can and most definitely should be involved. Unhappily there are many authorities that do not have a range of educational provisions so choices simply do not exist. The decentralisation of educational provision allows some education authorities to provide less than adequate facilities, and even permits them to say 'He is a deaf child, we have a school for the deaf, that is where we will place him,' when he may benefit far more from placement in a normal school with suitable support. Undoubtedly the whole future of some hearing impaired children is being affected in this way. We are all for local provision of educational facilities, but we think it is time that the government laid down minimum standards of provision to bring the least satisfactory authorities into line. Parents can be influential in pressurising local authorities and the government to provide facilities of the required standard.

Qualities of the ordinary school, and how these may affect the deaf child

Schools are by no means even in quality, and even physically they vary greatly. Some school buildings are new, others old, some have open plan and others separate classrooms, some cater for fewer than one hundred children, others for more than two thousand.

Further, there is a variety of philosophies which underlie the way a school is run. Head teachers in the United Kingdom have a large degree of autonomy, and while some aim for high academic standards others offer a broader range of subjects in less depth; one school may have very firm discipline, while another is very liberal. The actual organisation within the school can also vary greatly, with one school organised on vertical groupings (i.e. children of different ages in the same class – often found in smaller schools) while others have an age-related structure. In some schools classes are unstreamed, in others they are streamed either on a general basis (i.e. the brightest children all in the same class irrespective of subject variability), or according to the child's ability in particular subjects (so the child may be in the 'A' group for Maths, but in the 'C' group for English Language) – this is called 'setting'. Clearly these factors will have some effect on placement decisions.

Noise levels are a prime consideration for the hearing impaired child, and many ordinary schools have no acoustic treatment. This results in high background noise levels, a point we have already stressed as being undesirable from a hearing aid user's point of view. In such situations a child may find it impossible to cope even with a radio hearing aid system, which we see as a prerequisite in such an environment.

As is often the case in matters relating to education, a decision is not simply a question of adding together all known factors and arriving at the ideal school. Within the same structural conditions, an individual teacher can greatly affect the child's educational environment. For example, we could suggest that for hearing impaired children separate classrooms are better than open plan from a noise point of view. However, the teacher in the open plan class may adopt a very individualistic approach to her children, enabling the handicapped child to thrive on this treatment (and perhaps get more of it than his 'fair' share); whereas the teacher in the separate classroom may believe that she has quite sufficient 'problems' in her class with slow or under-stimulated children, without having handicapped children as well. (She may believe that they should be taught by specialists, or survive in her classroom without extra help from her.) We have polarised the situation as much as we can, but readers will see the possibility of teaching style affecting placement decisions. It will be worth while at this point to outline some of the teaching techniques that may be helpful to hearing impaired children.

When the teacher is group teaching, it will be helpful if she repeats, rephrases or summarises replies to her questions from pupils other than the hearing impaired child, particularly if she is using a radio transmitter. She will be able to give a much better signal through her microphone than the child will receive free field from the other children. It is also helpful if she can give her instructions clearly and carefully, and check that hearing impaired children have started on the right track. Good use of the blackboard or an overhead projector as a means of instructing for new work, or summarising work just completed, can be an invaluable aid. Hearing impaired children also benefit from being allowed to work and co-operate with other children. The degree to which this is encouraged will also depend on teaching style; some teachers are keen for children to work on their own, others happy to encourage working together.

Some people have noticed how normally hearing pupils will take steps to see that their hearing impaired classmates keep up with the work. What is even more interesting to us is to see, as we have done, a hearing impaired child helping a normally hearing little boy with his sums!

In this section we have tried to stress that there are a number of variables to be considered when placing hearing impaired children in ordinary schools: factors related to the child, to the potential school, the potential teacher and her teaching style.

At this point we should consider the sort of thing the special teacher will do with and for a child who is placed in an ordinary school.

The peripatetic teacher and the ordinary school
I think we can safely say that there is often (but not always) good co-operation between peripatetic teachers and the schools they visit. However, we must say that the kind of response these teachers have been able to make to the hearing impaired child in the normal school has often been governed by excessively large case loads. Some teachers have more than 200 children on their case load, and however minimal the requirements of help for each, these numbers make a mockery of the term peripatetic teacher. Half an hour per child per week would be regarded as relatively good provision, but this is totally inadequate to provide good tutorial support. The service is expanding, more slowly now than formerly, but there needs to be substantial expansion almost everywhere if each child's progress is to be closely monitored, by testing and observation; if the more severely handicapped are to be provided with a programme of tutorials geared to their classroom work; and if the ordinary school teachers are to be provided with the support which they deserve if they are to take handicapped children into their classes.

There are huge numbers of young children who have minor hearing losses related to catarrhal conditions, and these have been shown to be prone to some educational retardation. But it is our view that, while these children may require medical monitoring and possibly some remedial teaching, they are diverting too much of the attention of peripatetic teachers away from their main role of supporting sensori-neurally deaf children in the normal school. Where case loads are too large, peripatetic teachers often see their role as reduced to that of assessment of hearing and monitoring of hearing levels. But we believe that their main role is to monitor educational progress and tutorial, remedial and advisory work. If services cannot be expanded, and we think that in this vital area they should be, they must be focussed on those with the most urgent needs. You as parents of hearing impaired children may need to use your political muscle to achieve an adequate level of support for your child.

We would like parents to understand that provision needs also to be made for ordinary class teachers to benefit from the skills and experience of the peripatetic teacher. Too often the advisory role of the peripatetic teacher is carried out whilst the class are working, and the class teacher is naturally finding it difficult to concentrate on what is being said. It would be much more helpful if the child's class teacher could be relieved in order to discuss problems with the peripatetic teacher. This would be to the ultimate benefit of the hearing impaired child placed in that class, and the teacher would also benefit by learning about the handicap of deafness, the use of aids, limitations of aids in noisy conditions and so on. One-day conferences can be very successful, but they need to be organised regularly if they are to cope with staff changes.

The most efficient system links the remedial teaching of the peripatetic teacher closely to the work of the school; and, at least in current circumstances, limits this support to the children whose need is for more specialised help than can be provided by an ordinary remedial service.

At the secondary stage, support work becomes even more complicated because of the increase in specialisation. The child will have different teachers (and classrooms) for each subject, so someone needs to be in overall charge of the hearing impaired children. In some very large secondary schools it has been found beneficial to attach a specialist teacher, give him a base classroom or unit, and make one of his responsibilities the monitoring of all the hearing impaired children in the school. It may thus be necessary in a particular area to concentrate the hearing impaired children in one secondary school rather than two or three.

Peripatetic teachers have in any case difficulties enough visiting secondary schools. If the school is set on more than one site, or its campus is widespread, it is difficult to find the children, and sometimes also to find space to work with them. Co-ordinating the teacher's and child's timetables causes more problems, and much valuable time and energy are wasted.

The peripatetic teacher often has in addition some responsibility for following up children who have been placed at units or schools outside the authority.

In the best services for hearing impaired children, there is close liaison between educationalists and other professionals. So the peripatetic teacher has an important role here, in relation to providing a link between the particular child and the services of doctors, psychologists, social workers, speech therapists and others. This role also applies at the end of the child's school career, when links between school and employment officers are crucial: teachers are conscious of the importance of maintaining contact with their children until they are settled in jobs.

There has been a National Study Group investigating provision of further and higher education for the hearing impaired. This is still a poorly developed area, but there have been some developments, and if you wish to assess the opportunities available for your child we suggest that you obtain up-to-date information from the British Association of Teachers of the Deaf (address in Appendix 3).

The peripatetic teacher is likely to be your child's first contact with the education system for hearing impaired children, and of course she meets your child at a vital time in his development. It is therefore vital that the teacher is well trained and suitably experienced. Unfortunately there are few, if any, special courses which cover in sufficient detail the tasks of the peripatetic teacher.

In particular, such a teacher often lacks any experience in work with babies and with the babies and their families in early counselling and guidance. And parent guidance is itself still often interpreted as essentially child teaching, rather than guiding the whole family. If this is your experience, ask and keep asking for tips on how to help your child at his particular stage of development; don't leave the teacher to work with the child alone. You should be benefiting from your interaction with the teacher and applying any new skills or ideas in your life with your child.

Teachers have shown great willingness to attend seminars and conferences on these topics but the government and educational institutions have simply not provided them with advanced training courses.

There is also a need for all the peripatetic services to be organised as a unified service with a hierarchy of posts. This would have benefits for the child in co-ordinating efforts to help him, preventing teachers from becoming professionally isolated and providing the staff with a career structure which would lead to more stability in the service. Though this will no doubt ultimately come about, what service you get at present will depend largely on where you live, and the personal qualities of the teacher attached to you.

The Partially Hearing Unit
The first four special classes or partially hearing units (PHUs) in ordinary schools were opened in London in 1947. Their establishment was the fruit of early diagnosis and use of hearing aids by *moderately* deaf children. The first PHUs were set up in primary schools, and the aim was that by the time the children reached secondary school age it would be possible to transfer them to normal classes without any specialist help. If they had not reached the required standards by the time they were of secondary age, they would be transferred to schools for the partially deaf (later partially hearing).

In an earlier part of this chapter we outlined the growth of partially hearing units and other forms of provision, but here we wish to provide a little more information on their function.

The *Education Survey No. 1*, Department of Education and Science, H.M.S.O., 1967 defined the term unit as a 'group of partially-hearing children which is being educated in any one school which also has children of normal hearing, and is under the care of one or more teachers of the deaf appointed for this purpose. A unit may consist of one class, several classes or a number of individual pupils distributed amongst the ordinary classes, who return to the special teacher for tutorial periods.'

The statutory maximum number of pupils in the early

classes was ten children. There is currently no *statutory* figure but ten children was quickly accepted as being too many when one took into account the often complex and difficult teaching circumstances of the unit. On the other hand whilst it is difficult to generalise, it is possible for the host school to be too small to accomodate a P.H.U., particularly if integration into ordinary classes is planned. Hearing handicap leads to heavy demands for individual attention from the class teacher, and normal classes could easily be over-weighted by partially-hearing children. However, in our view one of the aims of the P.H.U. in the ordinary school must be to assimilate the children into normal lessons as far as possible, while providing them with on-the-spot back up support from the specialist teacher and/or the opportunity for withdrawal for short periods for intensive tutorial work.

There is on occasion opposition from ordinary class teachers to having a handicapped child in an already overcrowded class. Class teachers also do not always understand the role of the unit, so unit teachers can help by being diligent, conscientious, hardworking members of the *whole staff* of the school. They are of course responsible to the headteacher of that school; however they also need to be closely in touch with the service for hearing impaired children so that there is no danger of professional isolation: isolated teachers can all too easily become outdated in their ideas, with consequently low expectations of their children.

Today, increasing numbers of severely hearing impaired children are being placed in P.H.U.s as a result of the superior levels of oral skill they are being enabled to attain. It might thus be useful at this point to look at the approach of one service for hearing impaired children which is recognized as being one of the best in the country.

In Leicestershire there are eight units, employing nine qualified teachers of the deaf. There has always been a strong commitment to integration, and all children spend at least 50 percent of their school day in ordinary classes. David Harrison, currently President of the British Association of Teachers of the Deaf and Head of the Leicestershire

Service for Hearing Impaired Children, reports that originally the units were seen as a means of providing daily the type of support available from a peripatetic teacher on a weekly basis, and the children so placed were normally classifiable as 'partially-hearing'. In recent years in Leicestershire however, with earlier diagnosis and efficient use of hearing aids, the team have seen big changes in the abilities of the children passing through the system. Over this period the staff came to regret the cushioning effect of the unit, so links with the unit for many of the children were gradually but deliberately weakened. This made it less easy for children to retreat from the challenges of the ordinary class. There was clear evidence of improved performance, and some children were returned to local authority schools and to the care of the peripatetic staff.

Alongside this development, the improved performance of the pre-school groups resulted in more severely handicapped children being considered for unit places instead of places in special schools. The result of all this is that currently children with losses of the order of 80dB HL are being placed directly into local schools, and the units are catering more and more for severe and profoundly impaired children who are showing evidence of being able to develop speech and language skills via their residual hearing. There has been an overall improvement in communication skills and academic attainments, and staff have noted that parents are somewhat more 'relaxed'.

The Special School for hearing impaired children
We have chosen to consider the special schools together, although there are at least three types: the school for partially hearing, the school for deaf and partially hearing, and the school for the deaf. Increasingly the last are being depleted in numbers, or are developing specialist roles within a wider service, say, catering for multiply handicapped hearing impaired pupils. Children traditionally regarded as being deaf are now being educated as partially hearing in normal schools, units or the first two types of special school. So some schools for the partially hearing are now admitting

children who, on an audiogram at least, are very severely hearing impaired.

In 1978 one of the present authors, investigating the effects of the then marked decline in the birthrate, predicted that by 1985 there would be a drop in the numbers of children being educated in special schools and units for hearing impaired children of at least 1700 children. This may sound a small number, but it is the equivalent of approximately seventeen special schools, schools which theoretically would no longer be required. This figure was predicted for 1985 and was related only to the factor of declining births. In fact, a survey has already reported (1980) that the numbers in such placement has fallen to just over 6000 children – a fall of 2800 children or about twenty-eight schools. Some schools have closed, more will be so doing, but nowhere near twenty-eight have been lost. Many are turning to the more handicapped, children with additional physical, mental or perceptual handicaps. In some urban areas there has been an actual increase in children, particularly where there are large numbers of foreign-born children (Asian for instance) who might be seen as additionally handicapped in the sense that they are deaf and are also being educated in a language environment different from that used in the home.

What we do note in the remaining schools is that the number of pupils per school has dropped from average of 92 in 1977 to 58 in 1979. This in part reflects the more favourable staffing ratio required to teach multiply handicapped children, but by any standards this fall is dramatic. One head teacher at least has complained that these numbers make it impossible to offer the breadth of curriculum traditionally available, to provide separate primary and secondary departments, or to offer adequate career prospects to the staff. Some authorities are trying to meet this problem by developing comprehensive services where the intention, at least at present, is to maintain a small special school in the overall scheme.

Contraction of the special schools is, in our view, inevitable and rationalisation within an overall framework vital. If the special school *is* maintained, but *without* a well developed service, your child is possibly at greatest disadvantage, because he may be placed in the special school because the school is there. If your child in the opinion of the professionals involved, in consultation with you, needs to be educated in a special school he should be placed in one because of its advantages to him, and not because it is the only form of provision available.

There are several advantages which advocates might apply to the special school. For example, there is a concentration of specialist staff and specialist facilities and equipment. These factors make it possible to apply a consistent education philosophy to the child. The very small classes, and less stressful, more protected environment can clearly be of positive advantage to some children. But along with these factors is always the danger that the school's isolation from the mainstream may make its aspirations lower. Some schools in urban areas are responding to this special challenge by forging very close links with local ordinary schools.

Another advantage of the special school is its ability, under appropriate leadership, to respond to specialist needs and develop in particular ways. Examples of this are the two specialist schools, the technical and grammar school for the deaf, Burwood Park and the Mary Hare Grammar School respectively.

In all of this, what is the parents' special role? We believe that in your child's interests you should be as well informed as possible. This will mean asking professionals lots of questions, but it will also mean finding out for yourself. Visit as many different types of establishment as possible, taking note of our advice in the Preparation for School chapter. If you and other parents believe that there is not an adequate range of provision in your area, use whatever pressure you have as a group to have the matter rectified (e.g. chat with your MP). However, please try to judge the attempts of the authorities in the light of competing demands of other groups of handicapped children and the non-handicapped.

Insist on being consulted at every stage in the educational life of your child, and try to prepare for 'decision times', as the professionals do, by having a searching look at your child and his educational needs and at the facilities which may be needed to help him.

Finally, parents of a hearing impaired child have every right and justification to have high aspirations for him; and we believe that they have also the right to work alongside the professionals to help him achieve his full potential.

Appendices

1 Book List for the Pre-School Child

When using the book list one must remember that the selection is largely a subjective one. There are many excellent books which space has forced us to omit.

Picture Books
Animal Book, Dick Bruna – Eyre Methuen
What Whiskers Did, Ruth Carroll – Wm. Collins
Jacko, John S. Goodall – MacMillan
Paddy's Evening Out, John S. Goodall – MacMillan
Changes, Changes, Pat Hutchins – Bodley Head
How Santa Had a Long and Difficult Journey Delivering His Presents, Fernando Krahn – Kestrel
A Flying Saucer Full of Spaghetti, Fernando Krahn – Kestrel
The Magic Balloon, Iela Mari – Angus & Robertson
First to Fifth Ladybird Picture Books, (One word per page.)

Alphabet Books
A Finding Alphabet, George Adamson – Faber & Faber
B Is For Bear, Dick Bruna – Eyre Methuen
A B C, John Burningham – Johathan Cape
Teddybears A B C, Susanna Gretz – Ernest Benn
ABC of Things, Helen Oxenbury – Wm. Heinemann
Dr. Seuss's ABC, Dr. Seuss – Wm. Collins
Teeny Tiny ABC, Richard Scarry – Hamlyn
ABC, Brian Wildsmith – Oxford University Press

Counting Books
Finding 1 to 10, George Adamson – Faber & Faber
Teddybears 1 to 10, Susanna Gretz – Ernest Benn
Now I Can Count, Dean Hay – Wm. Collins
Numbers of Things, Helen Oxenbury – Wm. Heinemenn
1, 2, 3, Brian Wildsmith – Oxford University Press

Colour
My Vest Is White, Dick Bruna – Eyre Methuen
Real Thing Colour Book, F. T. Fife – Philip & Tacey
What Colour Is It? A Head Start Book, Eileen Ryder – Burke
This Is My Colour (Series of 6 books), Derek and Lucy Thackray – Alexander

Days Of The Week
The Days of the Week, Beman Lord – Angus & Robertson
Topsy and Tim's Monday Book, Tuesday Book, etc , Jean & Gareth Adamson – Blackie

Christmas
The Christmas Book, Dick Bruna – Eyre Methuen
Babar and Father Christmas, Jean de Brunhoff – Eyre Methuen
Father Christmas, Raymond Briggs – Hamish Hamilton
The Twelve Days of Christmas, Brian Wildsmith – Eyre Methuen
Long Ago In Bethlehem, Massahiro Kasuya – A. & C. Black

Nursery Rhymes
The Mother Goose Treasury, Raymond Briggs – Hamish Hamilton
Treasury of Nursery Rhymes, Hilda Boswell – Wm. Collins
The Oxford Nursery Rhyme Book, Iona & Peter Opie – Oxford University Press
The Best Nursery Rhyme Book Ever, Richard Scarry – Hamlyn

Appley Dapply's Nursery Rhymes, Beatrix Potter – Warne
Cecily Parsley's Nursery Rhymes, Beatrix Potter – Warne

Fairy Tales

The Fairy Tale Treasury, Raymond Briggs and Virginia Haviland – Hamish Hamilton
Treasury of Fairy Tales, Hilda Boswell – Wm. Collins
At the Stroke of Midnight, Helen Cresswell – Wm. Collins
The Owl and the Woodpecker, Brian Wildsmith – Oxford University Press
The Hare and the Tortoise, Brian Wildsmith – Oxford University Press
Ladybird Easy Reading Books: e.g. Goldilocks and the Three Bears, Vera Southgate

Popular Series

The Little Red Engine, The Little Red Engine Goes To Market, etc., Diana Ross – Faber & Faber
The Tim Books: e.g. Tim All Alone, Edward Ardizzone – Oxford University Press
Topsy and Tim Books: e.g. Topsy and Tim Go Safely, Jean and Gareth Adamson – Blackie
Dr. Seuss Books: e.g. Great Day For Up, Dr. Seuss – Wm. Collins
The Bear Books: e. g. Bears in the Night, Stan and Jan Berenstein – Wm. Collins

Other Picture Story Books

The Flying Postman, V. H. Drummond – Kestrel
Laura and the Lonely Ostrich, V. H. Drummond – Kestrel
Rosie's Walk, Pat Hutchins – Bodley Head
The Wind Blew, Pat Hutchins – Bodley Head
Kate and Sam Go Out, Michael and Joanne Cole – Eyre Methuen
Alfie and the Ferryboat, Charles Keeping – Oxford University Press
Through the Window, Charles Keeping – Oxford University Press

The Spider's Web, Charles Keeping – Oxford University Press

Where the Wild Things Are, Maurice Sendak – Bodley Head

In the Night Kitchen, Maurice Sendak – Bodley Head

Hector Protector And I Went Over The Water, Maurice Sendak – Bodley Head

Wild Animals, Brian Wildsmith – Oxford University Press

The Story of Little Black Sambo, Helen Bannerman – Chatto & Windus

Harry The Dirty Dog, Gene Zion – Bodley Head

The Very Hungry Caterpillar, Eric Carle – Hamish Hamilton

Some Collections

The Youngest Storybook, Eileen Colwell – Bodley Head

Tell Me a Story, Eileen Colwell – Puffin

Tell Me Another Story, Eileen Colwell – Puffin

Time For a Story, Eileen Colwell – Puffin

The Read To Me Story Book, Dorothy Edwards – Eyre Methuen

My Naughty Little Sister (and others in the same series), Dorothy Edwards – Eyre Methuen

Stories For Under Fives, Sara and Stephen Corrin – Faber & Faber

Best Word Book Ever (a good book for looking at and talking about), Richard Scarry – Hamlyn

Others in the Collins series 'Beginning Beginner Books', and for older children, 'Beginner Books'; e.g. *Are You My Mother?*, P. D. Eastman

The Early Bird (and others in the Collins Early Bird Book Series), Richard Scarry – Wm. Collins

The Adventures of Dougal (and other titles in the series), Eric Thompson – Brockhampton

Captain Pugwash (and other titles), John Ryan – Bodley Head

Railway Series, e.g. Small Railway Engines, Rev. W. Awdry – Kaye & Ward

Little Book Series, e.g. The Blanket, John Burningham – Jonathan Cape

Winnie the Pooh, A. A. Milne, Illus. E. H. Shepard – Eyre Methuen

The House at Pooh Corner, A. A. Milne, Illus. E. H. Shepard – Eyre Methuen

When We Were Very Young, A. A. Milne, Illus. E. H. Shepard – Eyre Methuen

Now We Are Six, A. A. Milne, Illus. E. H. Shepard – Eyre Methuen

The Story of the Fierce Bad Rabbit, Beatrix Potter – Warne

The Tale of Mrs Tiggy-Winkle, Beatrix Potter – Warne

The Tale of Tom Kitten, Beatrix Potter – Warne

The Tale of Mr Jeremy Fisher, Beatrix Potter – Warne

The Tale of Two Bad Mice, Beatrix Potter – Warne

The Tale of Timmy Tiptoes, Beatrix Potter – Warne

The Tale of Peter Rabbit, Beatrix Potter – Warne

The Tale of Squirrel Nutkin, Beatrix Potter – Warne

The Tale of Jemima Puddleduck, Beatrix Potter – Warne

**Readers Choosing books for older children are strongly recommended to read *Choosing Books for Children*, by Peter Hollindale – Paul Elek Ltd.

2 Suggested Further Reading

Chapter 1
A Short Survey of Some Common or Important Ear Diseases,
H. Engstrom and B. Engstrom, Widex Publication, available from P. C. Werth Ltd., 17 Stratford Place, Oxford Street, London, W. 1.
Clinical Aspects of Hearing, R.N.I.D. Publication.
Deafness, John Chalmers Ballantyne, J. & A. Churchill Ltd., 104 Gloucester Place, London, W.1.
Hearing Loss In Children, Burton F. Jaffe, University Park Press, Baltimore, Maryland 21202, U.S.A.
Otologic Diagnosis and the Treatment of Deafness, David Myers, Woodrow Schlosser, Robert Wolfson, Richard Winchester and Norman Carmel, Ciba Clinical Symposia, 1970, Ciba-Geigy Corporation, Wimblehurst Road, Horsham, West Sussex, RH12 4AB
The Medical Aspects of Deafness in Children, N.D.C.S.

Chapter 2
Hearing Loss, Definition, Symptoms, Alleviation, Leif Sorensen, Oticon Ltd., Cadzow Industrial Estate, Hamilton, Scotland
Measuring Sound, Bruel and Kjaer, B. & K. Labs Ltd., 17 Cross Lances Road, Hounslow, Middlesex
Notes on Free Field Screening, Tests of Hearing for Children Under Five Years of Age, Josephine Dodds, B. Edsall & Co. Ltd. 1978
Neurological Mechanisms of Hearing and Speech in Children, Ian G. Taylor, Manchester University Press, Oxford Road, Manchester 13
Pitfalls In Audiometry, V. J. Brasier, Dept. of Audiology & Education of the Deaf, University of Manchester

Chapter 3

Our Deaf Children, Freddy Bloom – Gresham
The Challenge For The Family of a Child Born Deaf, Theodore Blumberg – Wm. Heinemann Medical Books
The Deaf Child and His Family, Susan Gregory – George Allen & Unwin
Learn To Understand Me, Aira Kankkunen – N.D.C.S.
Deafness – Let's Face It, T. H. Sutcliffe – R.N.I.D.
Christopher: A Silent Life, Margaret Brock. Written by the parent of a hearing impaired child – MacMillan London Ltd.

Chapter 4

How To Raise A Brighter Child, Joan Beck – Fontana
Our Deaf Children, Freddy Bloom – Gresham
Happy Children, Rudolf Dreikurs (with Vicki Soltz) – Fontana
Distress And Comfort, Judy Dunn – Fontana
What Every Child Would Like His Parents To Know, Lee Salk – Fontana
The First Relationship: Infant And Mother, Daniel Stern – Fontana
Mothering, Rudolf Schaffer – Fontana

N.D.C.S. Publications:

A Pre-School Service For Deaf Children And Their Parents, Winifred Tumin
Parents As Partners, Winifred Tumin
Help For Parents Of Deaf Children
A Guide To The Education of the Hearing Impaired Child, Jacqueline Young
The Screening of Hearing Impaired Children
Weekly Boarding – Why And How
Guidelines On The Educational Assessment and Placement of Deaf Children
A Parent's Guide, B. McCormick
Talk – The society's quarterly magazine

John Tracy – A correspondence course is available free of charge to parents on writing to John Tracy Clinic, 206 West Adam Boulevard, Los Angelos, California, 90007, U.S.A.

Chapter 5
Acoustics for Amplification, Phonic Ear International, from P. C. Werth Ltd. (see p. 224)
Current Hearing Aids, R.N.I.D.
Helping Your Deaf Child At Home, Christine Cheney, B.A.T.O.D.
Instructions for Manufacturing Individual Acrylic Earmoulds from the Impression, Oticon Ltd. (see p. 224)
The Oticon Technical Library Series, Oticon Ltd
TV/Radio Adaptors And The Loop System, R.N.I.D.
Hearing Aids – Questions And Answers, R.N.I.D.
TV/Radio Adaptors And The Loop system, R.N.I.D.
Installing A Loop System, R.N.I.D.
Home Made Hearing Harnesses, N.D.C.S.
Hearing, R.N.I.D.
Modern Portable Electricity, The Ever Ready Co. Ltd., 1255 High Road, Whetstone, London, N20 0EJ

Chapter 6
Talk To Me: A Home Study Programme Of Language Development for Hearing Impaired Children from Infancy to Pre-School, J. G. Alpiner, Carol F. Amon, Joy Gibson and Patti Sheehy – University of Denver Press
How Your Baby Grows, J. G. Alpiner, Carol F. Amon, Joy Gibson and Patti Sheehy – University of Denver Press
Your Deaf Child's Speech And Language, M. Courtman-Davies – Bodley Head
The Perceptual World Of The Child, Tom Bower – Fontana
Understanding Your Child From Birth To Three, Joseph Church – Fontana
Play School Play Ideas, Ruth Croft – B.B.C. Books
Play, Catherine Garvey – Fontana

Learn To Understand Me, Aira Kankkunen – N.D.C.S.
What To Do When There's Nothing To Do, E. M. Gregg and the Boston Children's Medical Centre – Arrow Books
The Deaf Child and His Family, Susan Gregory – George Allen & Unwin
Choosing Books for Children, Peter Hollindale – Paul Elek Ltd
Let Me Play, Dorothy Jeffree and Roy McConkey – Souvenir Press
Play With a Purpose for the Under Sevens, E. M. Matterson – Penguin
A Parent's Guide to Developmental Sequences and Suitable Play Activities for Hearing Impaired Children Between the Ages of Six Months and Five Years, B. McCormick – N.D.C.S.

Toy Libraries Association Publications;
Hear and Say _ Toys for Children With Hearing Speech and Language Difficulties
Encouraging Language Development
Do-It-Yourself. Ideas On How Parents Can Make Their Own Toys
Choosing Toys And Activities For Handicapped Children
For Busy Hands. Instructions On Making Noisy Play Material
Homo Loquens – Man As A Talking Animal, Dennis Fry – Cambridge University Press
Play It By Ear. Auditory Training Games, – Wolfer Publishing Co., Washington

Chapter 7
How to Raise a Brighter Child, Joan Beck – Fontana
Children's Drawing, Jacqueline Goodnow – Fontana
How Children Fail, John Holt – Pelican
Let Me Play, D. Jeffree and R. McConkey – Souvenir Press
The Highway Code for Children, R.N.I.D.
The Three Four Five Nursery Course, Three Four Five Publishing Company

Learning Together, A Magazine Poster Pack for parents and children, on subscription from Evans Brothers Ltd., Montague House, Russell Square, London, WC1B 5BX

Chapter 8
Toilet Training In a Day, Azarin & Fox – MacMillan
The Education of Hearing Handicapped Children, Thomas Watson – University of London Press
Educational Provision for Children With Defective Hearing, – B.A.T.O.D.
List of Schools, Units Etc., for Hearing Impaired Children, – B.A.T.O.D.

3 Voluntary Organisations Associated with Hearing Impairment

Breakthrough: 103 Ridgeway Drive, Bromley, Kent, BR1 5DB. Among other activities, Breakthrough organises family holidays.

British Association of the Hard of Hearing: 16 Park Street, Windsor, Bucks. Hearing impaired adults.

British Association of Teachers of the Deaf (B.A.T.O.D.): Rycroft Centre, Royal Schools for the Deaf, Stanley Road, Cheadlehulme, Cheshire.

British Deaf Association (B.D.A.): 38 Victoria Place, Carlisle, CA1 1EX. Hearing impaired adults, including school leavers. Biased towards non oral deaf.

City Lit. Centre for the Deaf: Keeley House, Keeley Street (off Kingsway), Holborn, London, WC2. Further education facilities.

Commonwealth Society for the Deaf: 83 Kinnerton Street, London, SW1.

Jewish Deaf Association, Julius J. Newman House, 90–92 Cazenove Road, London, NI6 6AB.

Link Centre for Deafened People: c/o Princess Alice Memorial Hospital, Eastbourne, East Sussex, BN21 2AX. Deafened adults catered for on short residential courses.

National Deaf Children's Society (N.D.C.S.): 45 Hereford Road, London. W2 5AH. All matters relating to deaf children. (Addresses of local associations of N.D.C.S. are available from above address. There are 67 associations.)

National Centre for Cued Speech: 16 Nassau Road, London, SW13.

National Council of Social Workers for the Deaf: 102 Manchester Road, Chorlton, Manchester.

Royal National Institute for the Deaf (R.N.I.D.): 105 Gower Street, London, WC1E 6AH. All technical information and other matters related to deafness.

4 Voluntary Organisations for Other Handicaps

Association for all Speech Impaired Children: Room 14, Toynbee Hall, 28 Commercial Street, London, E1 6LS.

Down's Children Association: Quinbourne Centre, Ridgacre Road, Quinton, Birmingham, B32 2TW.

Gingerbread Association for One Parent Families: 35 Wellington Street, London, WC2.

National Association for Deaf/Blind and Rubella Handicapped: 164 Cromwell Lane, Coventry, CV4 8AP.

National Society for Mentally Handicapped Children: 117-123 Golden Lane, London, EC1Y 0RT.

National Children's Bureau: 8 Wakely Street, London, EC1V 7QE.

National Deaf-Blind Helper's League: 18 Rainbow Court, Paston Ridings, Peterborough, PE4 6UP.

Spastics Society: 12 Park Crescent, London, W1N 4EQ.

Voluntary Council for Handicapped Children: 8 Wakley Street, Islington, London, EC1.

5 Toys

British Toy Manufacturers' Association: 80 Camberwell Road, London, SE5 0EG. (The association runs an enquiry service, and will provide lists of toy manufacturers, many of whom will send a free catalogue on request.)

6 Nursery Education

Pre-school Playgroup Association: Alford House, Aveline Street, London, SE11 5DH.

Opportunity Nursery Classes for Handicapped Children: c/o Dr. E. Faulkner, 1 Weston Road, Stevenage, Herts.

Toy Libraries Association: Seabrook House, Wyllyotts Manor, Darkes Lane, Potters Bar, Herts, EN6 2HL.

The Three Four Five Nursery Course: Three, Four, Five Publishing Ltd., Henley, Surrey, CR2 57S.

British Association for Early Childhood Education: Montgomery Hall, Kennington Oval, London, SE11 5SW.

7 Radio Hearing Aid Manufacturers

Phonic Ear, P. C. Werth, 17 Stratford Place, Oxford Street, London, W1N 0DH.

Radio Link, Cubex Hearing Centre, 324 Gray's Inn Road, London, WC1X 8DH.

Jessops, Jessop Acoustics Ltd., Unit 5, 7 Long Street, London, E2.

8 Auditory Training Unit (Speech Trainer) Suppliers

Amplivox, Amplivox Hearing Centres Ltd., 9–13 Grosvenor Street, London, W1.

Connevans, Connevans Ltd., 1 Norbury Road, Reigate, Surrey.

Kamplex, P. C. Werth Ltd., 17 Stratford Place, Oxford Street, London, W1N 0DH.

Linco, 163 Oxford Road, Reading, R91 7XP.

Peters, Alfred Peters & Sons Ltd., Wreakes Lane, Dronfield, Sheffield, S18 6DH.

Siemens, c/o Phonophone Acoustics Ltd., Acoustic House, California Estate, Aylesbury, Bucks, HP21 8HH.

9 Technical Information

R.N.I.D. Technical information relating to hearing aids, equipment and special aids for the hearing impaired.

British Radio Corporation, Lea Valley Trading Estate, Angel Road, London, N18. Loop Systems.

R. S. Components, 13–17 Epworth Street, London, EC2. Electrical components.

Pure Tone Audiometers:

Alfred Peters & Son Ltd., Wreakes Lane, Dronfield, Sheffield S18 6DH.

P. C. Werth, 17 Stratford Place, London, W1.

Medelec Ltd., Manor Way, Old Woking, Surrey.

Sound Level Meters:
  Castle Associates, Redbourne House, North Street, Scarborough, Yorks. YO11 1DE.
  N. Rose Ltd., 8 St. Chads Place, London, WC1 9HJ.
Acoustic Impedance Meters:
  P. C. Werth
  Alfred Peters & Son Ltd., Wreakes Lane, Dronfield, Sheffield, S18 6DH.

10 Grants and Allowances Available to Parents of Hearing Impaired Children

a) *Attendance Allowance.* This is available to parents of hearing impaired children over the age of 2 years. Further information from local offices of the Dept. of Health & Social Security.

b) *The Family Fund.* This provides help in the form of grants to families with severely handicapped children to relieve stress. Grants may cover items such as washing machines, or travelling costs but not educational or health aids. Joseph Rowntree Memorial Trust, P.O. Box 50, York.

11 National Centres for Audiological Assessment

The Director, Dept. of Audiology and Education of the Deaf, The University, Manchester, M13 9PL.
The Director, Nuffield Hearing and Speech Centre, Royal National Nose, Throat & Ear Hospital, Gray's Inn Road, London, WC1.
The Director, Institute of Sound and Vibration Research, The University, Southampton, SO9 5NH.

12 Films, Cassettes and Various Items

Films: (16 mm. with sound and colour in most cases are available on loan).
'An Early Start': A film for parents demonstrating early home training of hearing impaired children in natural oralism. From Metromed, 8–10 Neal's Yard, London, WC2.
N.D.C.S. films on various aspects of deafness available from: Concord Film Council Ltd., Nacton, Ipswich, Suffolk, IP10 0JZ.
'Give me a signal': Demonstrates techniques of testing the hearing of handicapped children. From Town and Country Productions Ltd., 21 Cheyne Row, Chelsea, London, SW3 5HP.

Cassettes:
'Singing Action Nursery Rhymes': Produced with hearing impaired children in mind, and includes a leaflet of words and actions. From Dept. of Audiology and Education of the Deaf, The University, Manchester, M13 9PL.
'Filtered Speech': Simulates different types of hearing loss. From Dept. of Audiology, Manchester.
'Sound through a Hearing Aid': Gives examples of the subjective quality of speech through various hearing aids in differing conditions. E.g. in the home, in playgroup, in school. From Dept. of Audiology, Manchester.
'Speech': Simulates different degrees of hearing loss. From R.N.I.D.

Various Items:
Electronic Toy Panda: The panda's eyes light up in response to sound. From R.N.I.D.

High Frequency Rattles: From Dept. of Audiology, Manchester.

High Quality Musical Chime Bars: From Dept. of Audiology, Manchester.

Battery Warning Indicator: Emits a bleeping tone and flashes a warning light when hearing aid battery needs replacing. From Dept. of Audiology, Manchester.

Index